CW01646232

The real voyage of discovery consists not in seeking new landscapes, but in having new eyes

– MARCEL PROUST

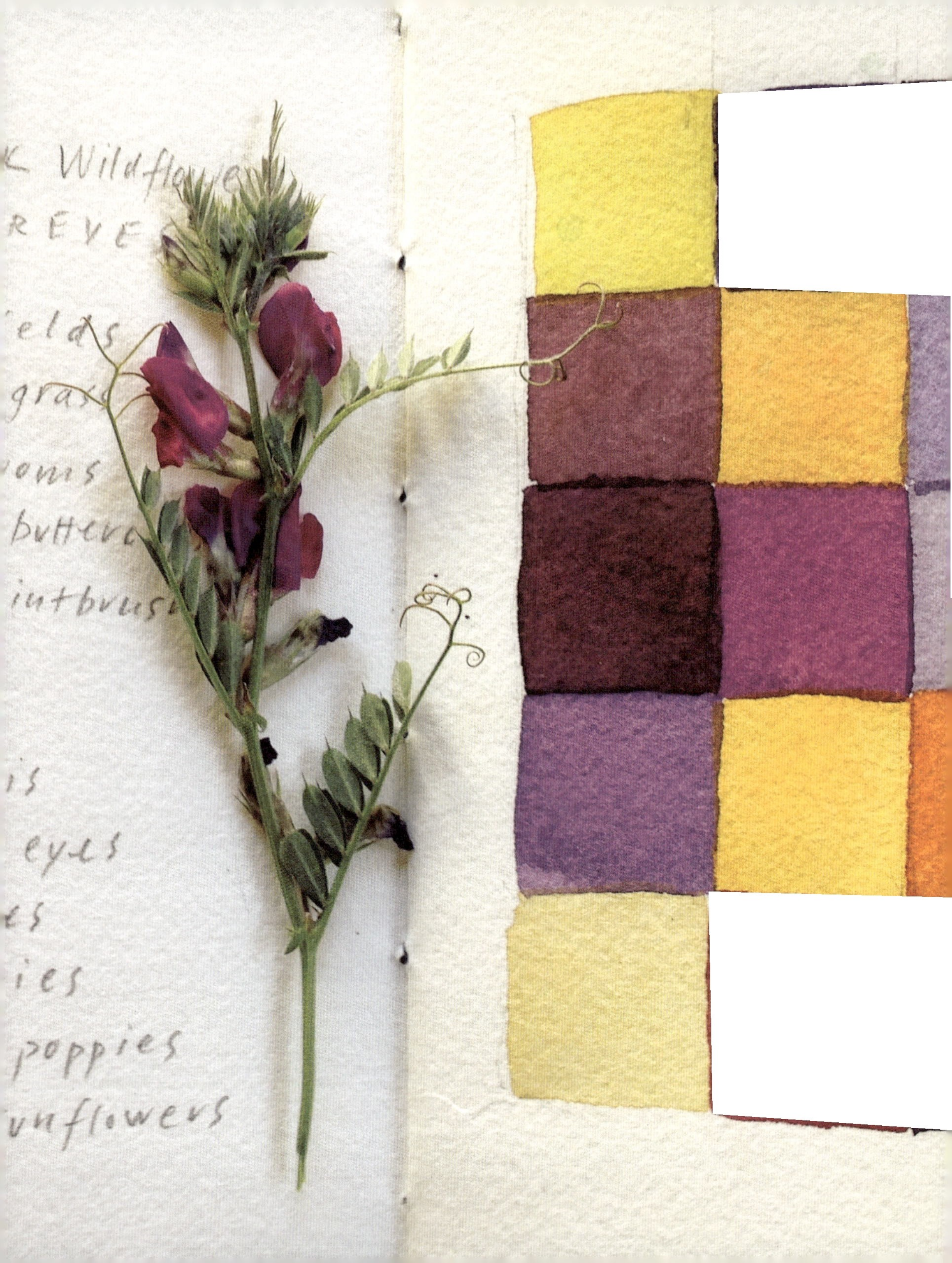
eyes
poppies

LOCAL COLOR

SEEING PLACE THROUGH WATERCOLOR

WITH 14 PRACTICES

MIMI ROBINSON

PRINCETON ARCHITECTURAL PRESS · NEW YORK

Published by
Princeton Architectural Press
202 Warren Street
Hudson, New York 12534

Visit our website at www.papress.com.

Printed and bound in China by C&C Offset Printing Co., Ltd.
21 20 19 5 4 3

Editors: Jennifer Lippert and Tom Cho
Designer: Mia Johnson

Special thanks to: Meredith Baber, Sara Bader, Nicola Bednarek Brower, Janet Behning, Megan Carey, Carina Cha, Andrea Chlad, Barbara Darko, Benjamin English, Russell Fernandez, Will Foster, Jan Cigliano Hartman, Jan Haux, Diane Levinson, Katharine Myers, Jaime Nelson, Rob Shaeffer, Sara Stemen, Marielle Suba, Kaymar Thomas, Paul Wagner, Joseph Weston, and Janet Wong of Princeton Architectural Press
—Kevin C. Lippert, publisher

Library of Congress Cataloging-in-Publication Data
Robinson, Mimi.
Local Color : Seeing Place Through Watercolor : 14 Daily Practices / Mimi Robinson.—First edition.
127 pages : color illustrations ; 22 cm
Includes bibliographical references and index.
ISBN 978-1-61689-297-5 (pbk.)
1. Watercolor painting—Technique. I. Title.
ND2130.R63 2015
751.42'2—dc23

2014039304

Acknowledgments

A special thanks to all of the people who helped bring this book into being: To my publisher, Princeton Architectural Press, for their vision; to Diane Chonette and Ann Hudner for their work on an earlier version of this book; to Steve Costa and Kate Levinson of Point Reyes Books, and Paloma Pavel, for their support and encouragement; to Kathy McNicolas and Kate Greene, who contributed color memories; to Robin Weiss for her superb eye; to Myn Ades for her masterful editing; and to Carla Robinson and Lily Reid for their help.
—Mimi Robinson

8 INTRODUCTION

10 CHAPTER ONE
Getting Grounded: My Backyard

28 CHAPTER TWO
Getting Started: Materials, Preparation & Techniques

36 CHAPTER THREE
Look Around You: Elements of Place
HABITAT · LIGHT · WEATHER · SEASONS

50 CHAPTER FOUR
World Color: Travel Journeys

88 CHAPTER FIVE
Wherever You Go: Field Studies
BIG PICTURE · DETAIL · SKY PATCH · TERRAIN · ROCKS · WATER
COLOR WALK · COLOR MEMORY · NAMING COLORS

108 CHAPTER SIX
Palettes to Painting: Some Places

118 CHAPTER SEVEN
Color Mixing: The Basics
HOW MANY GREENS ARE THERE?

126 FURTHER READING

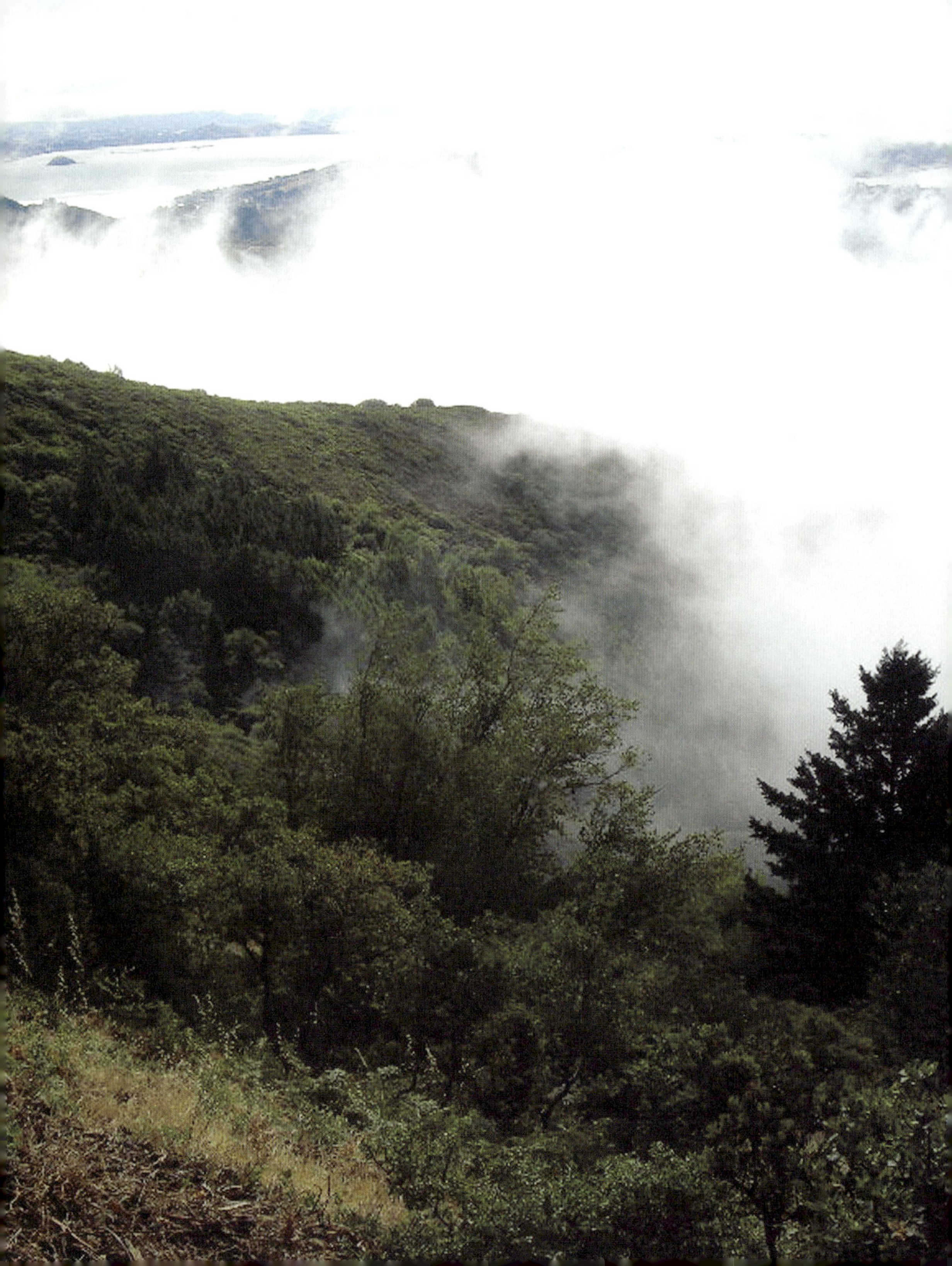

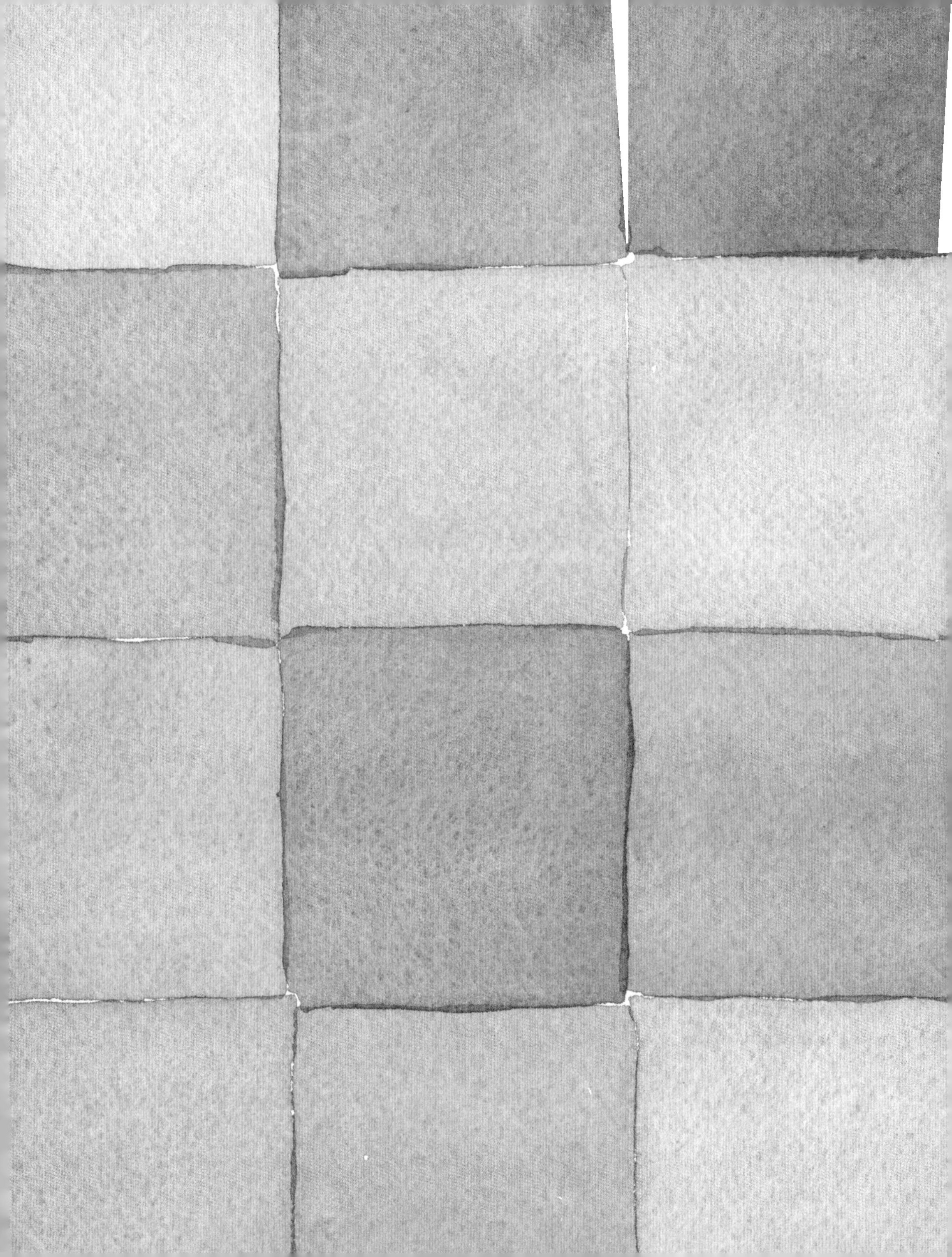

INTRODUCTION

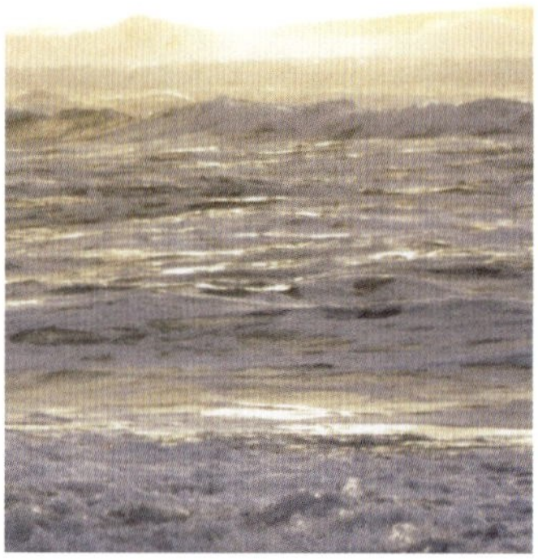

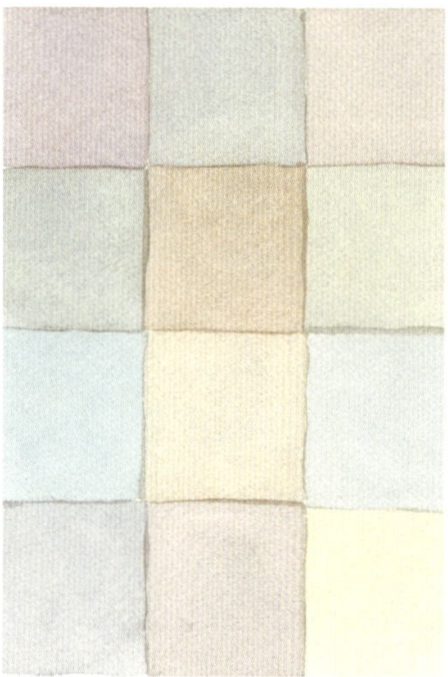

The color palettes I have created over the years have become a journal of my perceptions of place. Making them allows me to nurture a deep connection to the beauty of nature and the changing seasons as well as to local culture and history.

I have been greatly inspired by the artist Josef Albers's work in revealing the interactions and relationships of color. What we see in any given place reveals its special spirit through its collection of colors. Bringing your attention to the colors of a place, whether in your backyard or the places you've traveled to, allows you to slow down and really see what's in front of you.

I began making color palettes when I noticed that the color tests I made on scraps of paper, the process of trying to replicate the color of what I was observing, was an enjoyable and playful practice in itself. Throughout the years, I have used this visual form of journal keeping to document my interactions with color and locality. I also use this technique as a warm-up for when I go *plein air* painting (painting in the open air) to hone my perception of the colors before I use them to define a form.

Local Color: Seeing Place Through Watercolor invites you to train your eye to create your own color palettes using basic materials and through simple practices in watercolors. Watercolors have a beauty and magic of their own. You can achieve instant results or spend a lifetime perfecting the craft. Watercolors are well suited for capturing an impression, and they're portable. The tactile quality of holding the brush in your hand and mixing colors becomes another dimension of the experience.

The direct, hands-on practices I offer encourage you to open your eyes to things you may not have seen before and develop your color sense. Sharing my color journals from my own backyard and my travels around the world, I show how color palettes can capture the identity of a place. By introducing you to a few materials, techniques, and practices, I invite you to begin your own color explorations and collect a visual memory of your place in time.

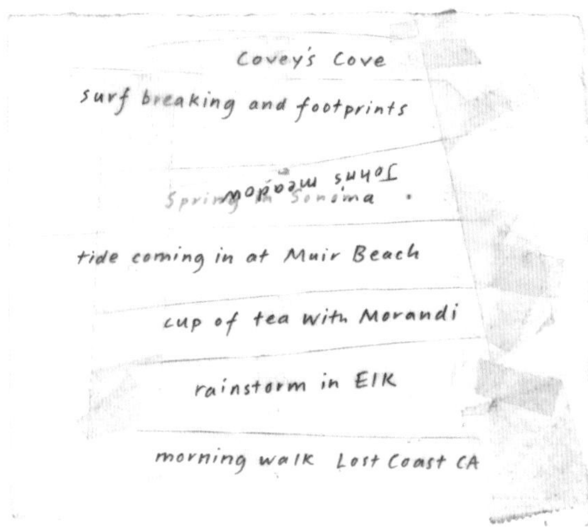

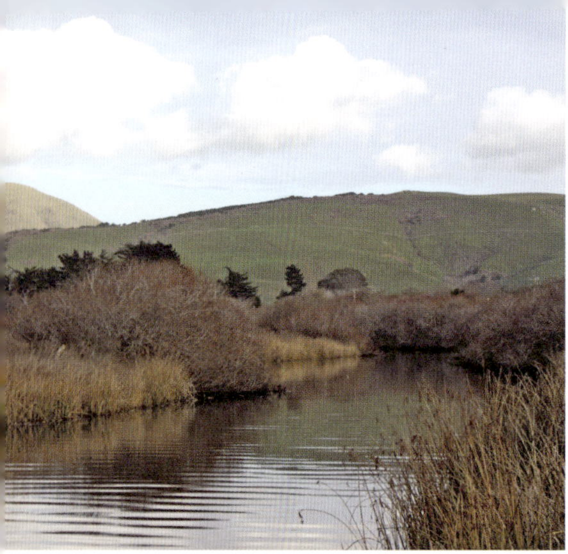
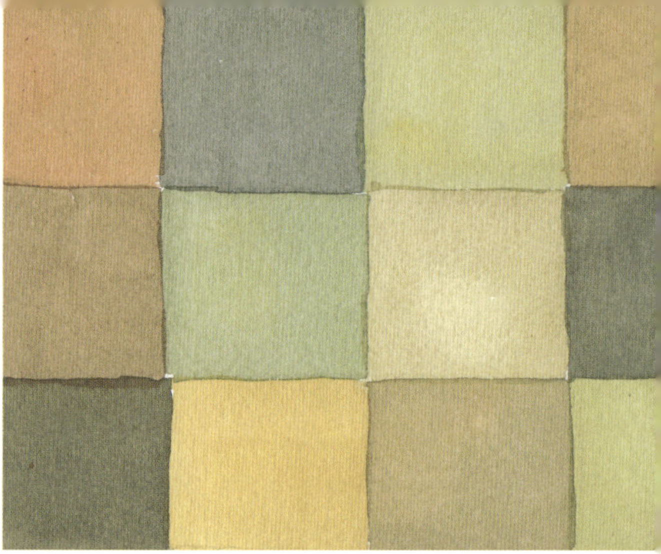
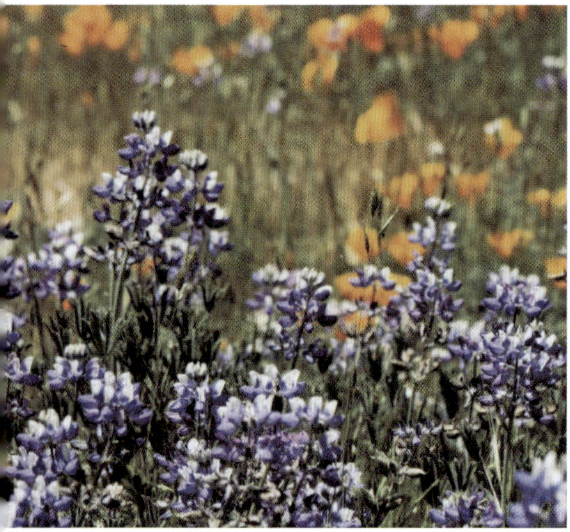
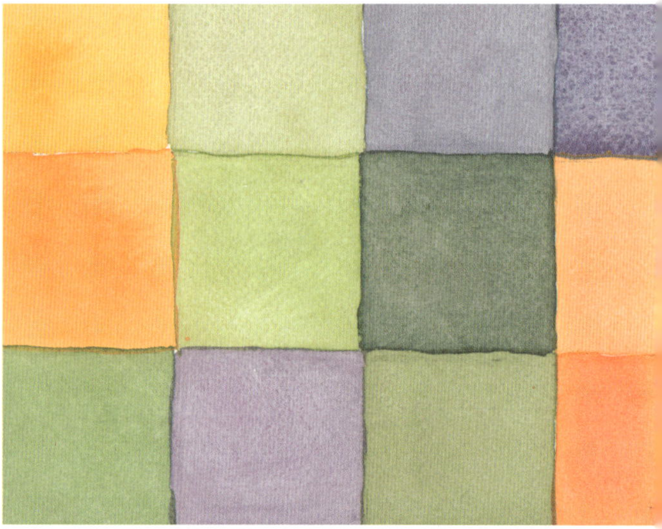
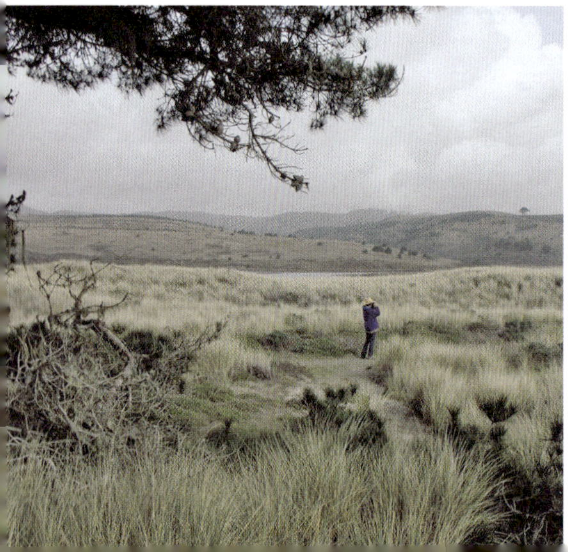
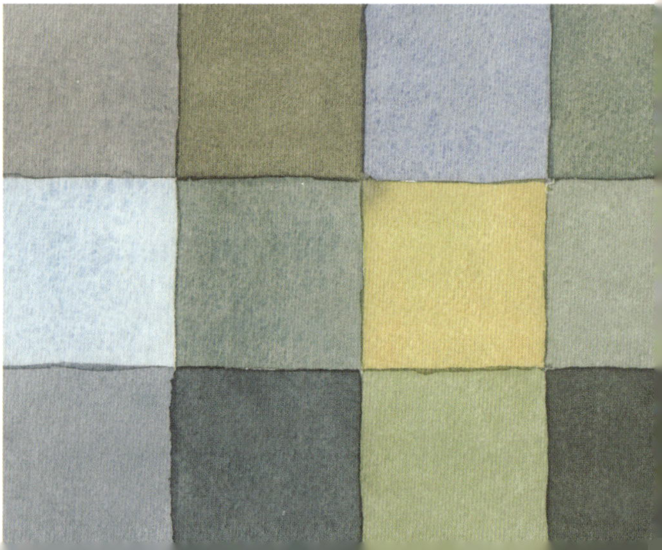

CHAPTER ONE

Getting Grounded: My Backyard

Point Reyes National Seashore, on the western edge of the United States, is a place that is very close to my heart and a short drive from where I live in Northern California. I think of it as my backyard. Over the past two decades, I have studied the coastal landscape of Point Reyes, exploring the area in detail. Nurturing my relationship with this extraordinary natural environment animates me as an artist and continually guides my work.

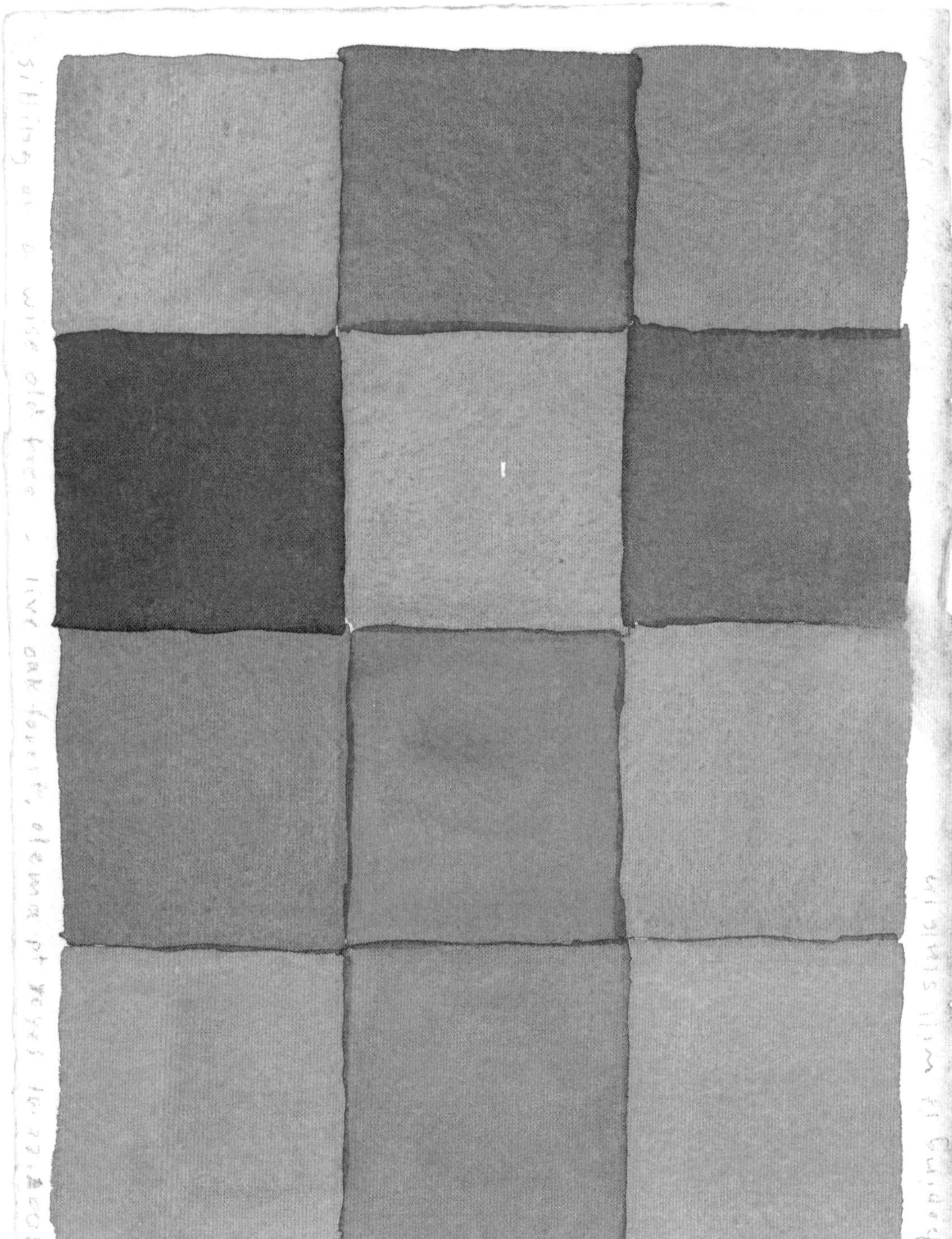

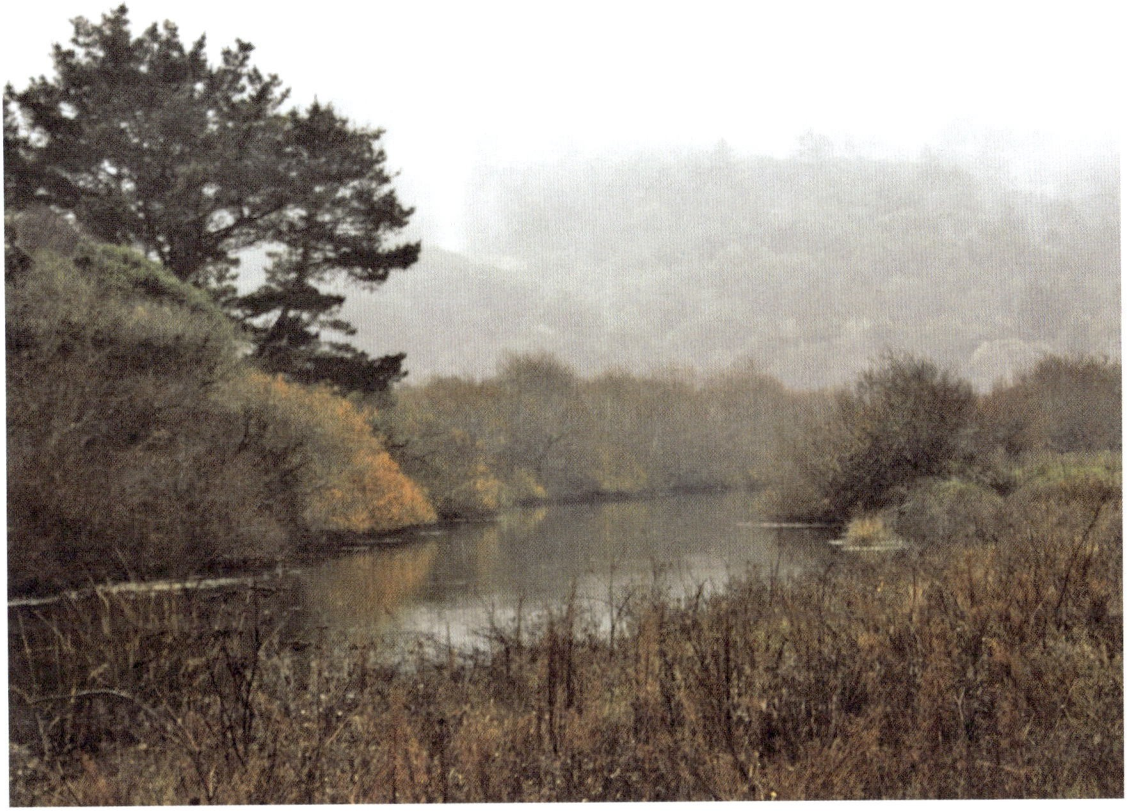

LANDSCAPE

The environment of Point Reyes, informed by the power of the Pacific Ocean, holds a rich diversity of habitats: dense forests, wild beaches, windswept cliffs, coastal dunes, marshland, and open pastures, all within close proximity. By observing color, I have developed a deeper appreciation for the ecology, the local plant life, and the windswept trees, along with the animal and bird life.

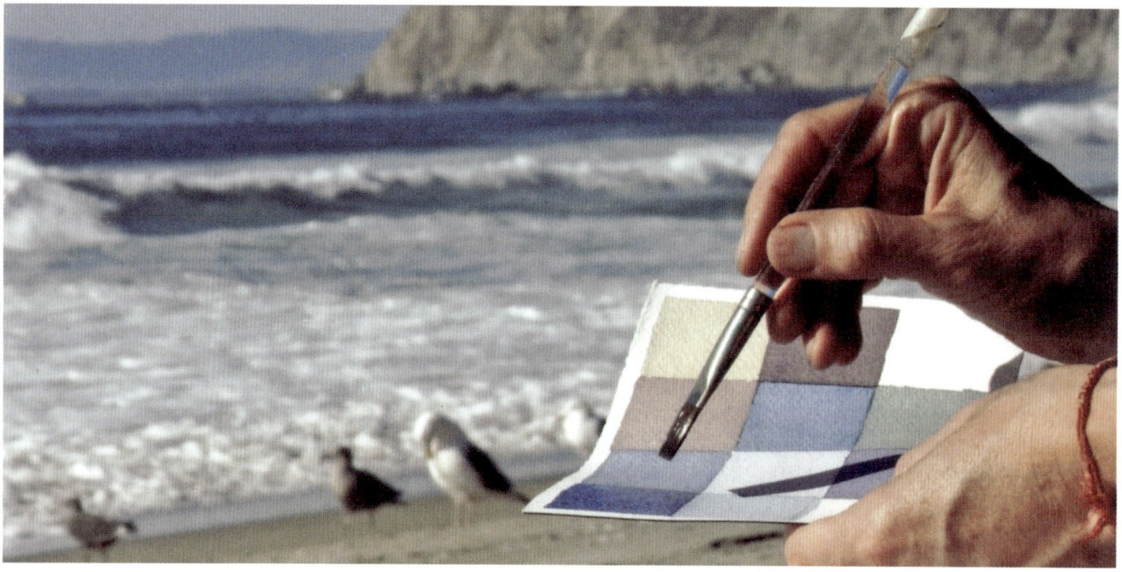

OCEAN/SKY

There is an exquisite quality to the afternoon light at Point Reyes, when the sun passes behind the clouds and shifts the colors in an instant. It's a reminder to me that everything changes. As I walk the muddy trails and coastal paths with wet feet and cold hands, Point Reyes awakens my senses.

Sunsets can be spectacular here, with the orange sun sinking into the Pacific Ocean. At dusk the ocean produces a light show of violet purples that change subtly and rapidly to orange, then red, and all shades in between. Waves catch the light, sand dunes glow, and grasses are illuminated like amber.

The beauty of the wild, frothy ocean stops me in my tracks, the salt spray flying and the colors of the beach changing in front of me. At other times, the in-between places of Point Reyes, the places I experience on my way to something else, inspire me the most. While driving one spring day, I saw big, fluffy, violet clouds low on the horizon. Suddenly the clouds opened in front of me and the sun came through, illuminating emerald green fields and mustard yellow meadows.

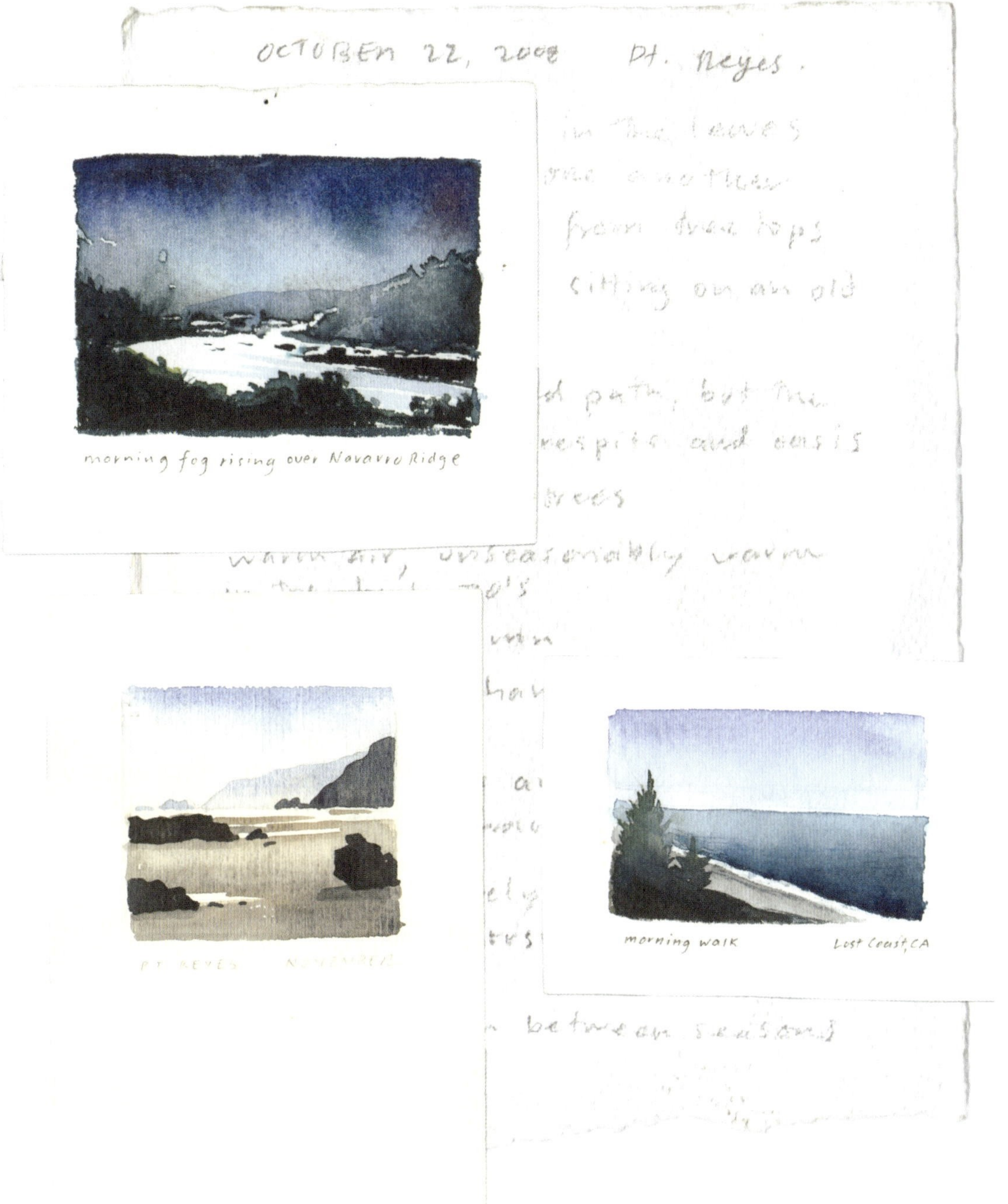
OCTOBER 22, 2008 Pt. Reyes.
in the leaves
from tree tops
sitting on an old
path, but the
respite and oasis
trees
warm air, unseasonably warm
between seasons
morning fog rising over Navarro Ridge
morning walk
Lost Coast, CA

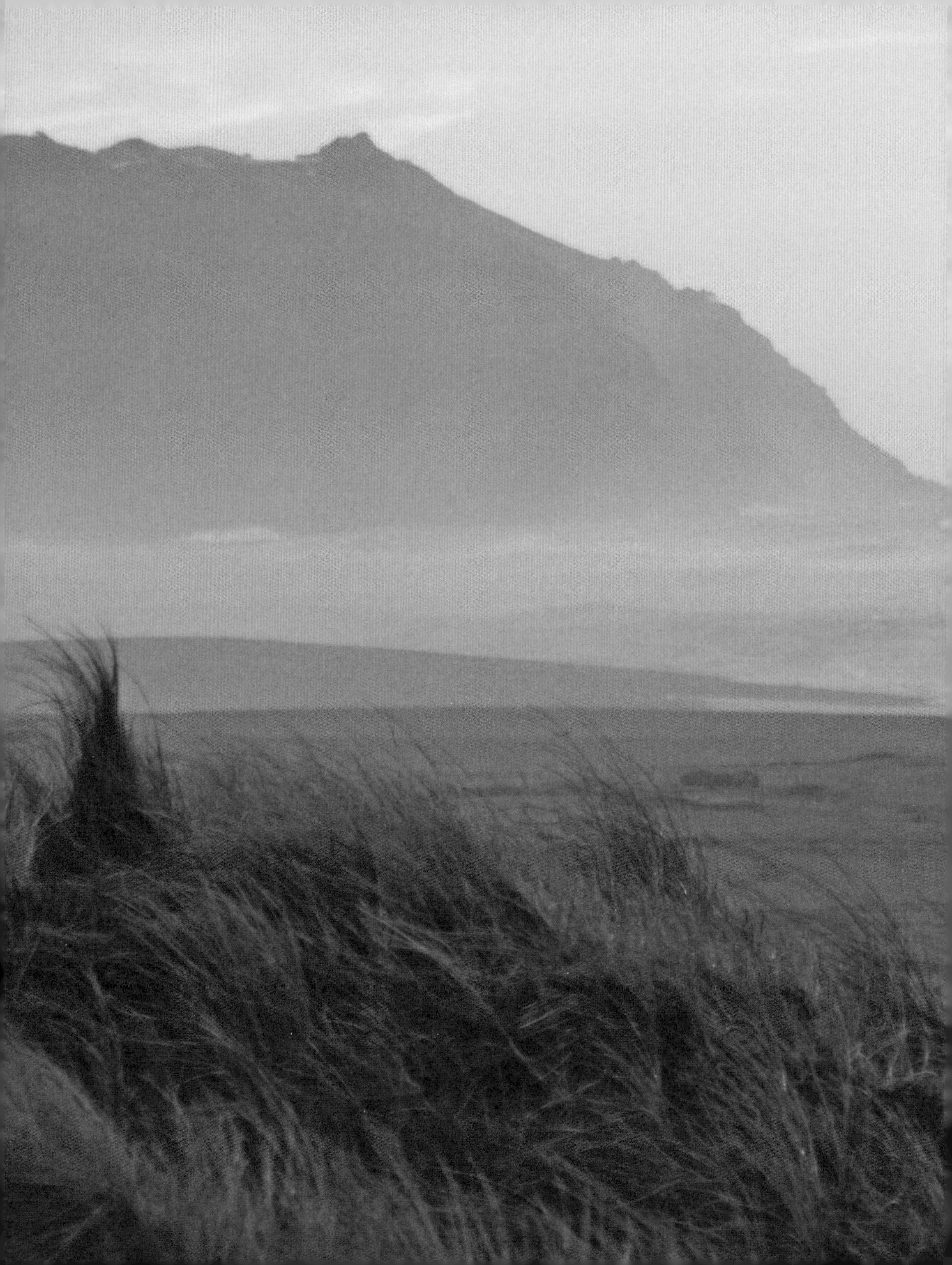

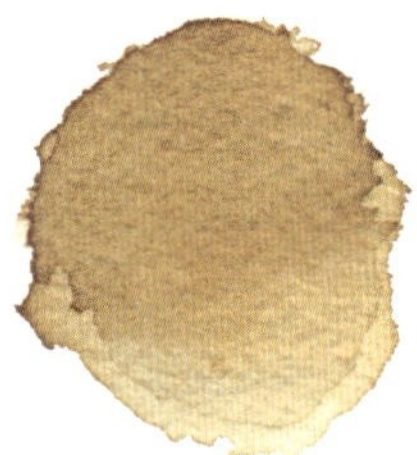

summer grasses

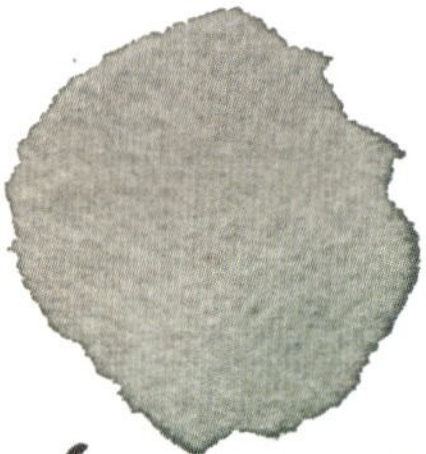

fog in trees

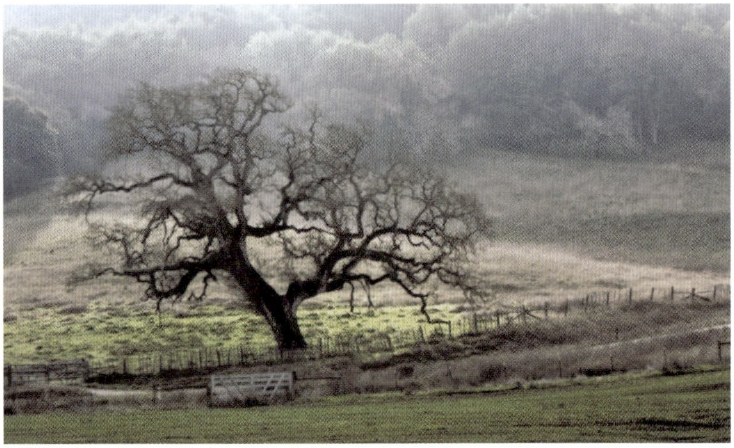

cliff at sunset

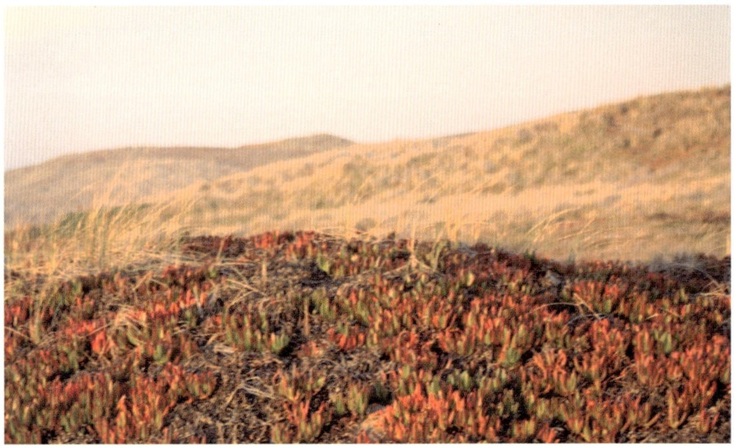

LIGHT

Light shifts throughout the days and the seasons. Early morning sunrises and evening sunsets, when the sun is low in the sky, typically create warmer colors, while high noon tends to yield cooler colors that are punctuated by stark shadows. In the winter, the light has a yellow quality. In April, there is a clear glow, ethereal in the morning, as the salt crystals from the ocean rise to meet the sky.

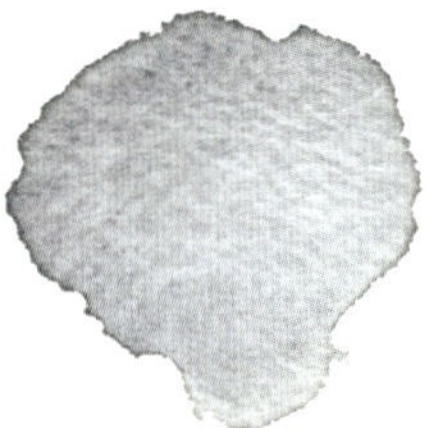

rain

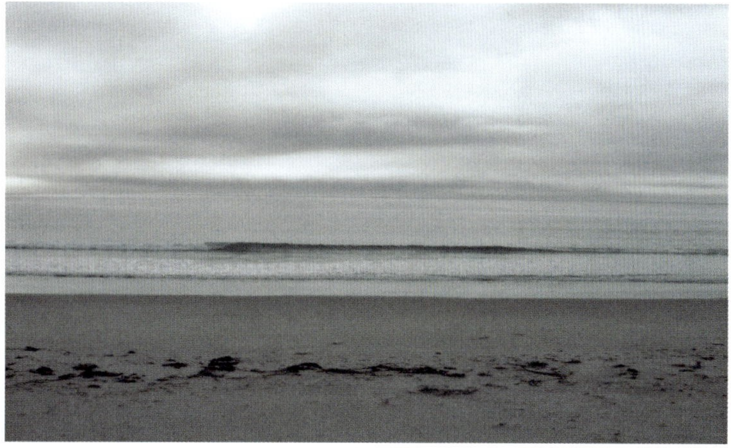

seaweed

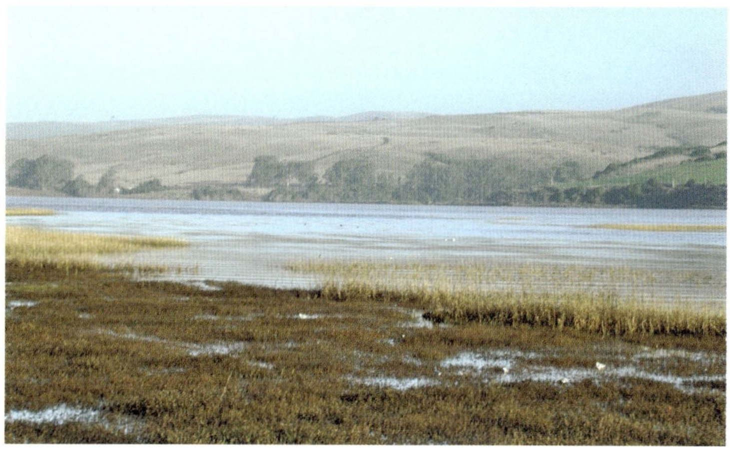

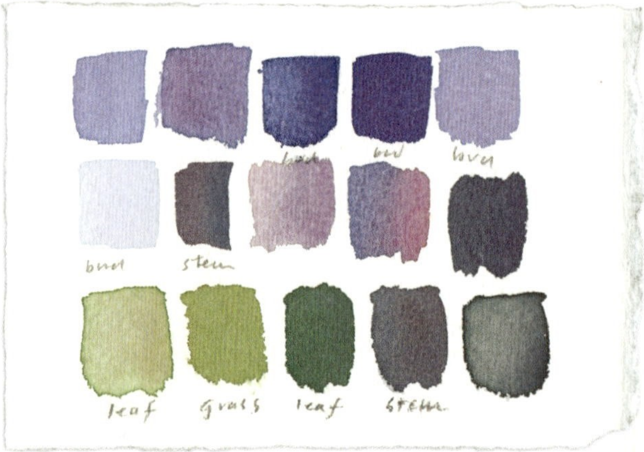

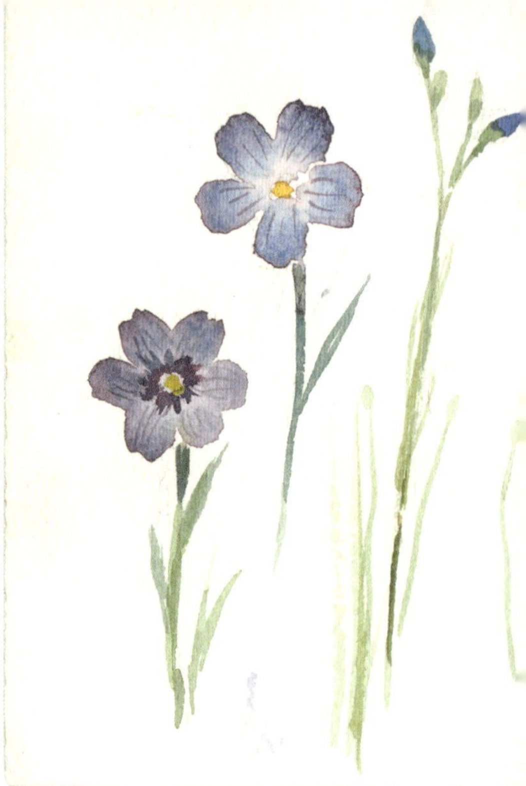

More often than not I invent new names for colors — I want the colors to evoke a more personal connection to the place. Take back your colors!

WILDFLOWERS

From January through August, depending on the mix of spring rain and sun, you can witness a show of wildflowers in Point Reyes. The bright orange splashes of California poppies and deep purple of Douglas iris are always a vivid surprise.

Coastal lupines—yellow, purple, and white—line the walking trails through the meadows. My favorites are the lavender ones as they stand against the backdrop of the ocean.

In a pasture of grass where cows graze off in the distance, the field appears to be all grass, but upon closer inspection, delicate little flowers are mixed in—worlds within worlds. They say that color can change your mood. Try sitting in a field of wildflowers in the spring and see how you feel.

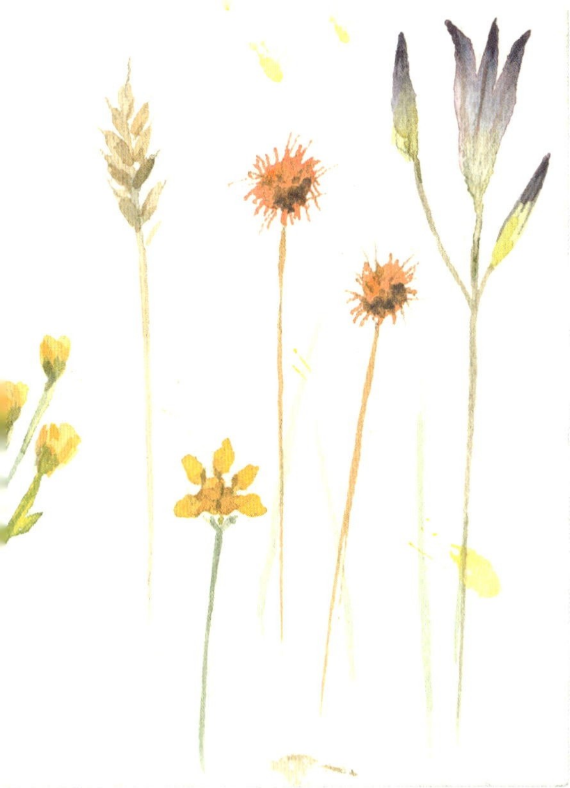

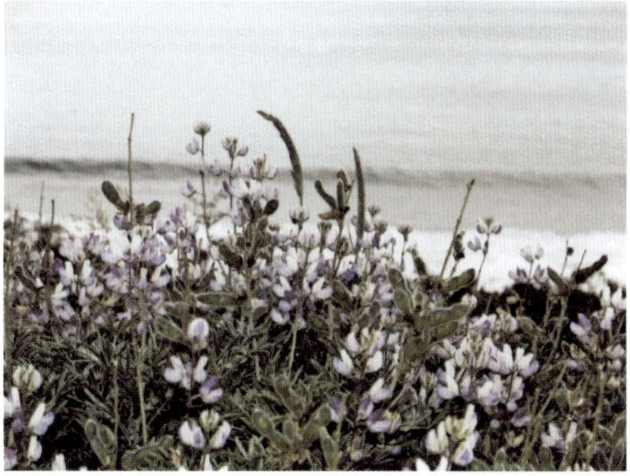

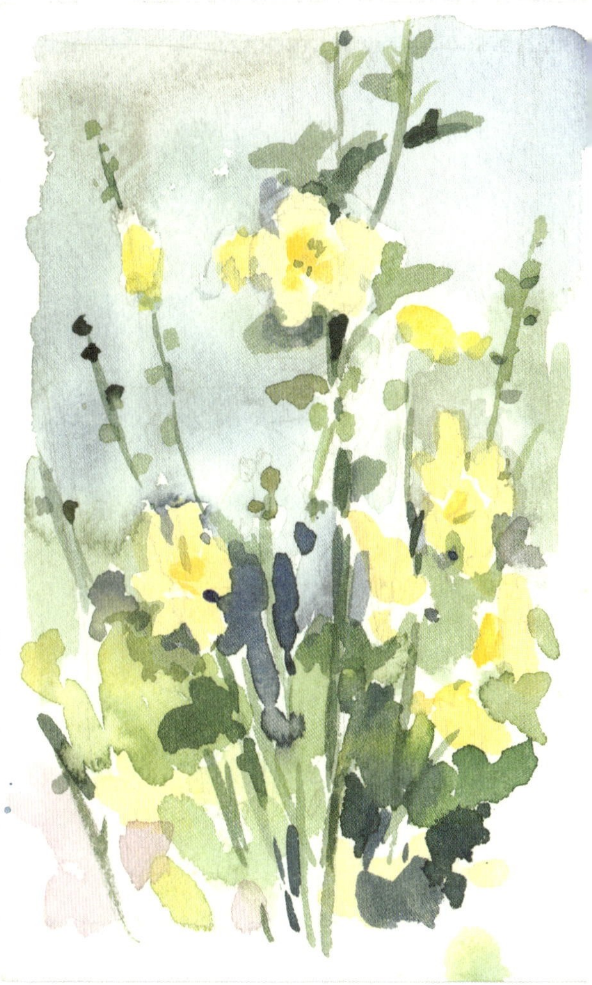

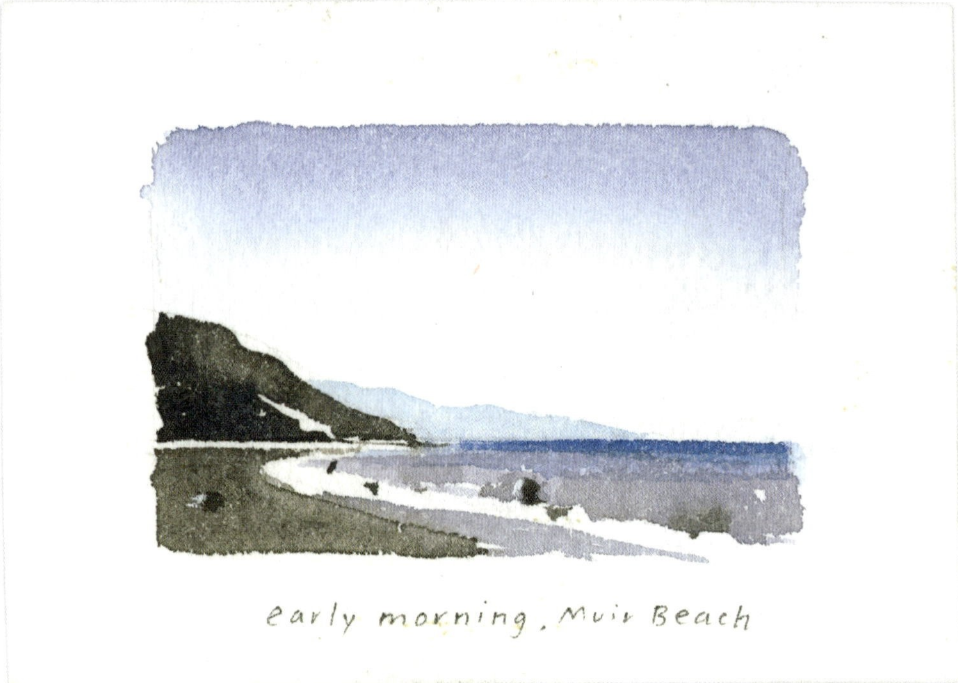
early morning. Muir Beach

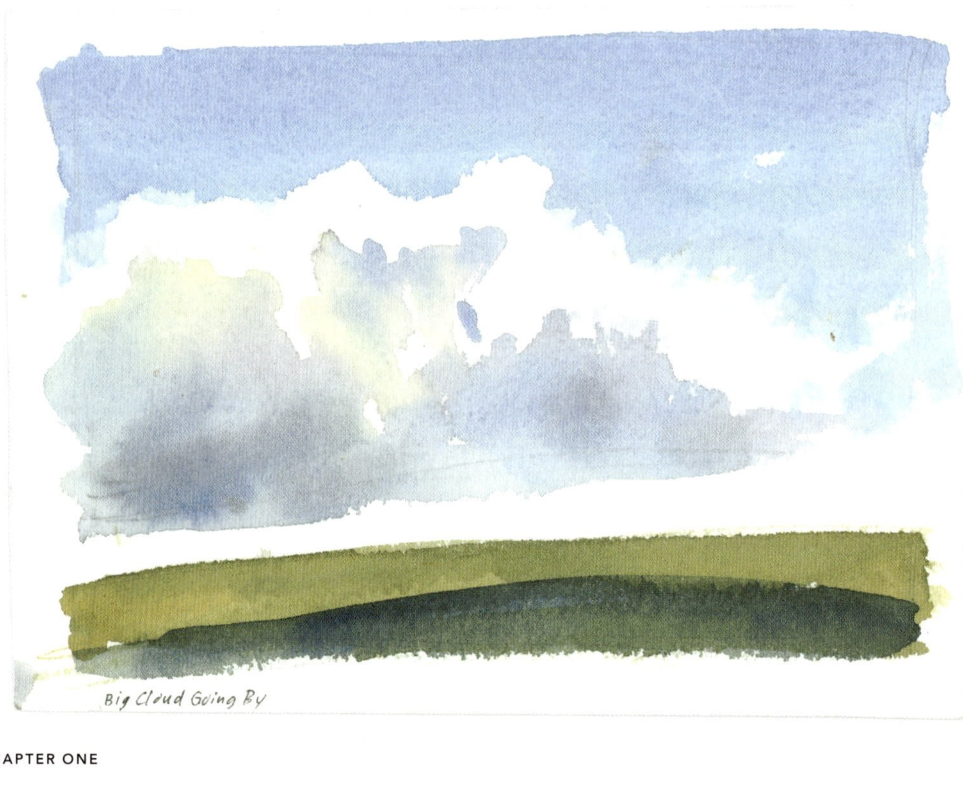
Big Cloud Going By

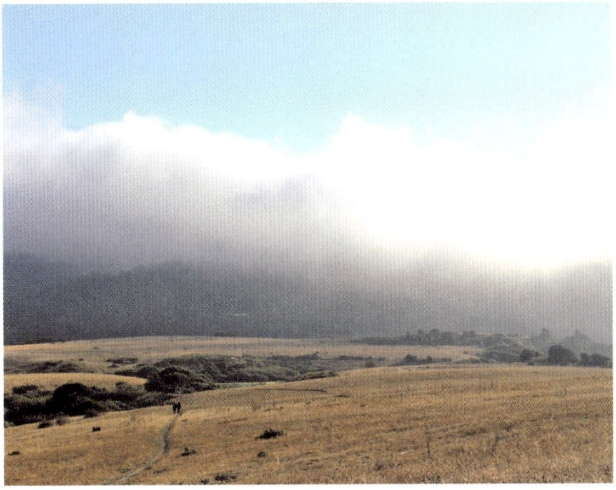 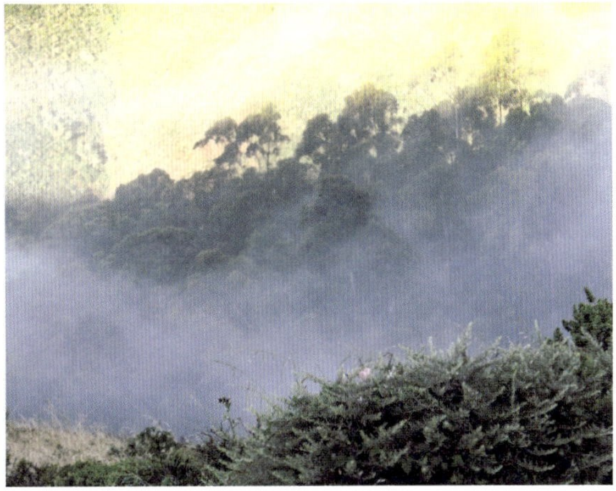

FOG, MIST, AND HAZE

What is the color of fog? How do you capture the color of mist as it rolls in and out?

Fog and mist are made from tiny suspended water droplets, and they usually form at night, when the air is too cool to hold its humidity. Fog is considered a low-lying cloud that captures moisture as it rises from the ground. Mist is less dense and usually stays close to the ground.

Haze is composed of dust from the land and salt from the sea suspended in the air. It makes distant dark objects appear blue and distant white objects appear yellow. In coastal areas, salt crystals form in the air from the evaporation of wave droplets. These small, invisible crystals are largely responsible for the blue color in the atmosphere, and they are the reason the ocean sky is often bluer than the sky over land.

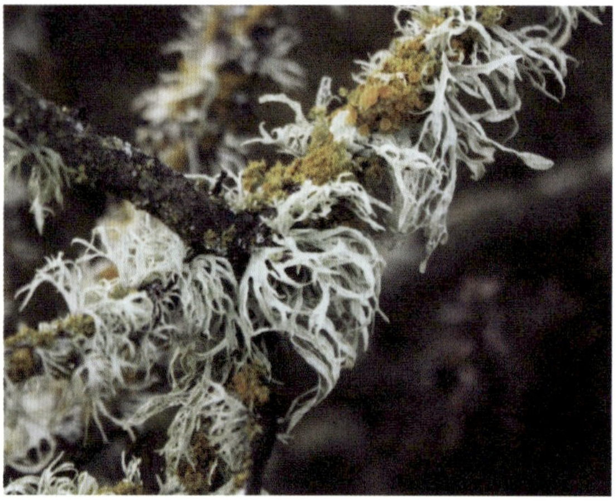

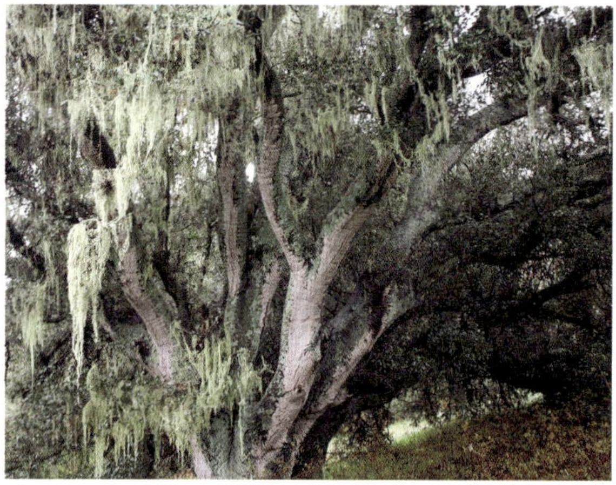

FOREST, LICHEN, AND MOSS

One of my favorite places in Point Reyes is a grove of coast live oak in a woodland forest on the eastern ridge. In the presence of the silent oaks, time slows, and my awareness of the unseen life of the forest around me increases. Fog lingers in the canopy. A squirrel takes a flying leap in search of acorns. Tree limbs weave together into arches. Lichen drips from the branches, and moss crawls up the trees. A vast network of roots stretches underneath the soil.

I observe the colors of the grove through dappled light—a mosaic of greens, silvers, and grays. A shaft of light illuminates a brilliant transparent green leaf. Lichens, mosses, and bark create an intricate patchwork of color and texture. An abundance of water in early spring makes sponge-like moss come alive with intense chartreuse and neon green. In late fall, the colors fade to ochre-tinged green and russet brown. It is an ever-changing, living palette.

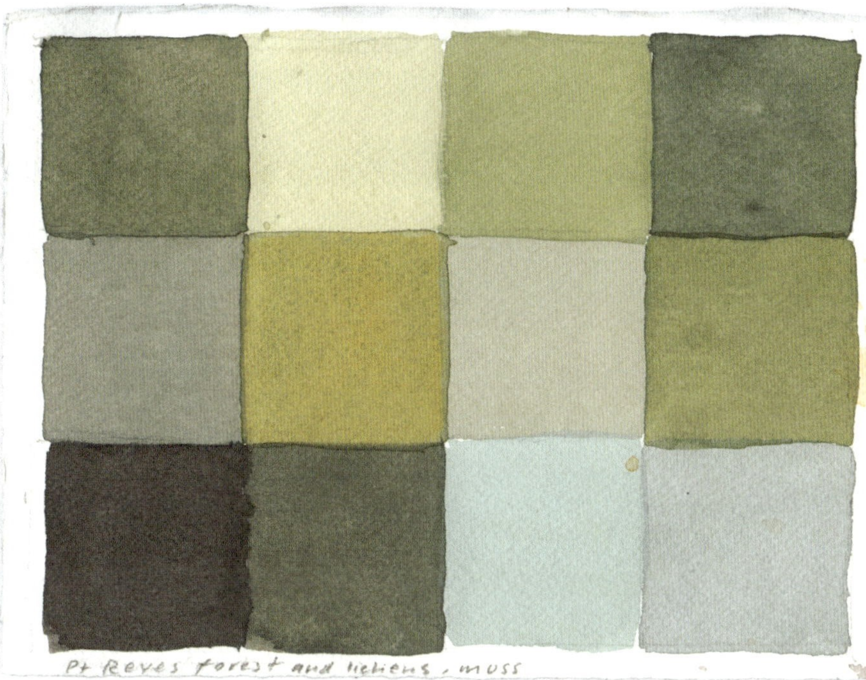
Pt Reyes forest and lichens . moss

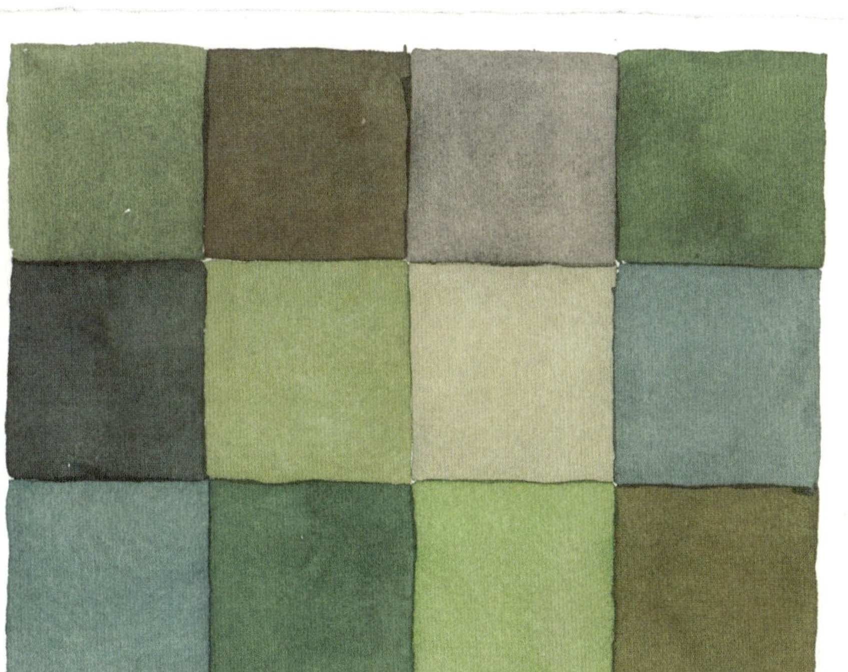
Point Reyes
Pine forest
July 2006

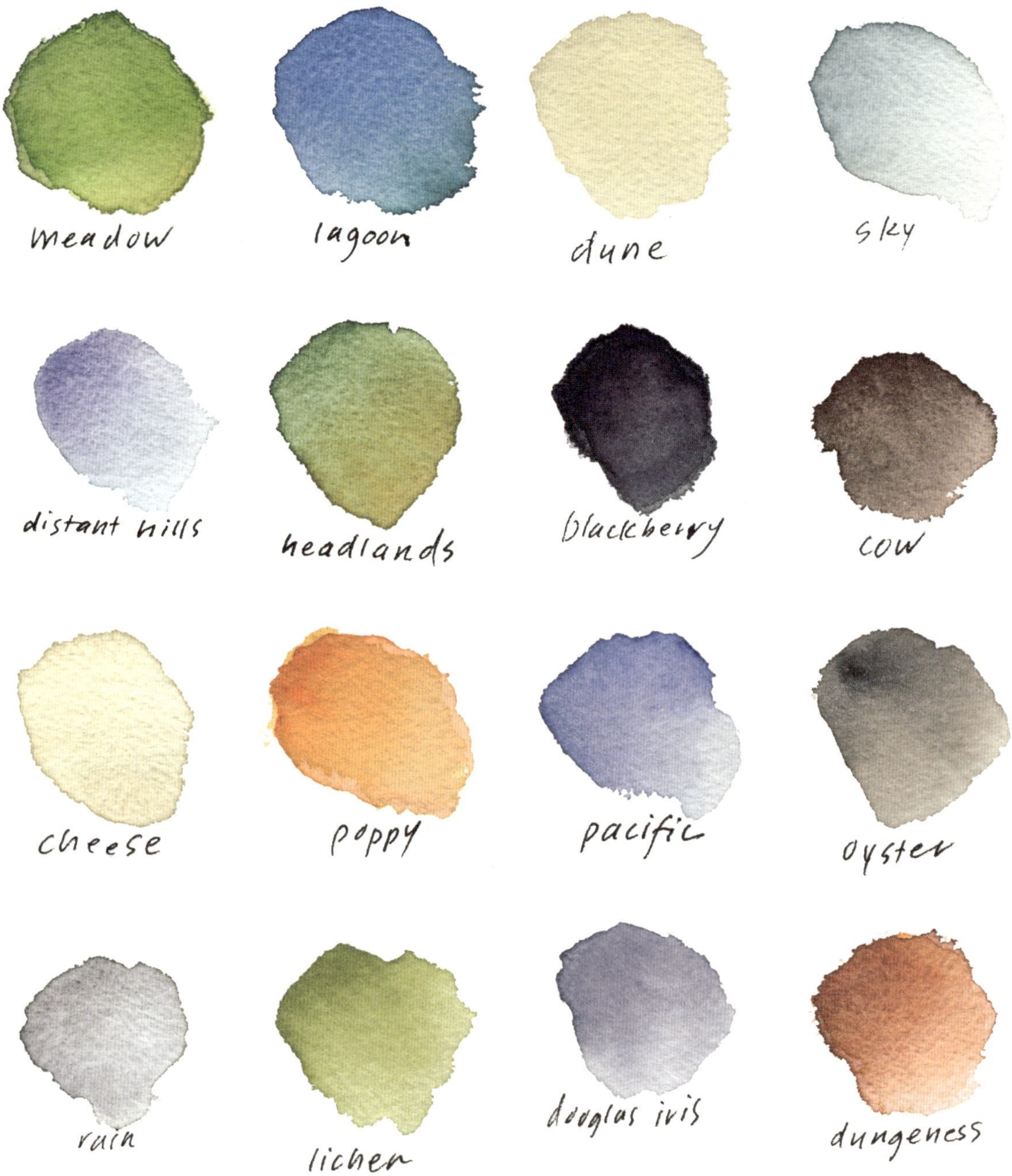
meadow
lagoon
dune
sky
distant hills
headlands
blackberry
cow
cheese
poppy
pacific
oyster
rain
lichen
douglas iris
dungeness

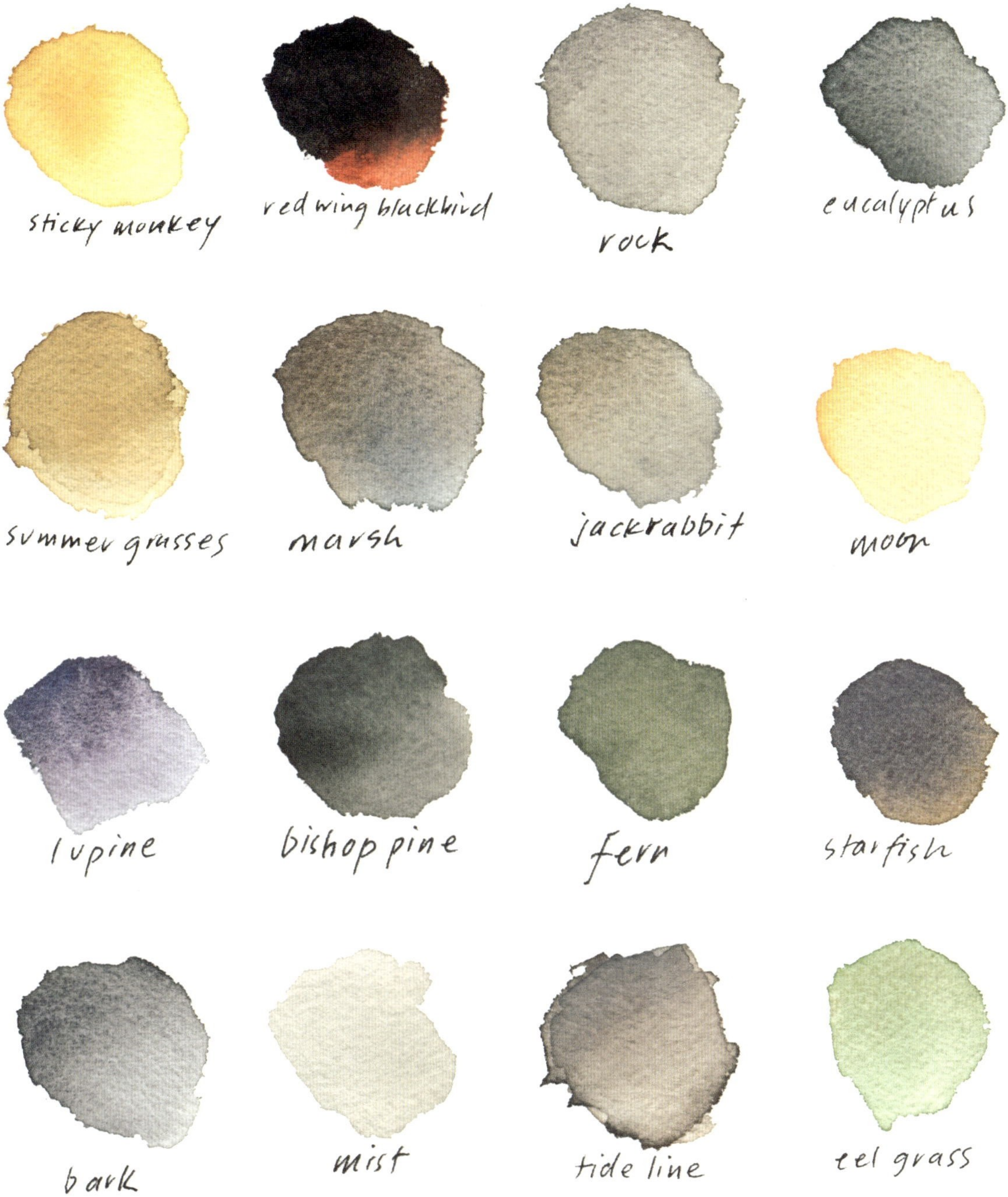
sticky monkey
red wing blackbird
rock
eucalyptus
summer grasses
marsh
jackrabbit
moon
lupine
bishop pine
fern
starfish
bark
mist
tide line
eel grass

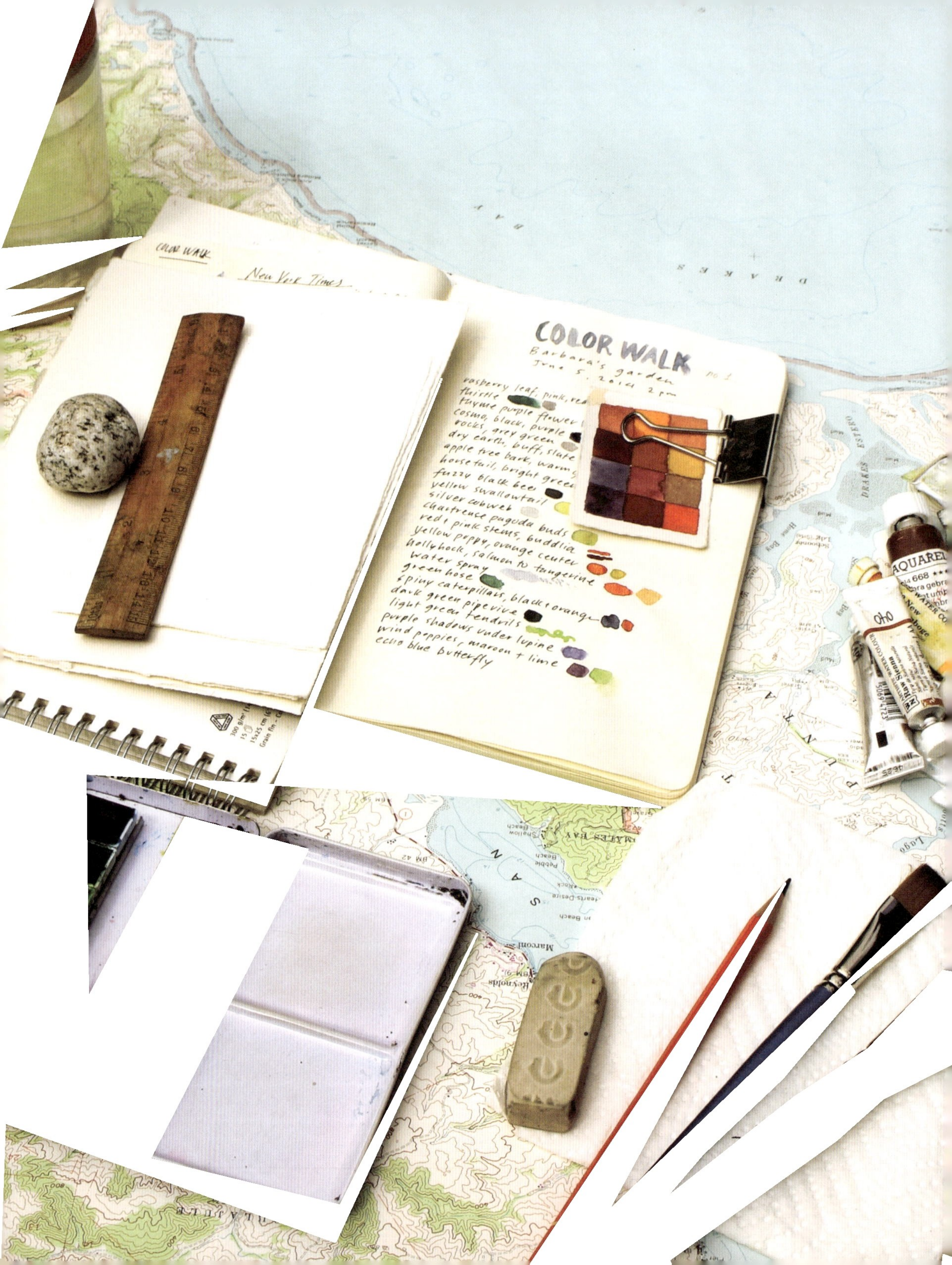
COLOR WALK
New York Times
COLOR WALK
Barbara's garden
June 5, 2014 2pm
no 1
raspberry leaf, pink, red
thistle
thyme purple flower
cosmo, black, purple
rocks, grey green
dry earth, buff, slate
apple tree bark, warm
horsetail, bright green
fuzzy black bee
yellow swallowtail
silver cobweb
chartreuse pagoda buds
red + pink stems, buddlia
yellow poppy, orange center
hollyhock, salmon to tangerine
water spray
green hose
spiny caterpillars, black + orange
dark green pipevine
light green tendrils
purple shadows under lupine
wind poppies, maroon + lime
echo blue butterfly
AQUAREL

CHAPTER TWO

Getting Started: Materials, Preparation & Techniques

A few essential materials and techniques are all you need to get started with watercolors and create color palettes. The quality of the papers, pigments, and brushes makes a big difference, so buy the best you can afford. Simple but high-quality materials can create wonderful results.

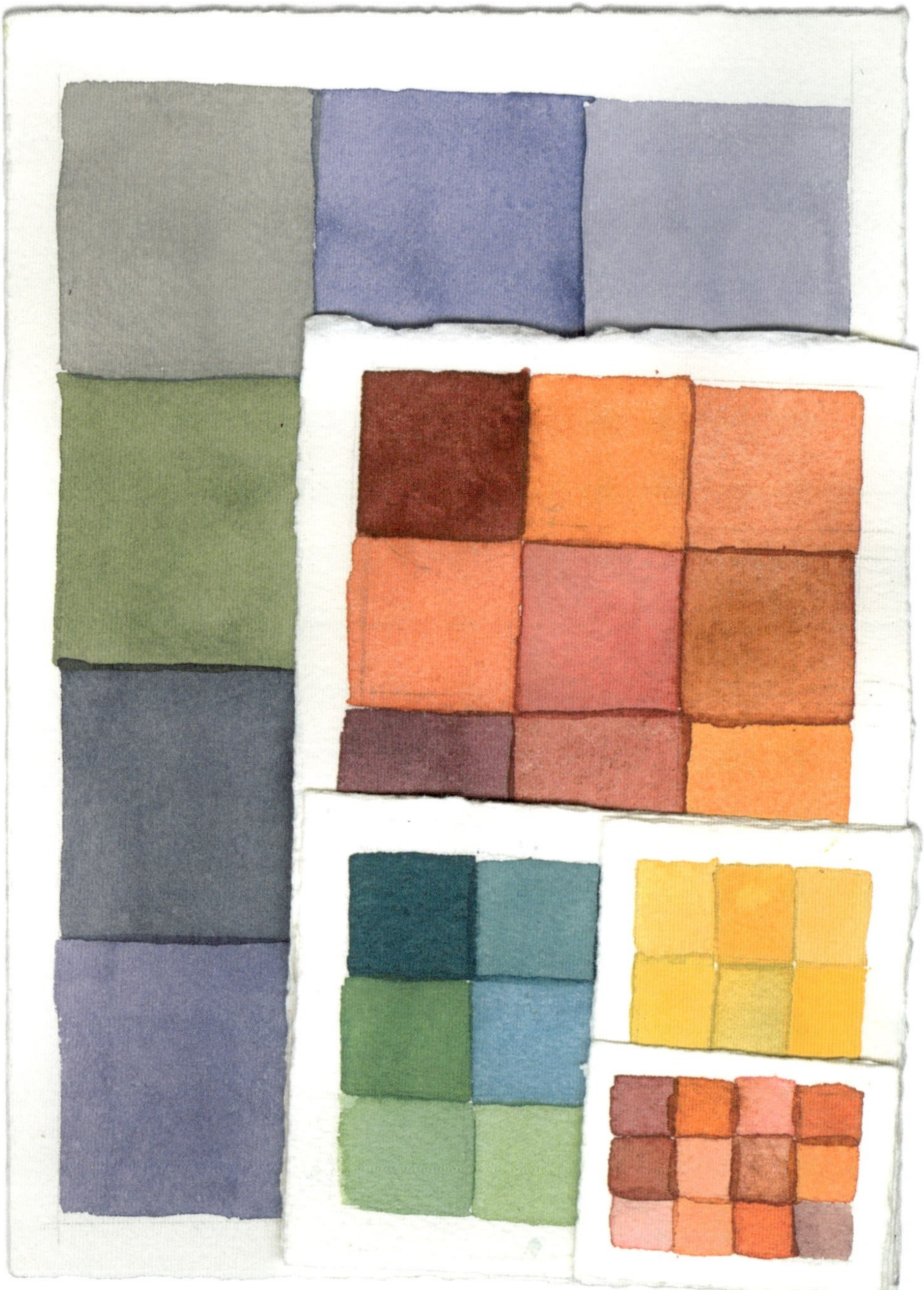

One 20" x 30" piece of watercolor paper can yield a variety of sizes to work with.

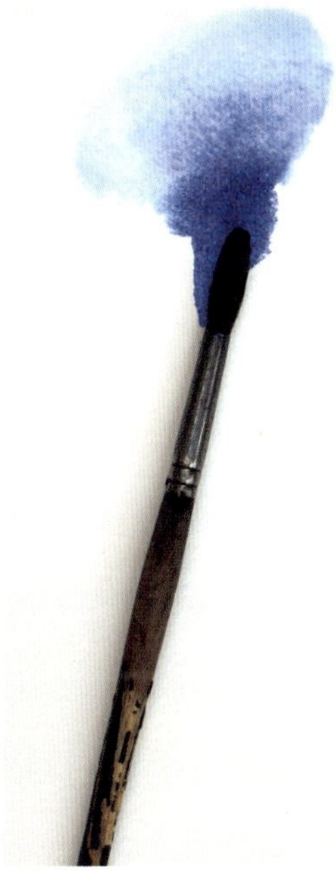

MATERIALS

Essential Equipment

- A pencil and pencil sharpener
- Kneaded or white eraser
- 0.5" and 0.75" flat brushes (inexpensive synthetic brushes are fine)
- Cold press 140 lb. watercolor paper (Arches or Winsor & Newton brands are good) or a bound watercolor journal
- Watercolor tubes (Winsor & Newton and Sennelier are good quality) or pans of 8 or 16 colors (Prang or the Winsor & Newton travel set are good). These are the color tubes I use:

* Permanent alizarin crimson	Cerulean blue
** Cadmium red light or medium	Yellow ochre
Permanent rose	* Lemon yellow
* Ultramarine blue	** Aurelian yellow
** Pthalo (or Prussian) blue	Burnt sienna
Cobalt blue	Burnt umber

  To start with just a few colors, use Triad 1 (*) for a bright palette and Triad 2 (**) for a versatile palette (see chapter 7, Color Mixing).
- Portable drawing board
- Clips or tape for securing paper onto the board
- 2 small water jars with watertight lids: one for mixing, one for cleaning
- A portable watercolor palette for mixing colors (if using a paint box, you can mix on the inside of the cover)
- Paper towels

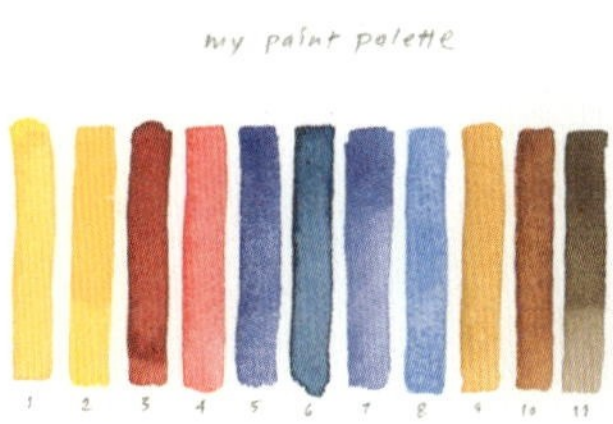

Optional Equipment

- Medium-size travel brushes with water reservoir in handle
- Size 8 round brush
- Bone folder
- Ruler
- Field stool

PREPARATION

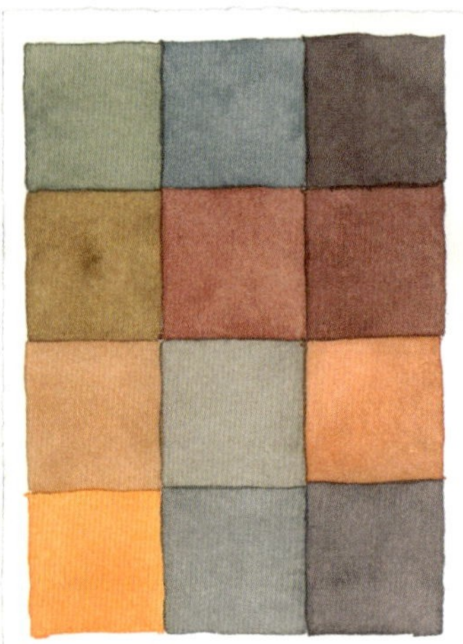

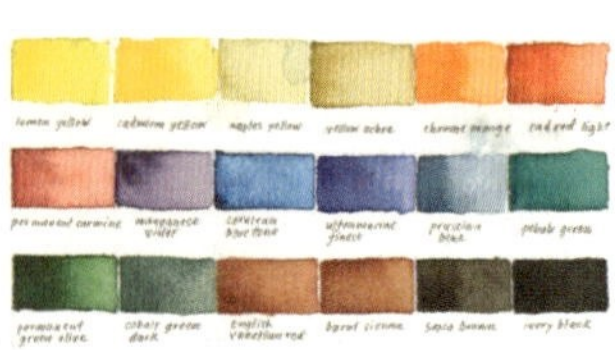

Paper Size & Grid

I like to use a 5.5" x 7.5" sheet of paper when painting a color palette. A 20" x 30" piece of watercolor paper is a good place to start for a variety of paper sizes; fold it in half, creasing with a bone folder a few times, then tear. Keep folding and tearing until you have the sizes you want.

On one of the pieces, lightly pencil in a frame about a half-inch from the edge to leave room for notes, and draw a 12-box grid. A grid allows you to create a replicable structure so you can compare palettes over time. Experiment with your own dimensions and grid.

Pigments & Color Theory

Whether you are working with tube or pan pigments, there are hundreds of colors to make by mixing paint. Start by painting swatches of all your colors so you know what you are working with.

From color theory we know that any three primary colors, a triad, can make many colors that will be harmonious. I work with a variety of triads—various blues, reds, and yellows—to achieve a larger range of bright and subdued colors. I sometimes use an even more limited palette of just two colors, but I'm also quick to bend the rules and experiment with other color mixes. Mixing color and water in different proportions can create thousands of colors. Different palettes are useful for different subjects and views.

The beauty of working with tubes is that you can customize your own palettes. I know painters who bring different sets of colors with them, depending on where they are traveling: for example, in the American Southwest where there are warm, subdued earth colors, or in India, with its riot of color.

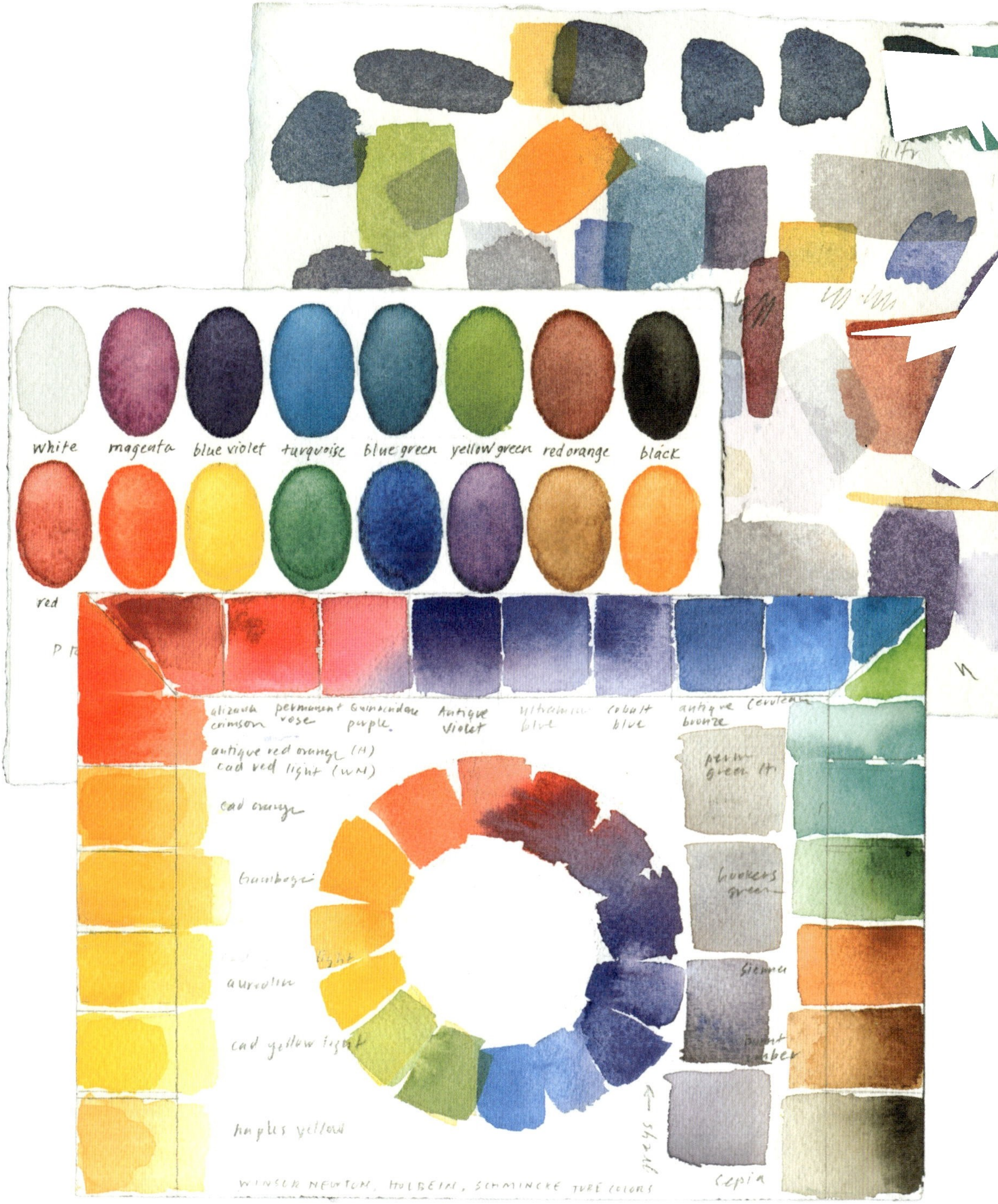
white
magenta
blue violet
turquoise
blue green
yellow green
red orange
black
red
alizarin crimson
permanent rose
Quinacridone purple
Antique violet
ultramarine blue
cobalt blue
antique bronze
cerulean
antique red orange (H)
cad red light (WN)
cad orange
Gamboge
aureolin
cad yellow light
naples yellow
hookers green
sepia
grays
WINSOR NEWTON, HOLBEIN, SCHMINCKE TUBE COLORS

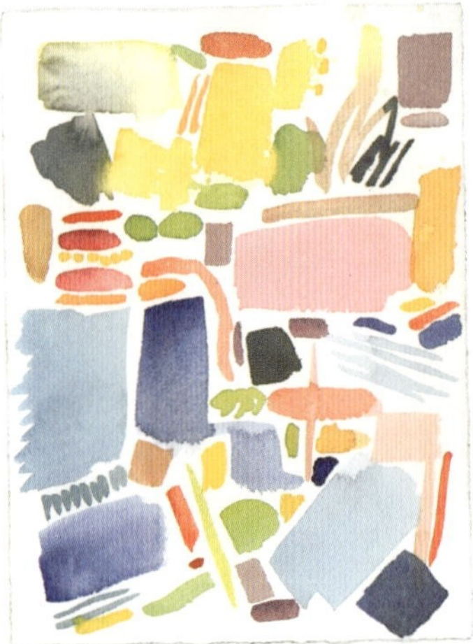

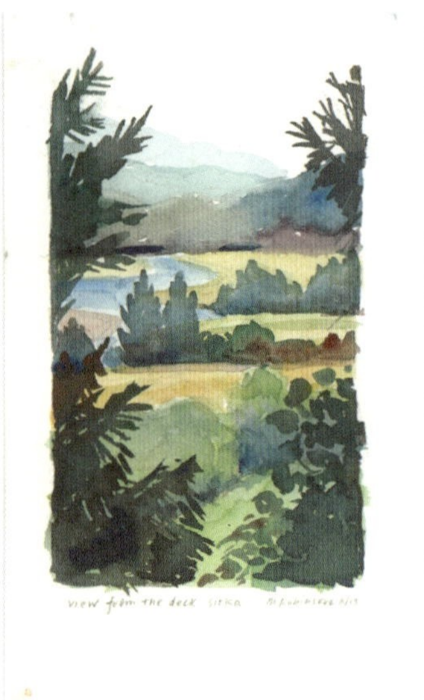

TECHNIQUE

Brush Marks

Get to know your brushes and explore the marks they make. Hold the brush lightly; think of it as an extension of your hand. Use large brushes to encourage a sense of freedom. Whether a square or a line, thin or fat, blob, blip, or spatter, making marks is an expressive part of painting—your vocabulary. Marks contain energy: some are quick and gestural while others can be slow and detailed. Some marks are brimming with pigments while others hold only trace amounts of color. Use a lot of water and lots of pigment to explore a variety of marks.

Painting

Watercolors are both evocative and surprising. Embrace their dynamic and spontaneous nature, as they lend to painting quick impressions. Transparent layering and overlapping of colors can create a multitude of subtle effects.

Make sure your paintbrush is clean before you reach for another color (blot on a paper towel).

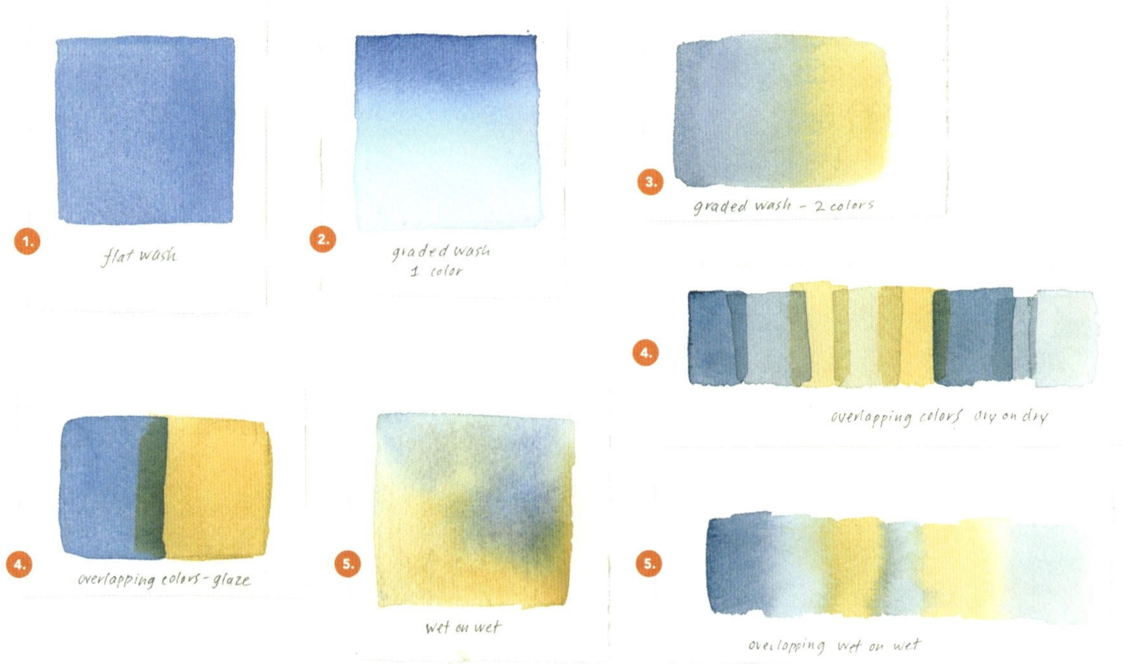

1. Flat (one-color) wash

Dip your brush in water, pick up some pigment, and lay it down on the page. For the next stroke, pick up more water and pigment and overlap the edge of the wet mark you have just painted. Tilt the paper as you apply the color. To overlap colors, apply a second pigment over the dry wash.

2. Graded wash

Start with a dark band of color. With each stroke, use more water to lighten the color as you go down the page.

3. Two-color graded wash

On damp paper, lay a band of color on one side and then a band of color on the other side, and let the colors run into one another in the middle.

4. Glazing

Apply a thin layer of color over a dry wash to produce a new color.

5. Wet on wet

Wet the paper with your brush, wait a moment, then drop in colors from a brush charged with concentrated paint.

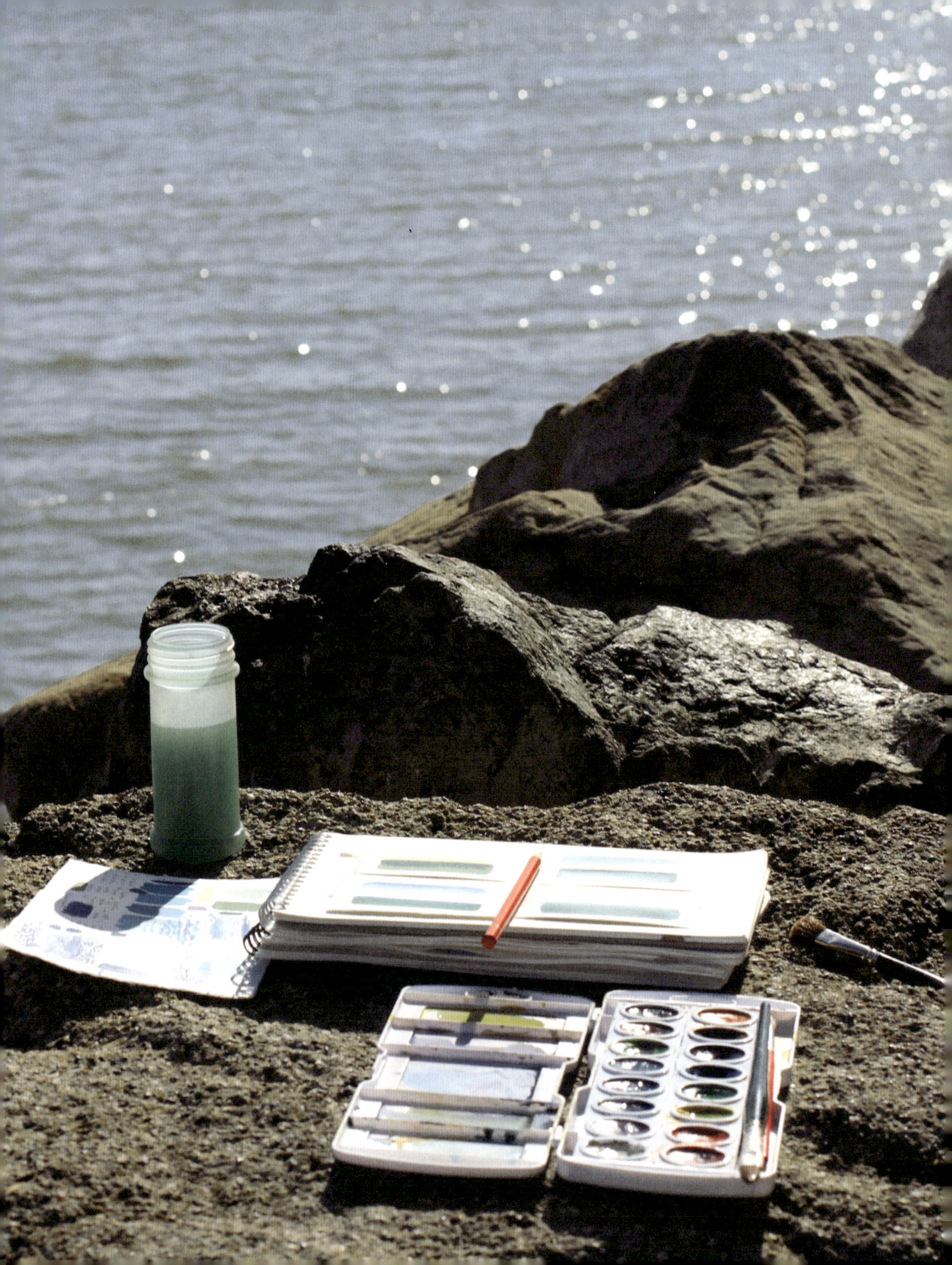

CHAPTER THREE

Look Around You: Elements of Place

The practices in this book open the door to looking at color, engaging with it, and experimenting as you go. This is about a process. Have fun with these practices and jump in!

Here's what I do in the field. I sit down and tune into my senses—sight, sound, touch. I may close my eyes, then open them again and take in the view, finding something I like. I look at one color and try to match it with paint, trying out color mixes on test paper. When I'm satisfied, I put that color down on my palette.

Focus on the elements of place: habitat, light, weather, and season. They will help ground you to wherever you are. They are all interconnected and influence one another in unique ways depending on the time of day or within a season.

Pick a color and try to match it. If the first mark doesn't look quite right, keep mixing, making it warmer or cooler, darker or lighter, adjusting the color until you find what you want, then put that one down on the palette as well and move on to the next color you see. Once you've made your mark, resist the temptation to go over it and you'll have cleaner colors.

Consider working on more than one color palette at a time. That way, the paint can dry on one while you shift your attention to another—perhaps another view or another set of colors from the same view.

A NOTE ON THE PHOTOGRAPHS

The photographs are here for reference, so you can see where my color palettes come from. I much prefer to work directly from nature. I sit and absorb a place. The color relationships between land, sky, water, weather conditions, quality of light, time of day, and the angle of the sun and shadows—all of these add up to fully experiencing your surroundings and being truthful to the moment.

HABITAT

Wherever you are—whether in a meadow or a city—you can observe and paint the colors of the local habitat. Habitat is just what you see around you: from sidewalk, floor, or path to buildings, trees, or mountains. The angle of the sun. The clouds in the sky. Each habitat is a collection of colors.

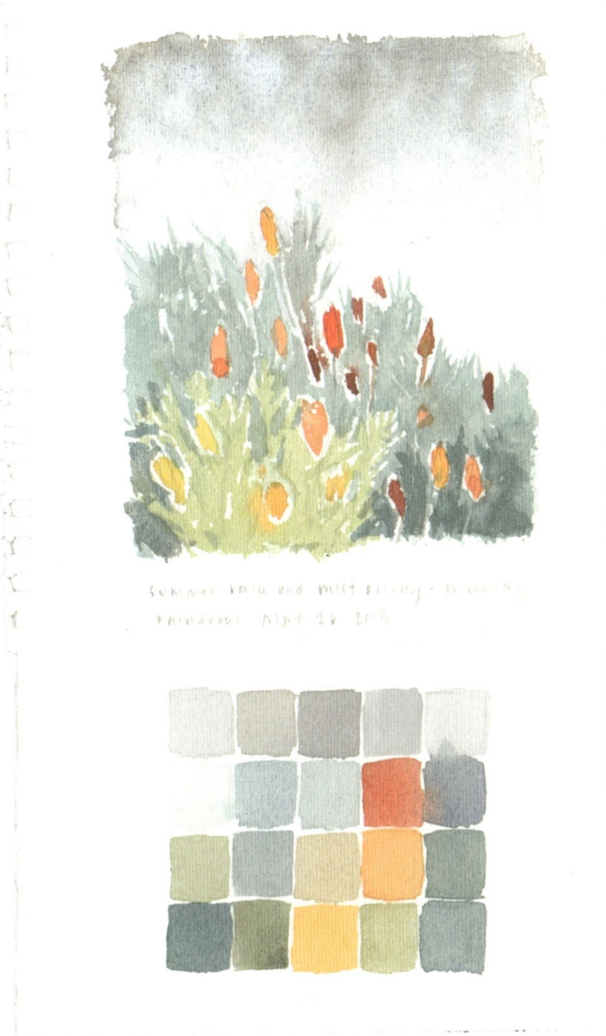

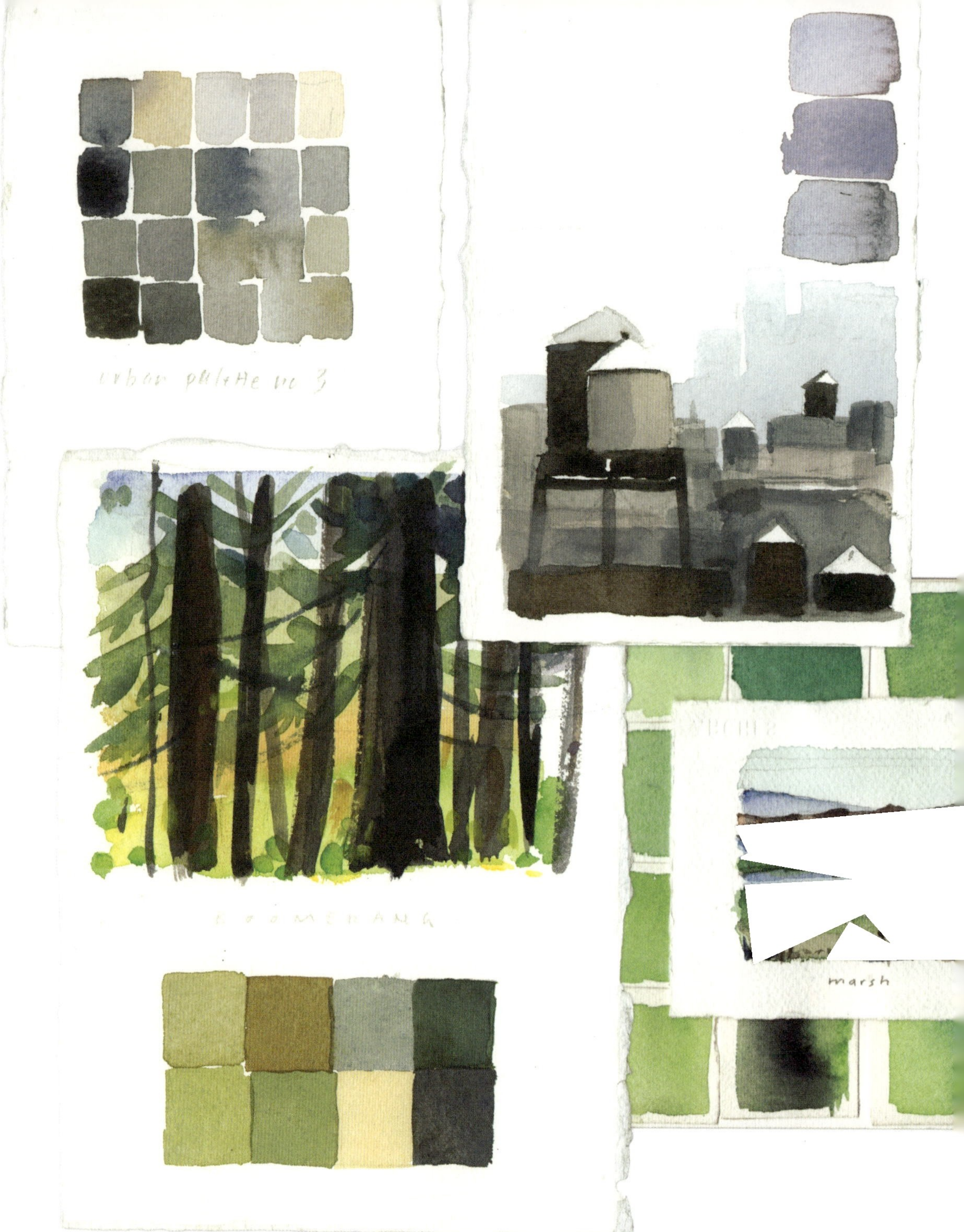
urban palette no 3
BOOMERANG
marsh

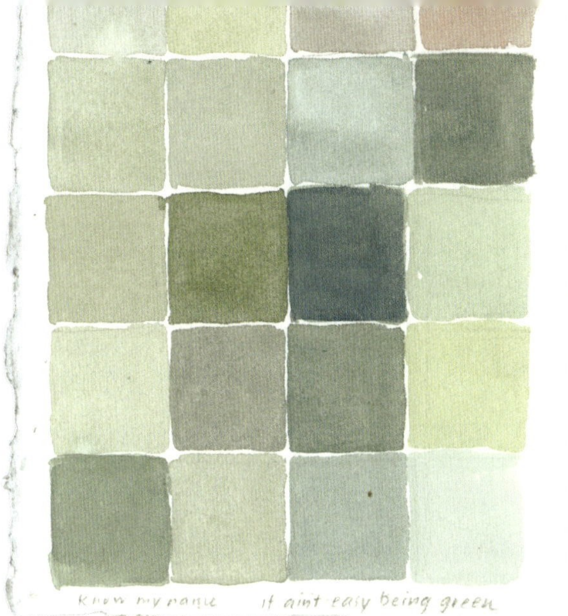

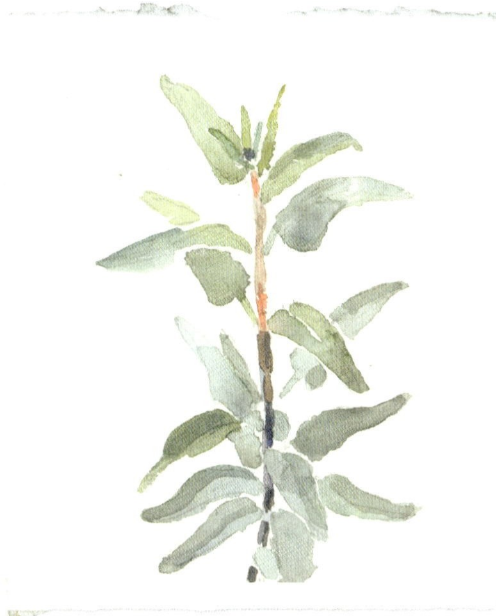

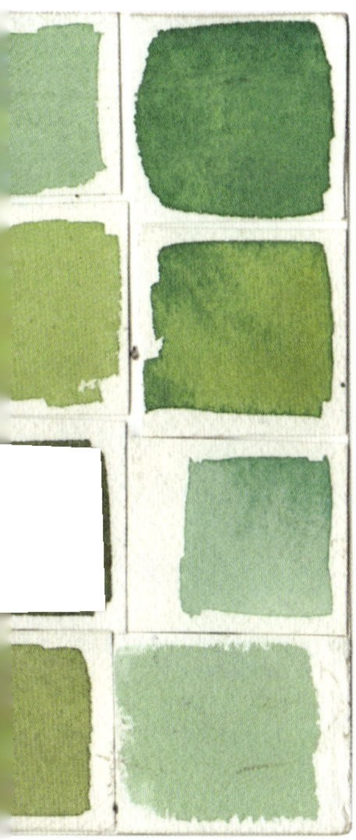

PRACTICE

- Bring your paints and find a comfortable place to sit. Take a moment and allow yourself to drop into this place. Close your eyes and open them—what colors do you see? Now look more closely. What are the colors beneath your feet? What are the colors at eye level? Overhead, do you see sky, tree branches, clouds, or the tops of high buildings? Notice the time of day and where the sun is in the sky. Can you see the moon? What is the season?

- Take your piece of paper and start with the color you see most of. What color sits next to that color? What color do you see traveling across a leaf or up the side of a building?

- Next, what color do you see least of? What proportion of the scene does each color take up? Notice how color takes on different forms—a version of gray may present itself as cloud, granite, or bark. Notice the feeling of the brush in your hand as it moves across the paper. As I am painting, I often think, "In through my eyes and out through my hand."

- Shift your perspective. If you are sitting, do a color palette while standing; if you are standing, try one sitting. What differences do you see?

- Begin a color library of your local habitat, cataloging the spectrum of colors and how they change throughout the seasons.

LIGHT

Light gives birth to color. Notice where light lives—on the facade of a building, on the back of a bird flying through the sky, in a sunflower tracing the path of the sun. Some colors are naturally light in feeling (yellow) and others are dark (purple, ultramarine blue). Light colors seem to float, while darker colors feel rooted.

Light changes subtly as the sun shifts with the time of day and the seasons. My favorite times to catch the color of a place are in the early morning, later afternoon, and at sunset, when colors take on more depth. Low in the sky, the sun sends out a warm golden glow and the long shadows add rhythm and texture. Summer days are wonderful for painting outdoors because of the long hours and abundance of light.

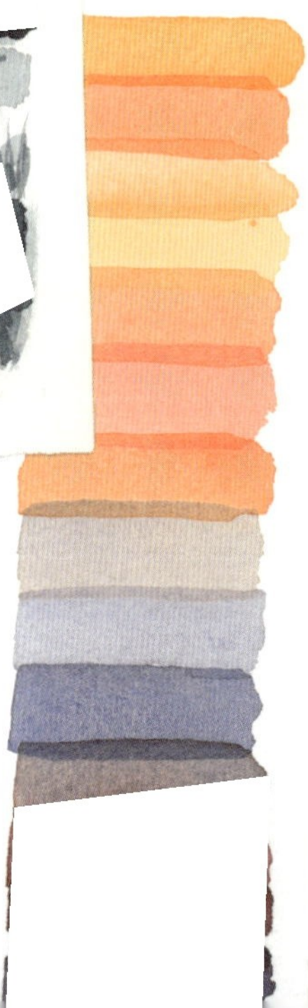

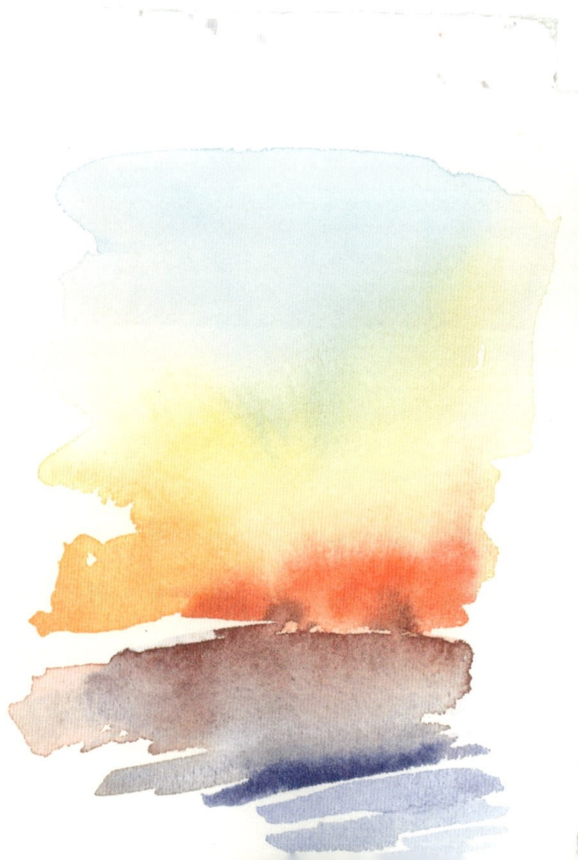

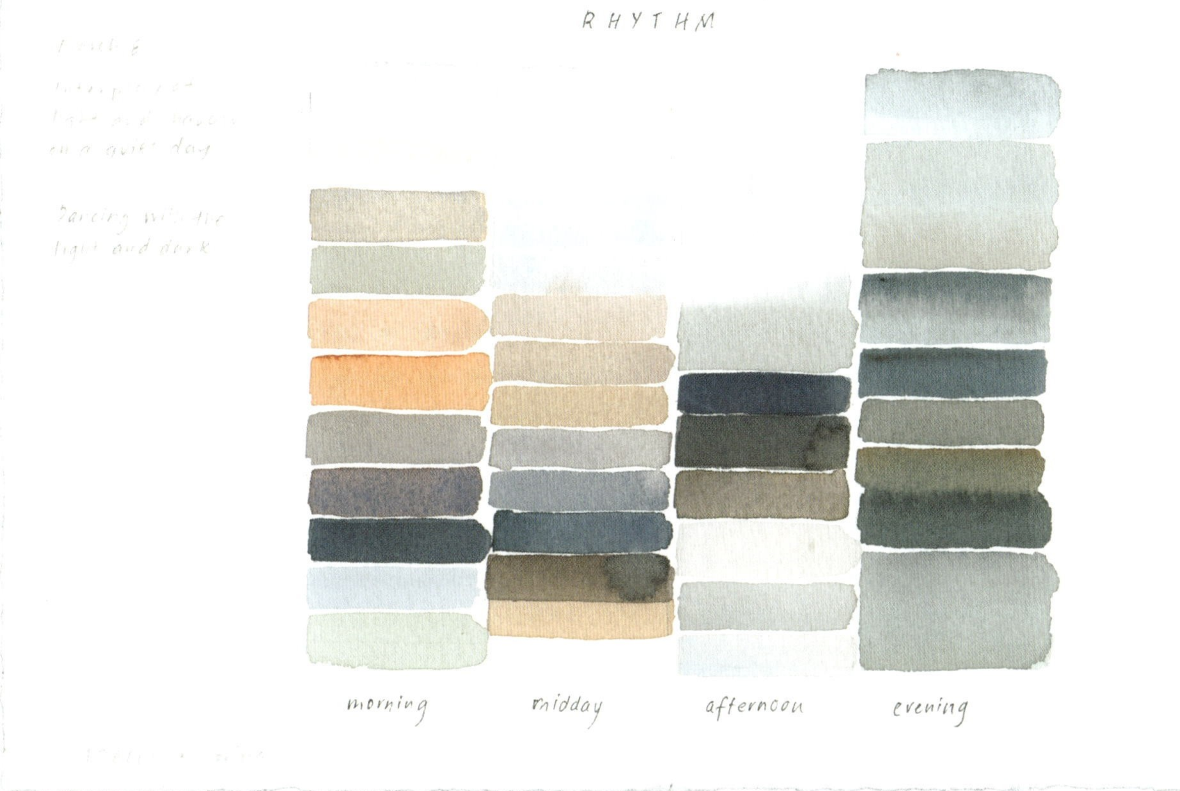

PRACTICE

- Paint a series of palettes at the same time each day—either the first hour of light after sunrise or the last hour of light before sunset (both called the "golden hour"). In the city, observe the color in the shadows cast by the buildings. Work quickly, as the light changes fast. Try to capture the patterns of light and dark. Don't worry if you don't get it right—it will come back again tomorrow.
- Track color throughout the day, making a connection to the rotation of the earth. Be aware of warm and cool tones and the interplay of light and shadow. Select a simple view and create palettes at early morning, midday, and evening. On a sunny day, colors are typically warmer in the morning and shift to cool as the sun arcs overhead, then back to warm as the sun is setting. Even on foggy or cloudy days, you can sense a brightening and the movement of the sun.

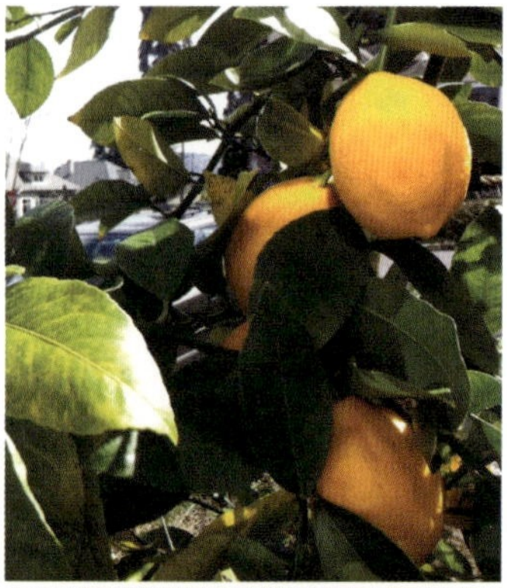

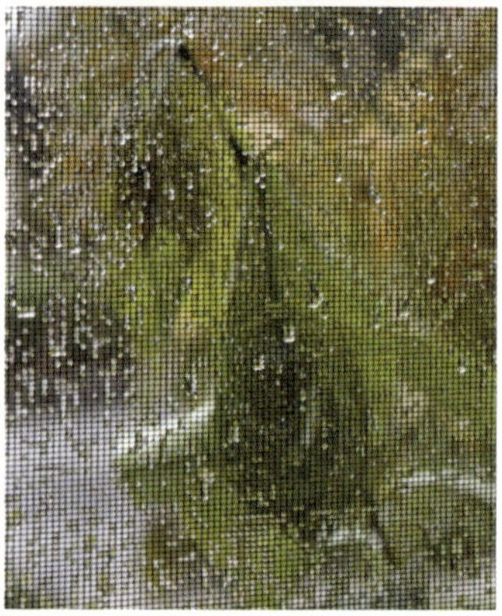

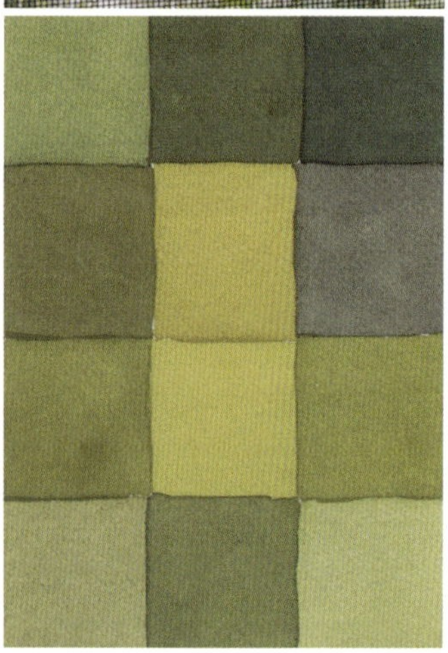

WEATHER

Imagine a hot, dry sun in the desert, a blizzard in Chicago, or spring rain along the coast. Rain, snow, sleet, sun, wind—how do they change what you see in a place?

During a winter storm in Inverness, California, rain, mist, and fog soften the view, creating muted notes of harmonious color. This is the day to paint wet on wet. Painting with more water can capture the feeling of a rainy day, accentuating place and mood. The light is soft and the colors run together. There are no edges.

In New York City, I expect to paint monochromatic cityscapes but wake up to deep snow. Today, the world is brilliant white, blue, and purple. Bright sun brings out the color and the contrasts: the inky black of tree bark and branch against white snow. Water towers have little white triangular snow hats. I see drifts of snow and the yellow blur of taxis.

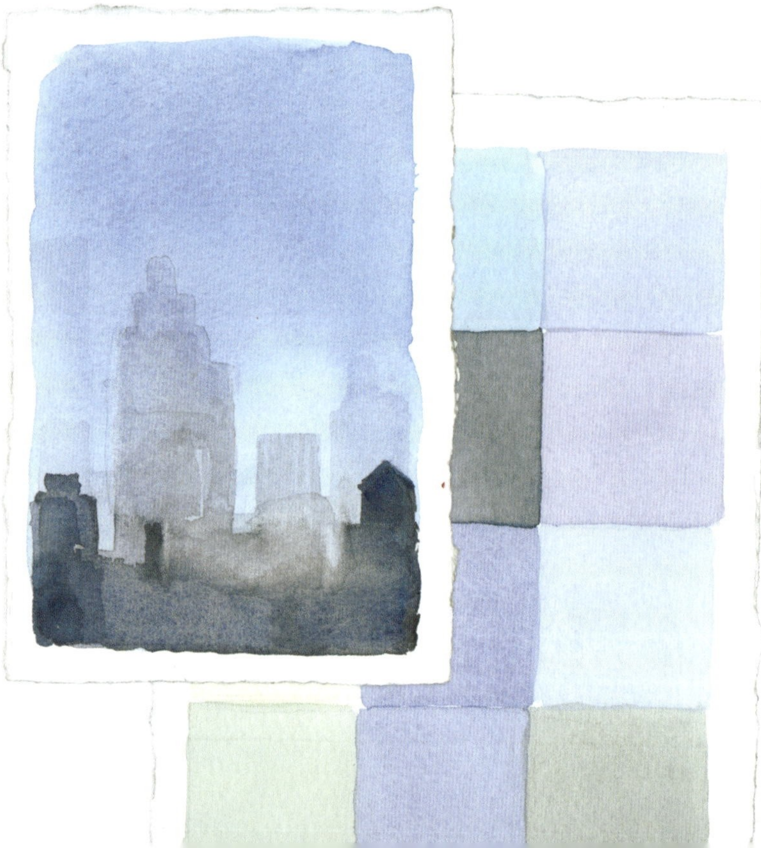

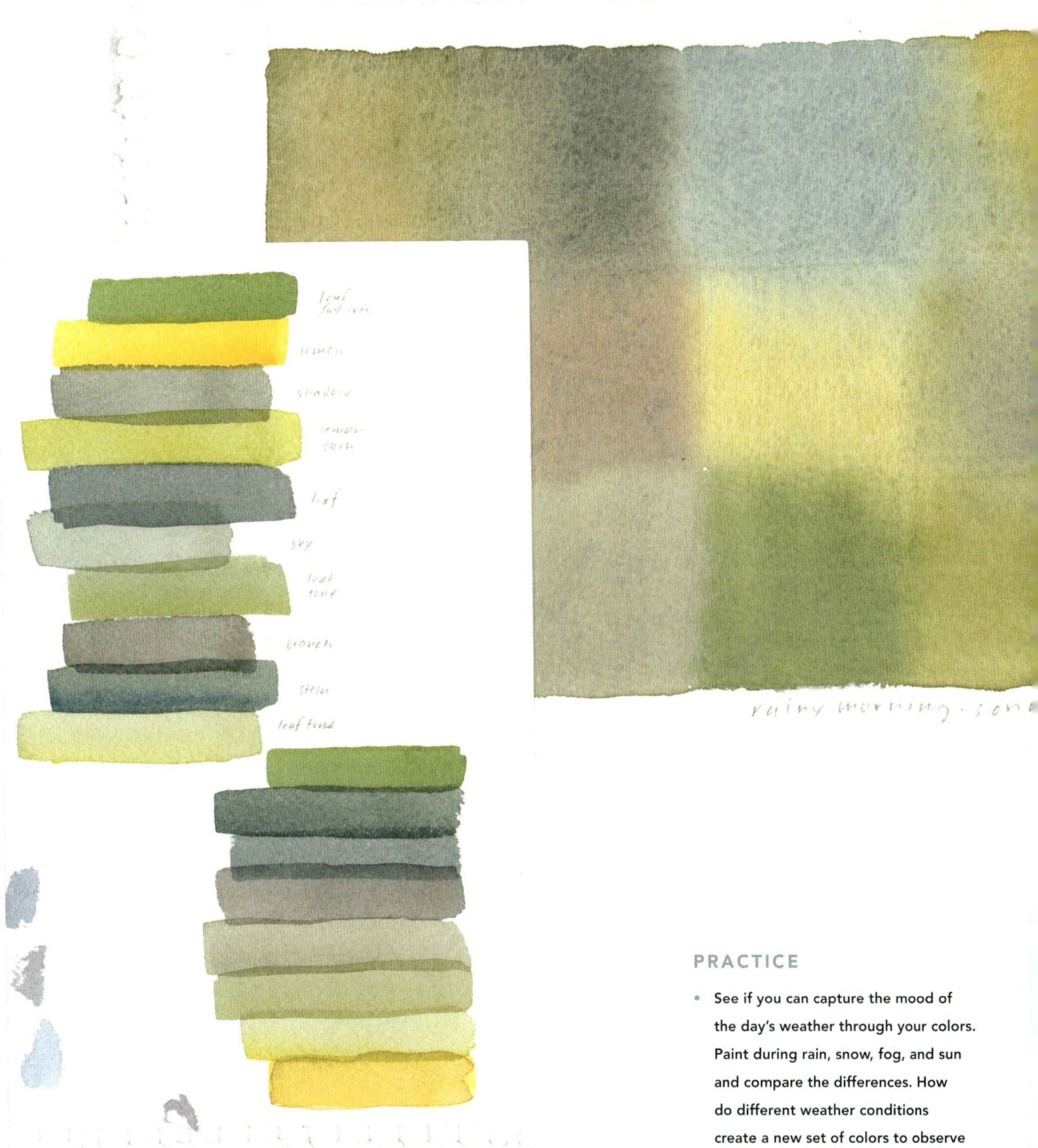

PRACTICE

- See if you can capture the mood of the day's weather through your colors. Paint during rain, snow, fog, and sun and compare the differences. How do different weather conditions create a new set of colors to observe and paint?

SEASONS

Years are marked by time and the shift of seasons as the Earth travels around the sun. On a cold dark February evening, I look at vibrant color palettes I created on a summer day sitting on a rock in the Sierra Nevada Mountains, and I can almost feel the warmth and light of that moment.

Each season has its own colors, and places have their own seasons. Making seasonal color palettes encourages you to consider time in a different way—in rotations around the sun rather than around the clock.

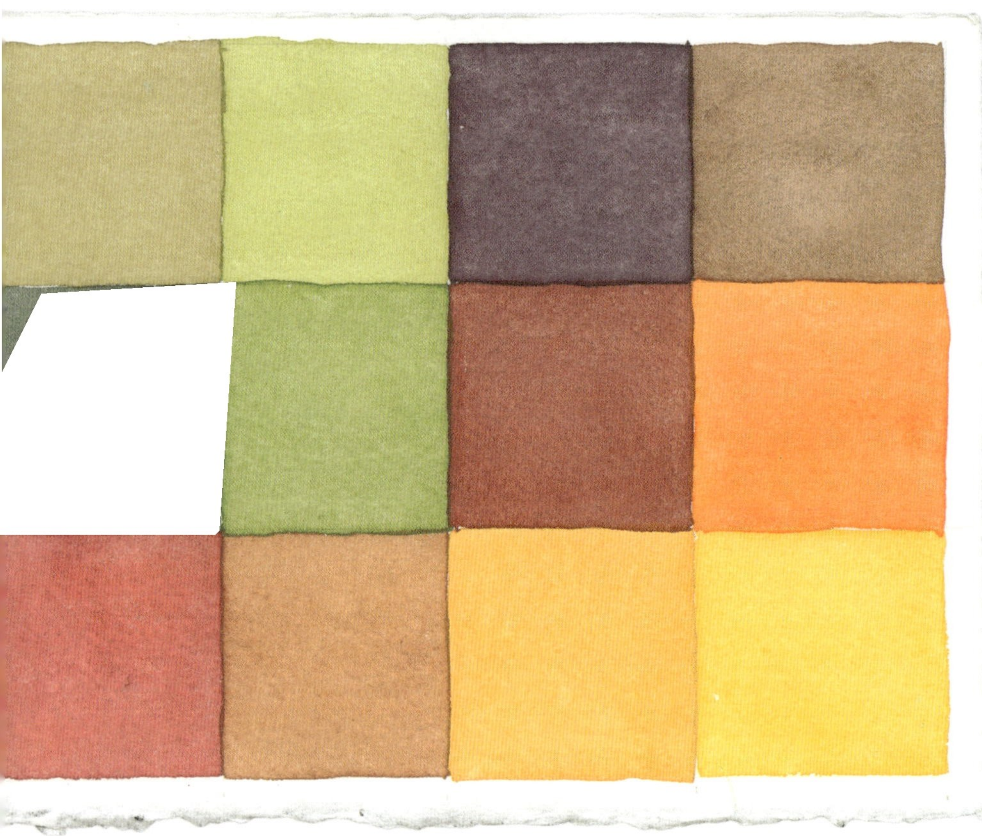

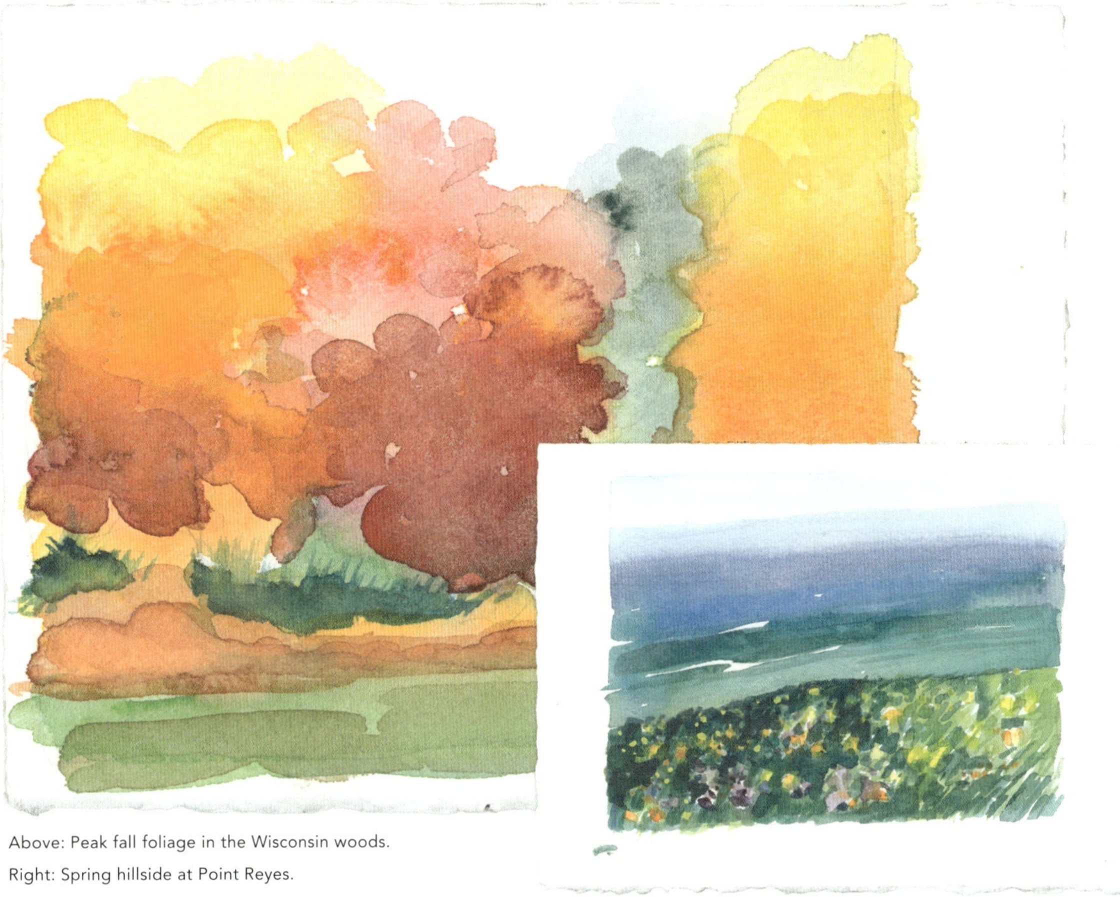

Above: Peak fall foliage in the Wisconsin woods.

Right: Spring hillside at Point Reyes.

PRACTICE

- Immerse yourself in one season. What are the colors that come to life in this season, in this light? Are colors brightening or fading? Every few days or weeks, make a palette of a scene or object that speaks to you of this season. It could be a bright new apple in fall, the view out your window in winter, or the sharp green growth of spring.
- Track a year in color, creating a color palette for each season. When you're done, look at the palettes together: How did the colors change with the seasons and the different effects of weather and intensities of light? What colors emerged in each new season as flowers bloomed and faded, grasses grew and died, snow or rain came and went?

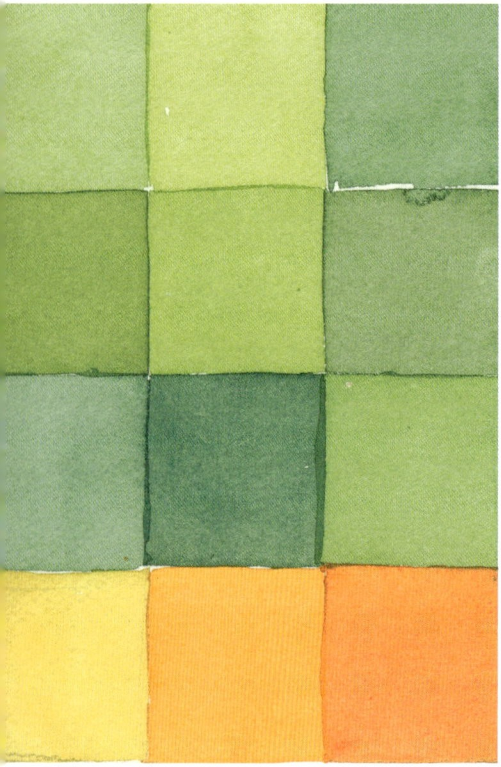

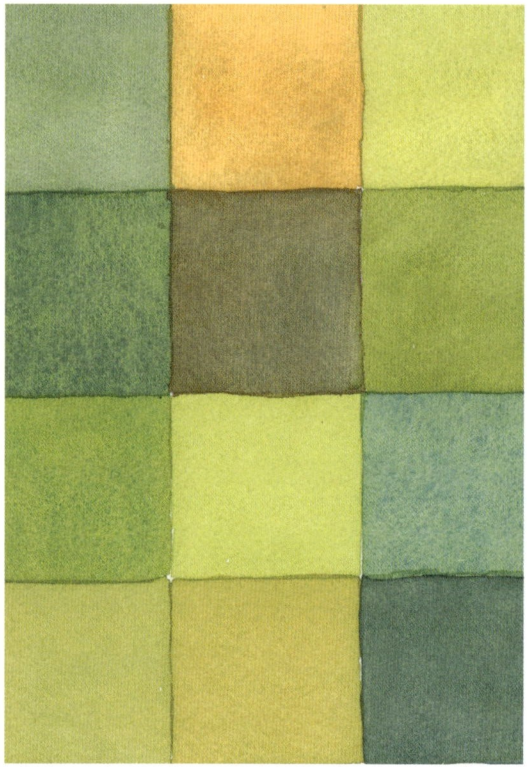

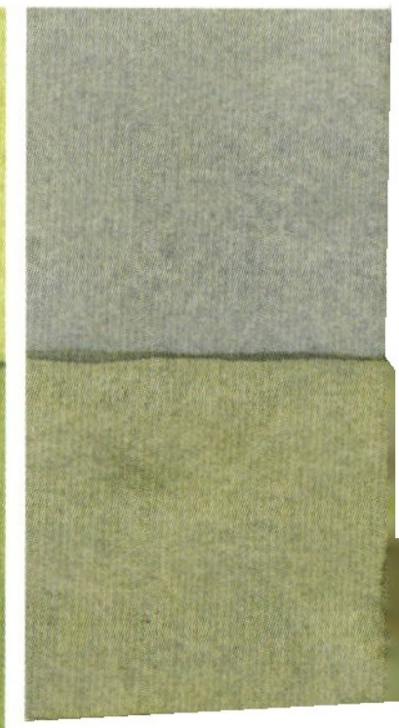

SEASONS: A YEAR IN COLOR

As an experiment, I decided to chart the colors of the specific landscape of Point Reyes over a period of a year to see what I might learn. I asked myself, How do colors change with the seasons and with the different effects of weather and intensities of light? What are the color relationships in the spring, when the hills are blanketed with the intense velvet green of new growth? Or in January, when the rising ocean mists and clear nights illuminate the hibernating grassland? What colors emerge from the parade of wildflowers? How are the colors of this place different from those of other places?

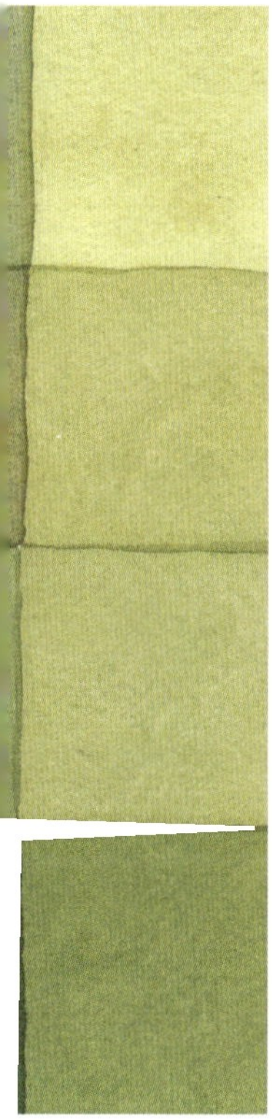

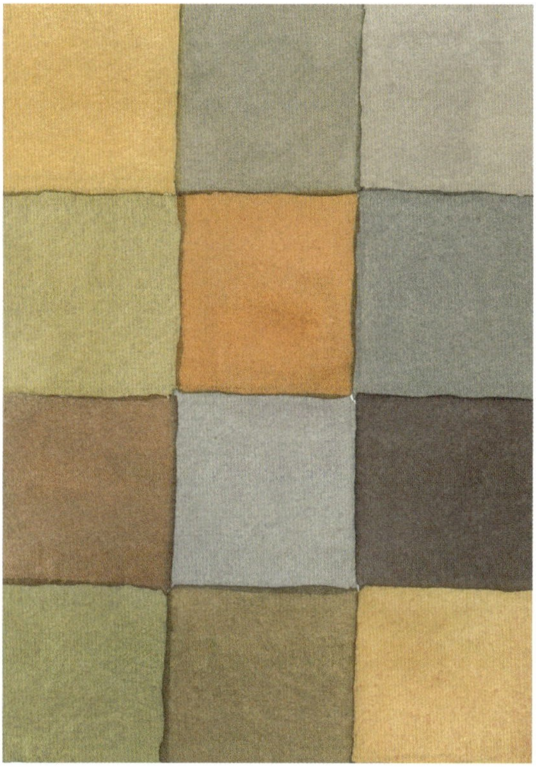

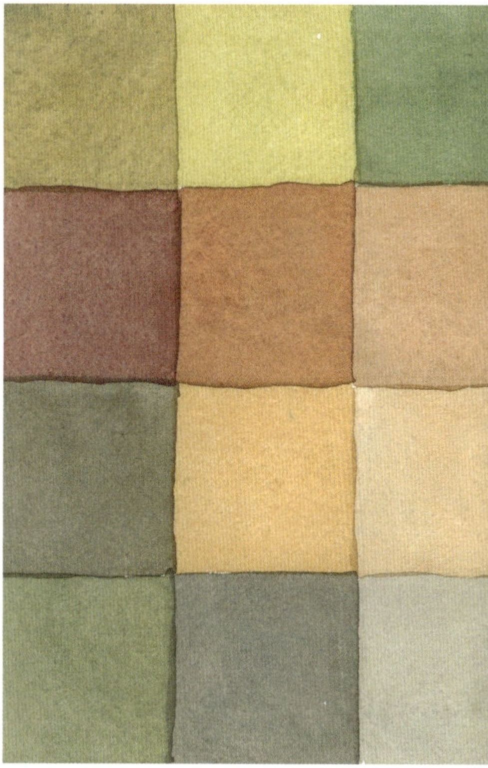

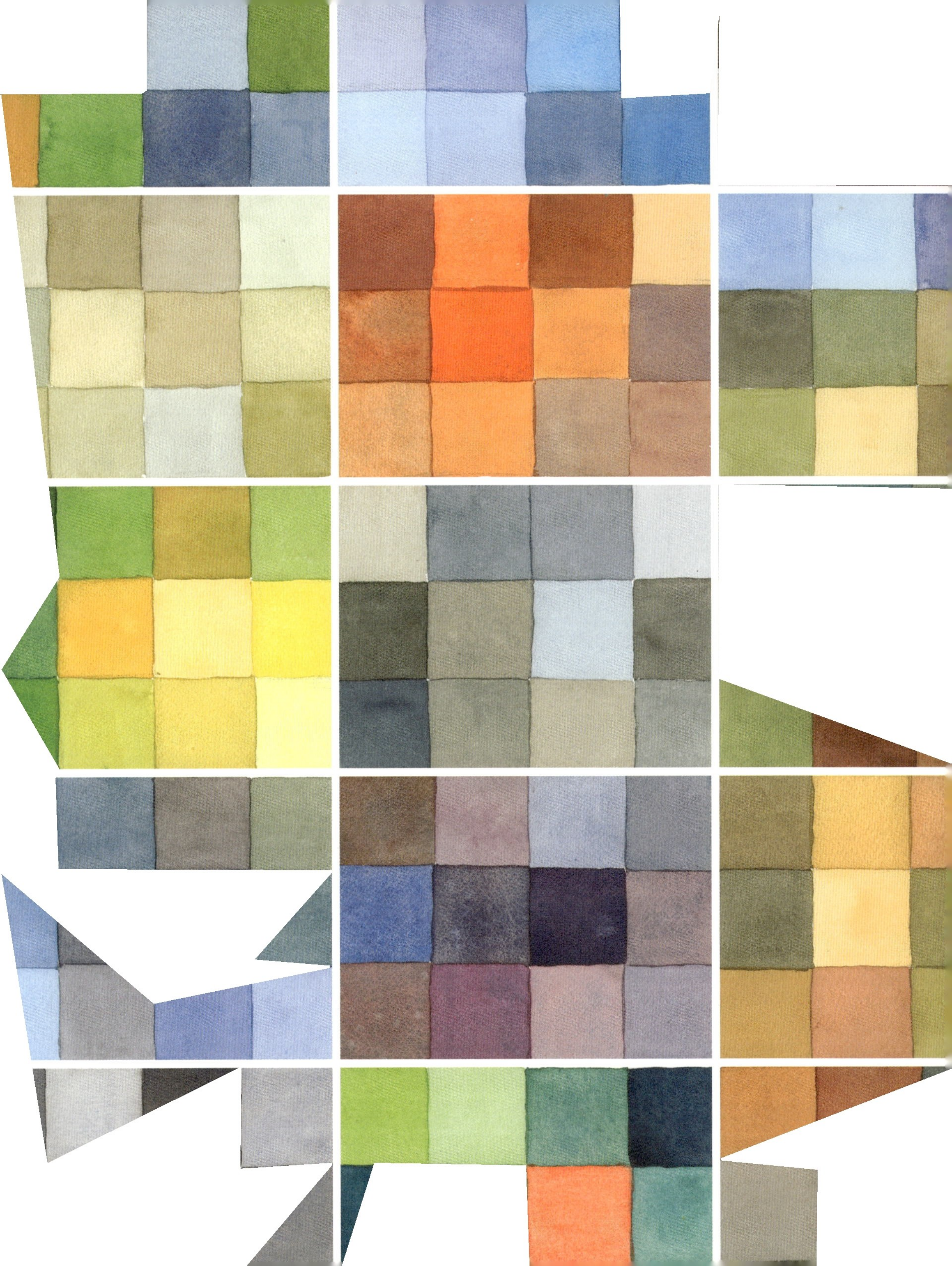

CHAPTER FOUR

World Color: Travel Journeys

As I've traveled the world, I've come to realize that I can take the process of observing place with me wherever I go. I slow down and become receptive to what I see, hear, and smell. In each location I visit, I wonder, what is the spirit of this place? And whether I am painting in my own backyard, on the edge of the ocean, in a small pueblo in Mexico, in the mountains of Kyrgyzstan, or in a corner of Portland, Oregon, I find that the active process of observing color and creating color palettes grounds me and allows me to engage with each unique place in a more substantial way.

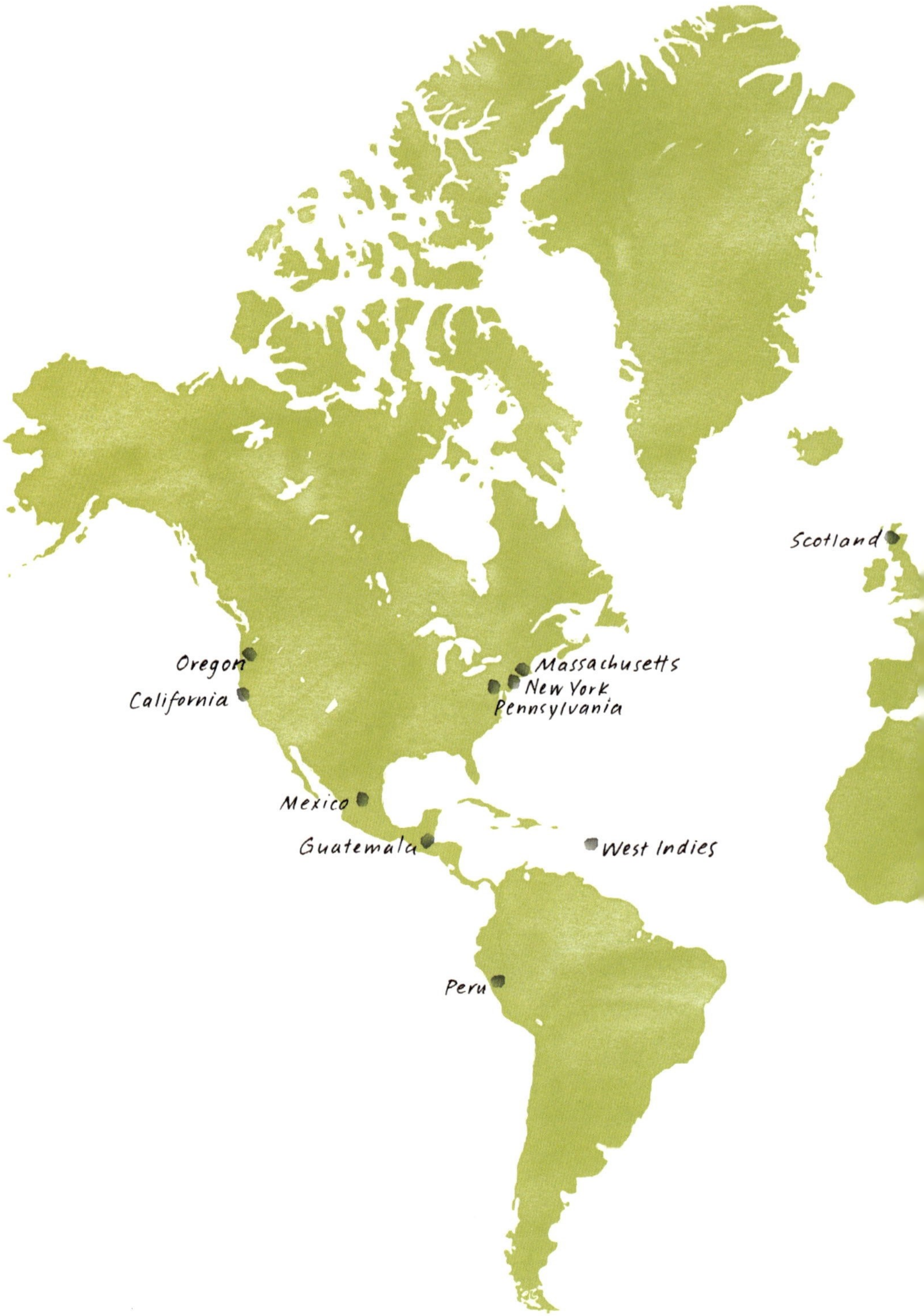
Scotland
Oregon
Massachusetts
New York
California
Pennsylvania
Mexico
Guatemala
West Indies
Peru

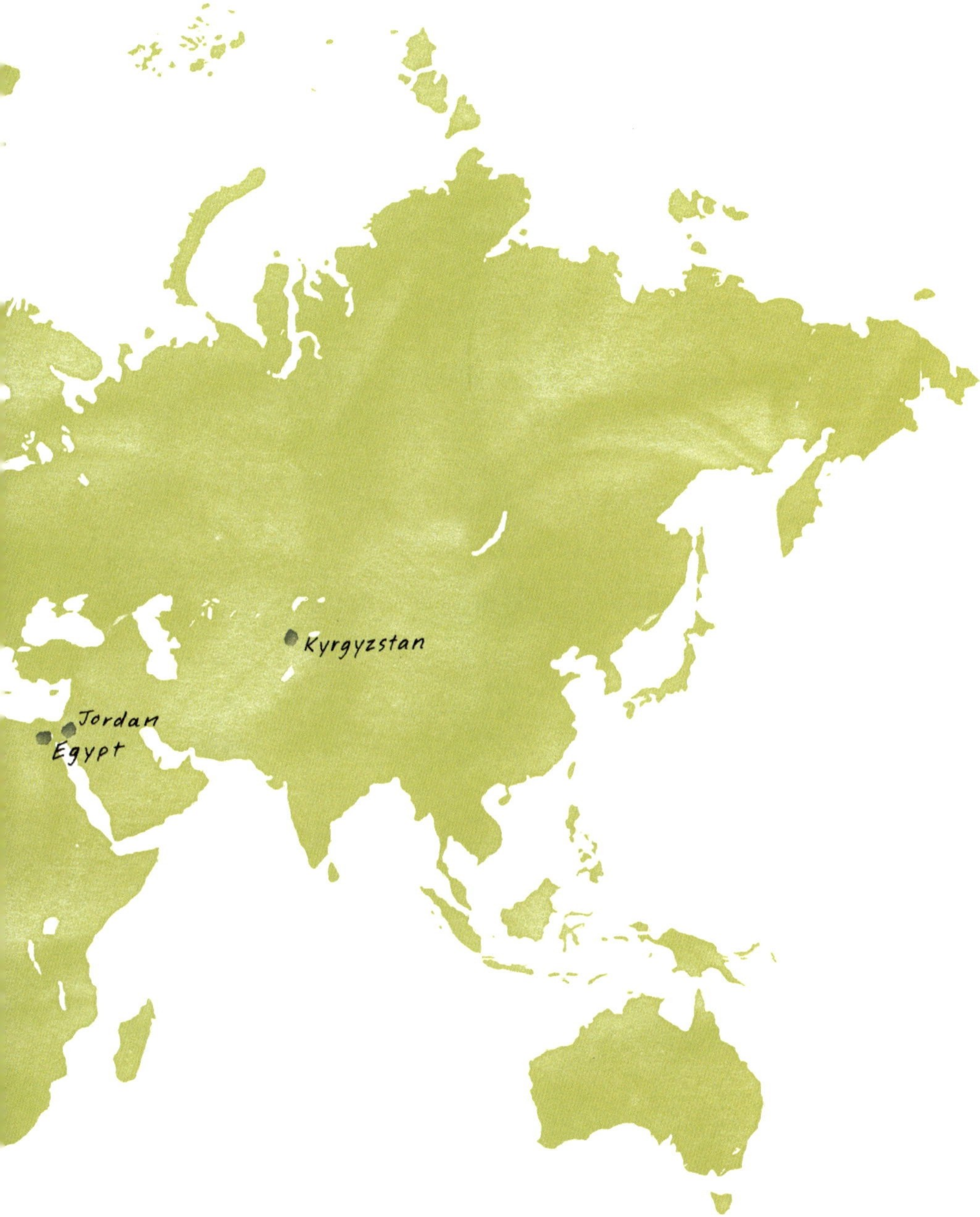
Kyrgyzstan
Jordan
Egypt

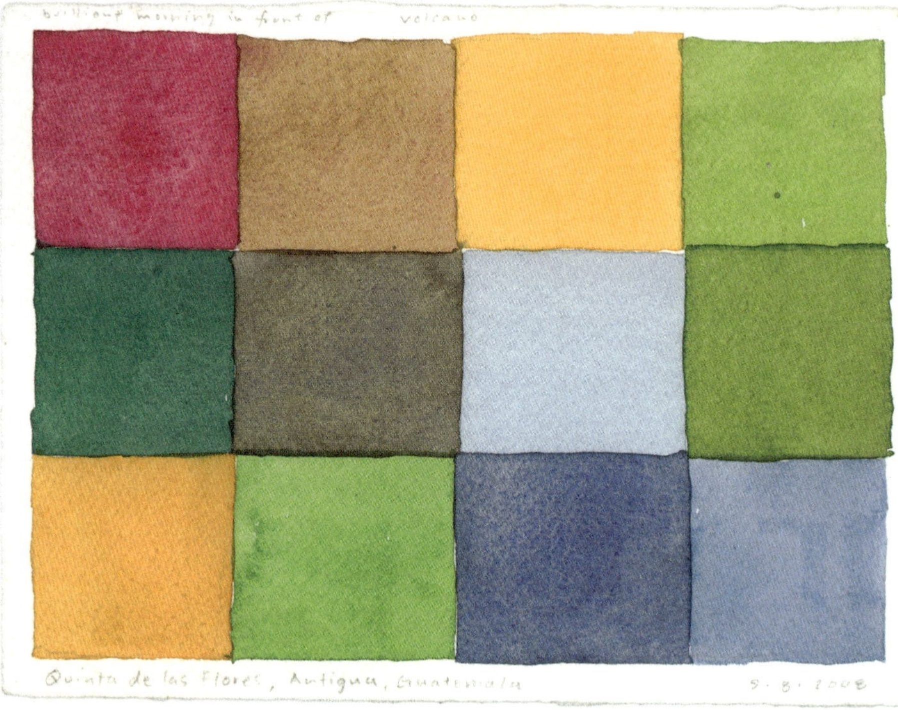
brilliant morning in front of volcano
Quinta de las Flores, Antigua, Guatemala
5 · 8 · 2008

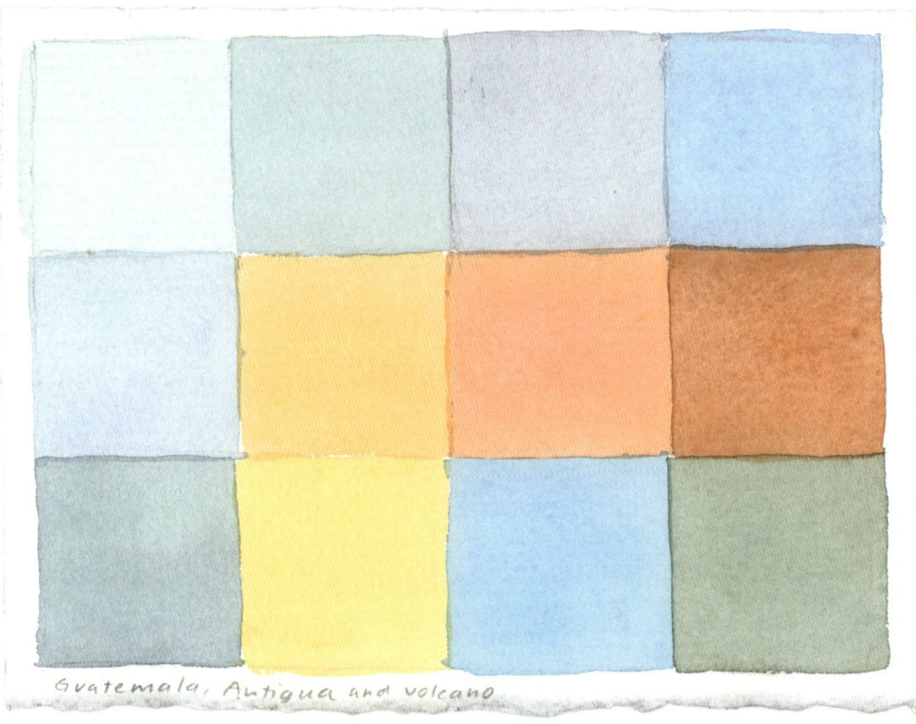
Guatemala, Antigua and volcano

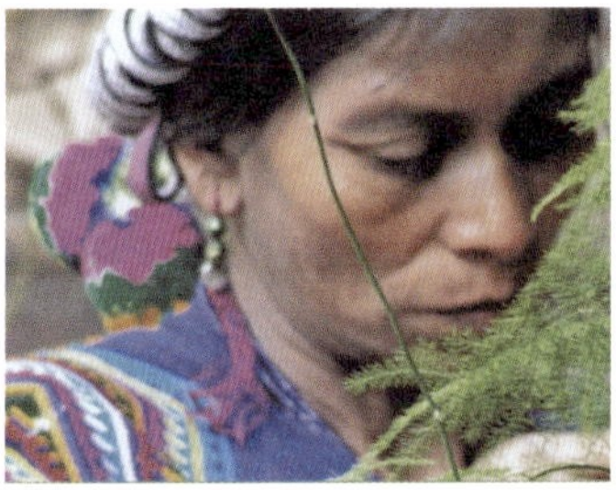

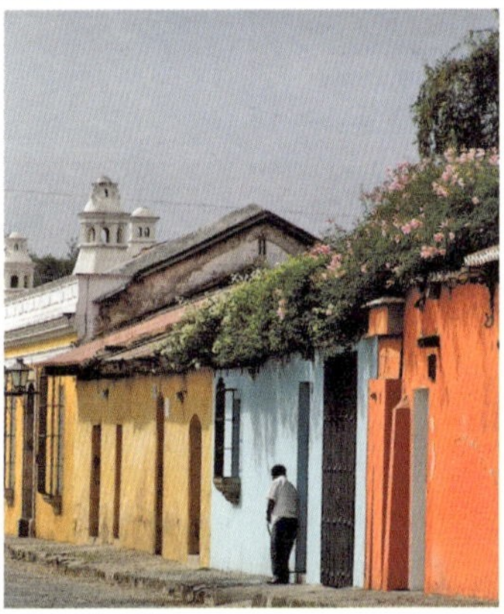

ANTIGUA, GUATEMALA

There is no fear of color in Guatemala. I am often amazed by the vast array of colors that I never thought would work together but somehow do here: olive green and hot pink, coral and turquoise blue, lilac and chartreuse, indigo and electric green.

Situated in a highland valley and nestled beside three volcanoes, Agua, Acatenango, and Fuego, Antigua is one of the best-preserved colonial cities in Central America. If you are lucky and look long enough, you can see a cloud of smoke escape from one of the active mountains. The morning mist hangs pale violet and gray on their sides. Colorful buildings are painted in a lively variety of bright pastels, tangerines, sun-drenched yellows, and cerulean blues.

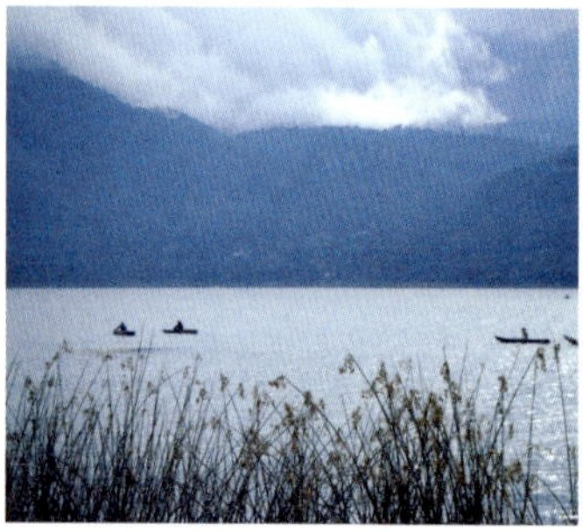

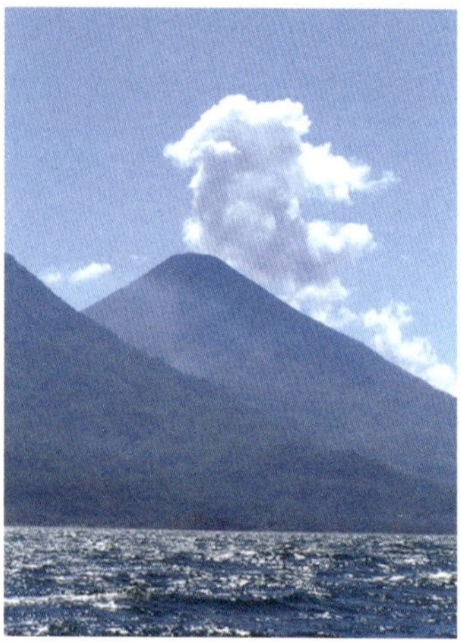

LAKE ATITLÁN, GUATEMALA

Lake Atitlán is a volcanic lake in the western highlands, a mile above sea level, that seems to float in the sky. It is considered one of the deepest lakes in the world. In the Mayan language, Atitlán translates as "place where the rainbow gets its colors."

Under a clear sky and bright sun, the dark blue of deep water shifts to lighter values in the shallows. Closer to the shore, where the clay gets stirred by the tide and the sunlight shines back off the seaweed, light-green and gray tones emerge.

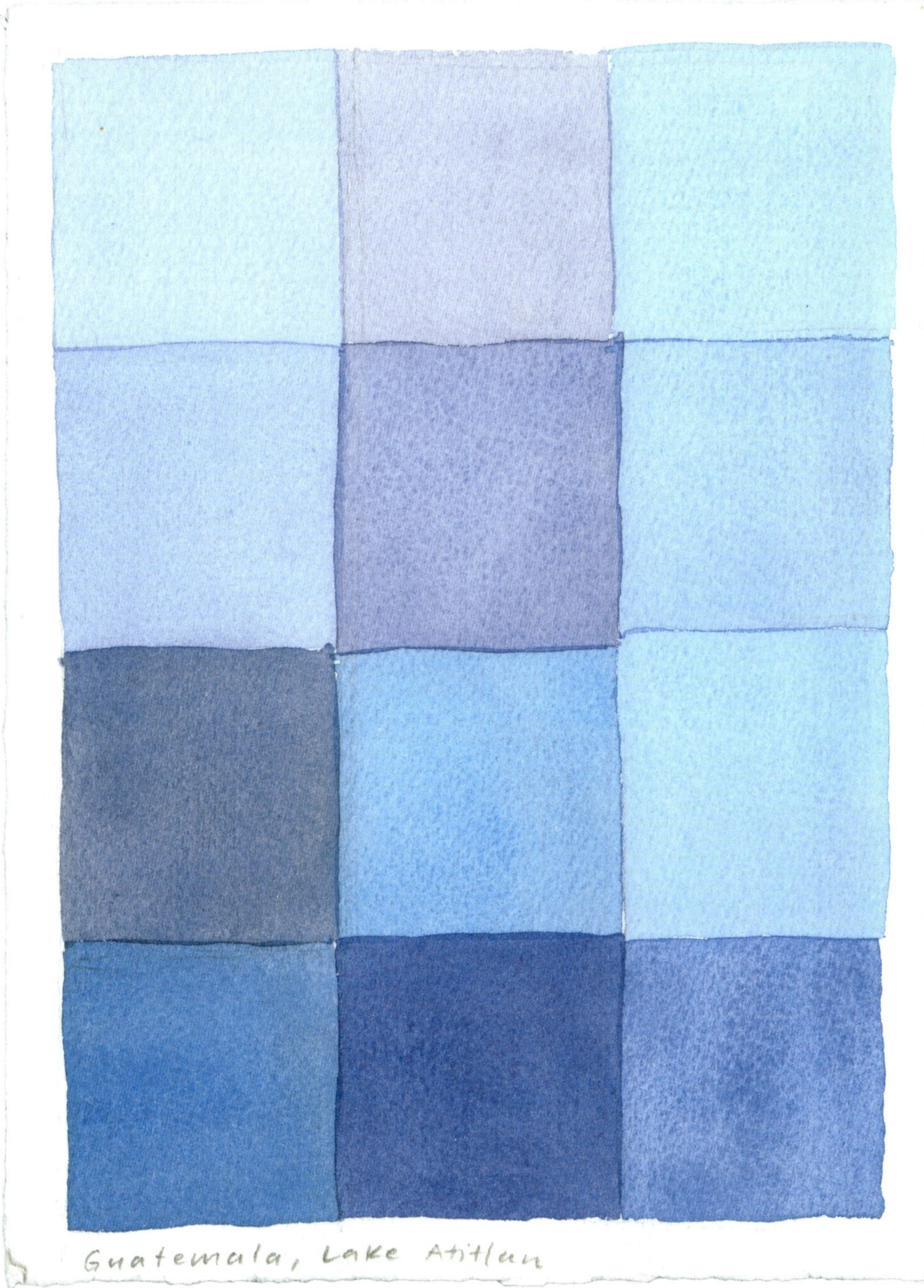
Guatemala, Lake Atitlan

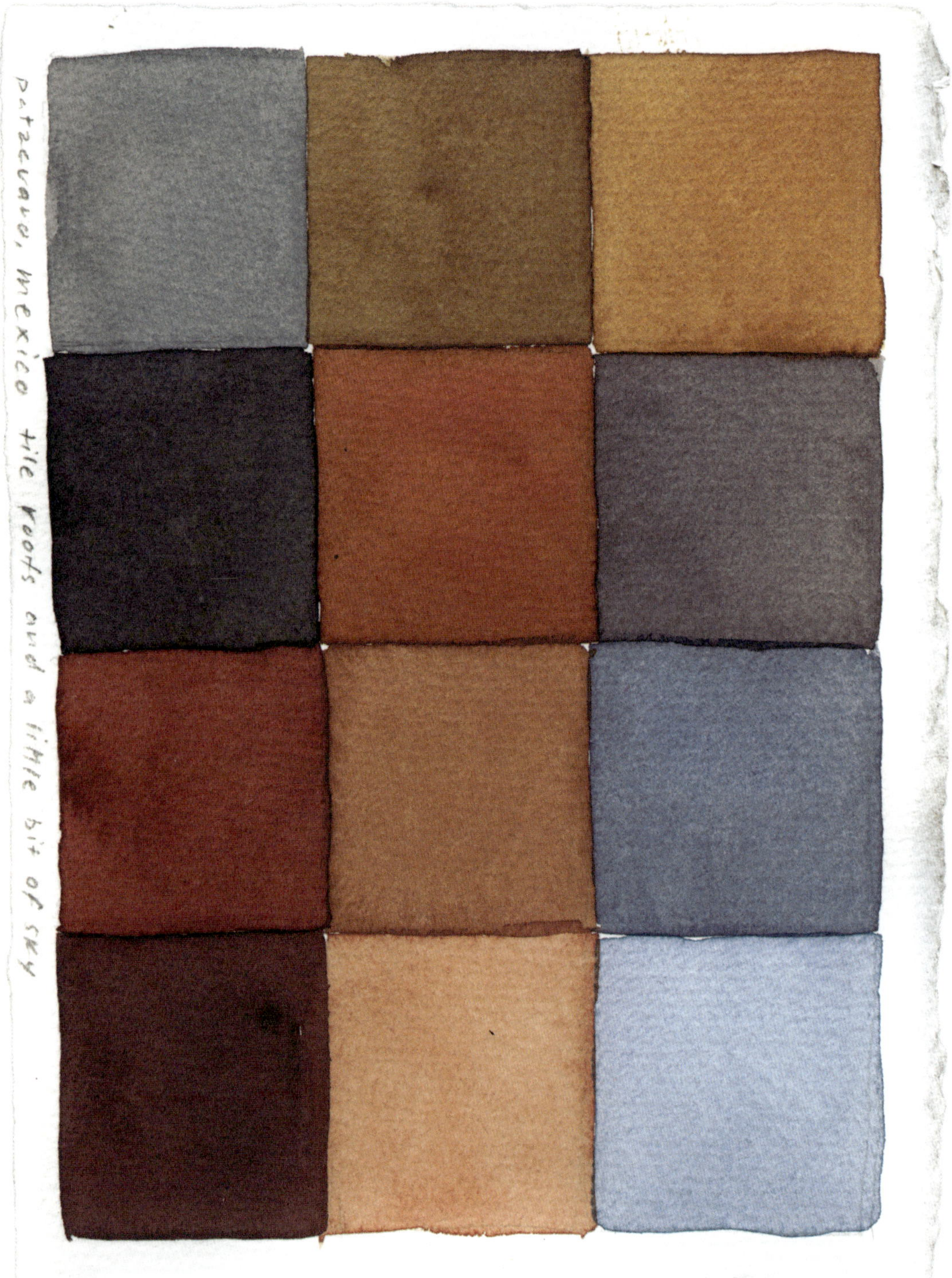
Patzcuaro, Mexico tile roofs and a little bit of sky

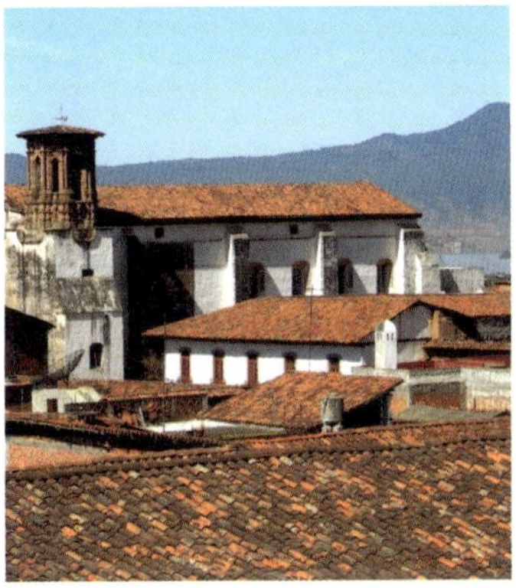

PÁTZCUARO, MEXICO

Pátzcuaro, a designated World Heritage Site, is located in the central part of the Mexican state of Michoacán and is situated high in the mountains at an elevation of 7,130 feet. Pátzcuaro, which means "place of stones" in the Purépecha language, is a small colonial town that has retained its authentic character. With very little intervention from tourism, it feels as if the town has gone back in time.

The day here starts early with the ringing of church bells. There is a symphony of birdcalls, the clacking of carts going down the cobblestone streets toward the market, and the smell of fresh tortillas.

Sitting in the central *zocalo*, the "public square or plaza," with my paints, I experience the gentle rhythm of the town as it wakes. I begin to record the colors of the early morning light as it shifts across the buildings: rosy reds, cadmium oranges, and every shade of warm brown.

The predominant colors in Pátzcuaro are highlighted by its architecture. A sea of terra-cotta roof tiles catches the light and casts a warm glow that is punctuated by the whitewashed buildings, which are set against the blue sky and the purple mountains rising in the distance.

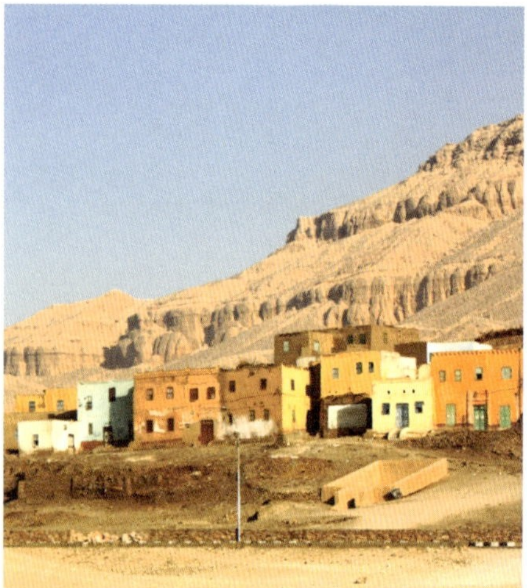

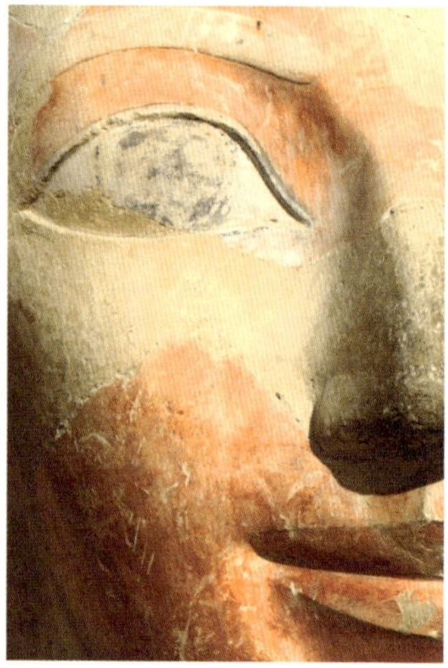

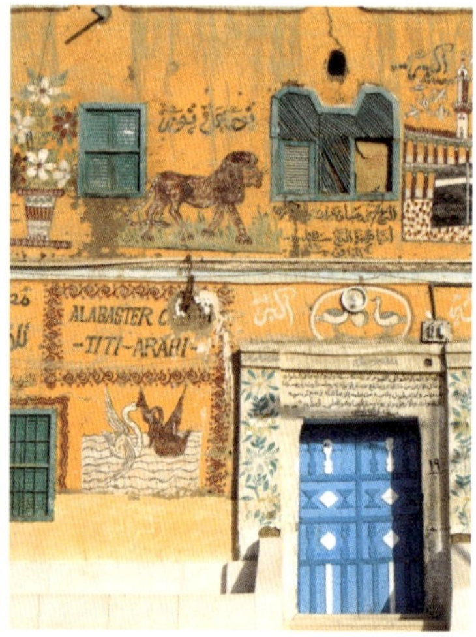

LUXOR, EGYPT

Luxor is the home of the ancient city of Thebes, located along the Nile River. During an early morning visit to the Temple of Hatshepsut in the Valley of the Queens, the sun beats down, blazing hot, accentuating the sharp contrast between land and sky. The color of sand and sun seems to define everything, reminding me that I am standing on the edge of the great Sahara Desert.

Contrasted against the browns of the hillside is a jumbled mosaic of dwellings saturated with bright colors. These naturally occurring pigments, extracted from locally found minerals and oxides, define the color of this valley. All around me I see the six basic pigments that early Egyptian artists used to create their palettes: red, green, blue, yellow, black, and white. The colors held many symbolic meanings, and as each object was painted, it was imbued with significance through color. Blues represented water, sky, and the celestial heavens, while yellow signified the sun and eternal life.

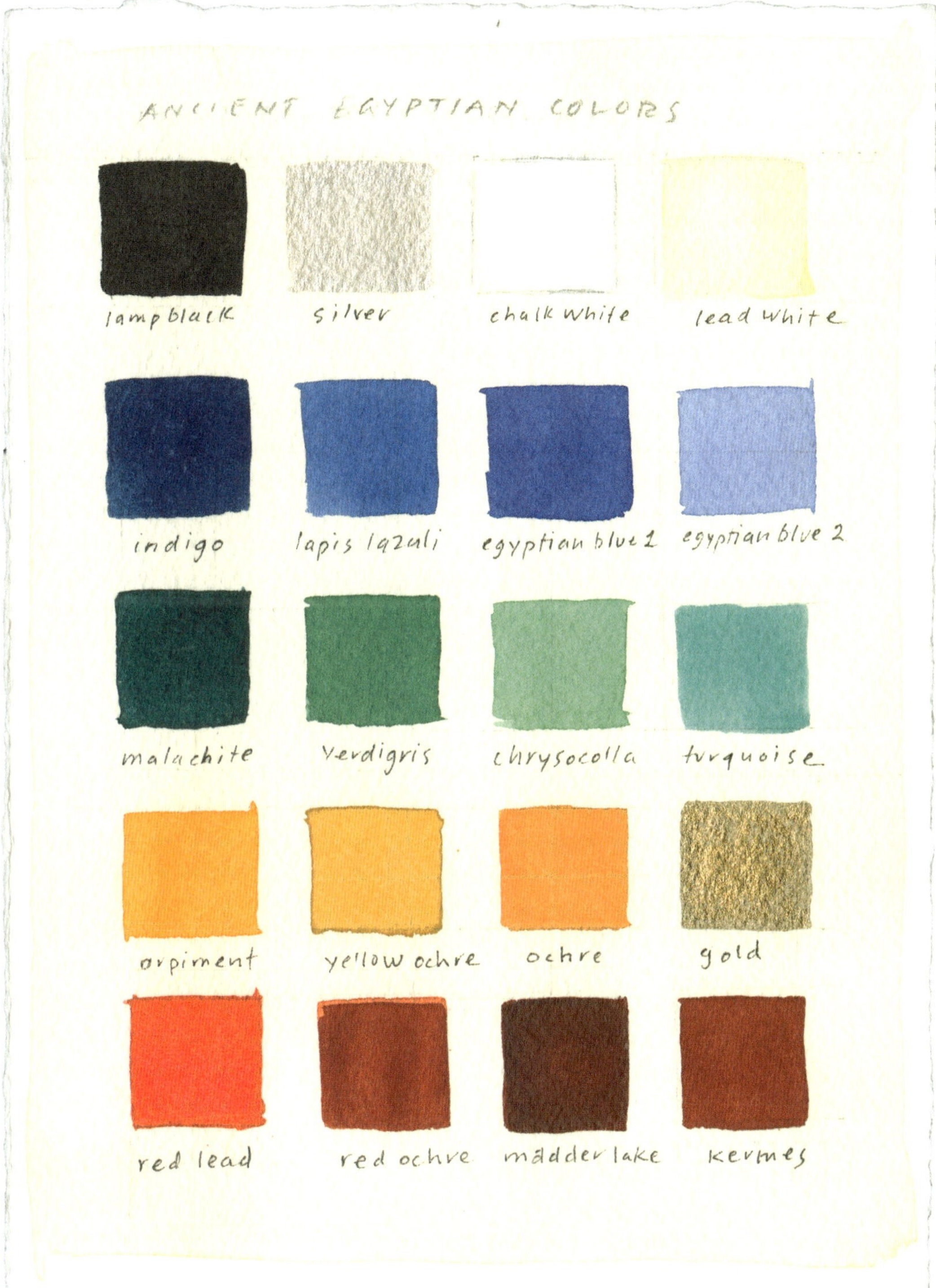
ANCIENT EGYPTIAN COLORS
lamp black
silver
chalk white
lead white
indigo
lapis lazuli
egyptian blue 1
egyptian blue 2
malachite
verdigris
chrysocolla
turquoise
orpiment
yellow ochre
ochre
gold
red lead
red ochre
madder lake
kermes

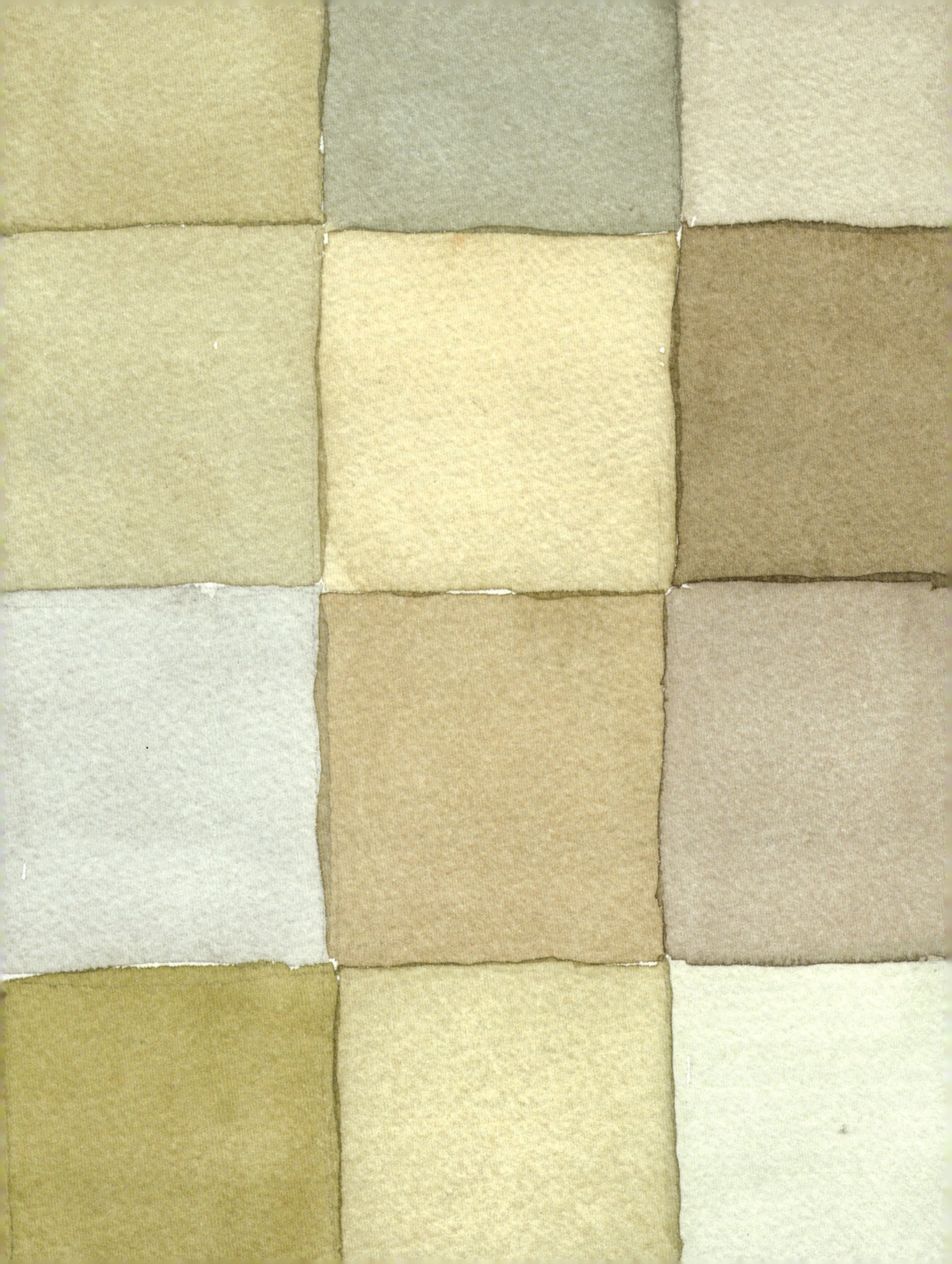

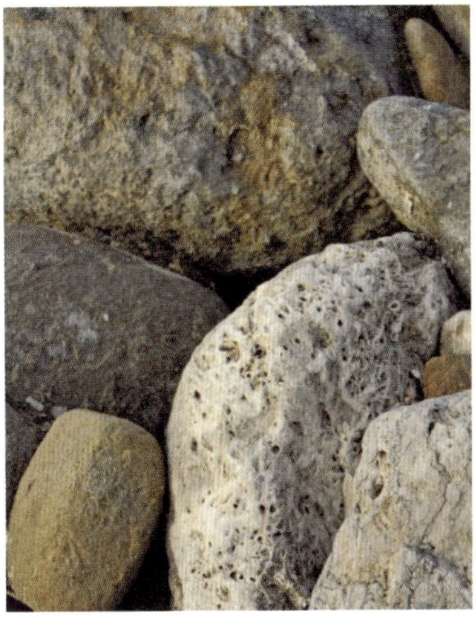 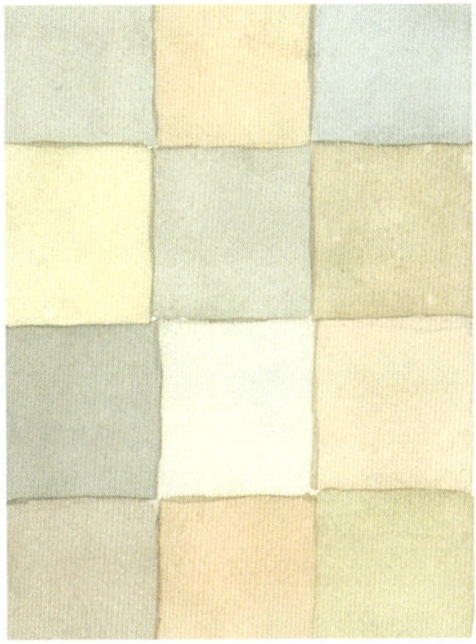 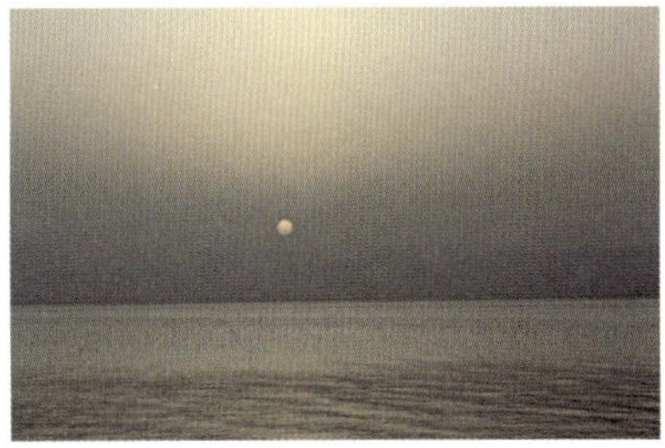 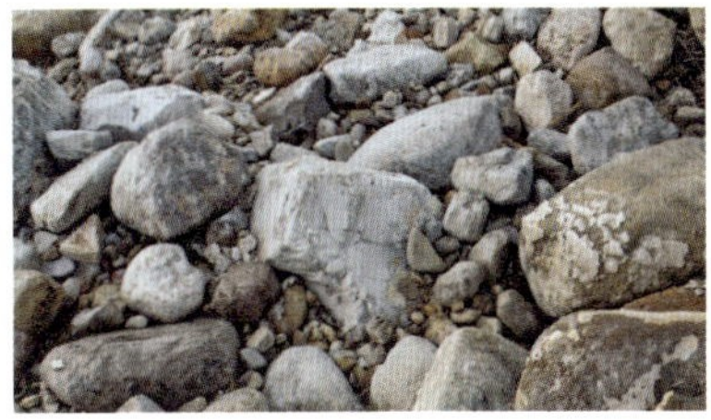

THE DEAD SEA, JORDAN

The Dead Sea, which sits at 1,300 feet below sea level, has the lowest elevation on Earth. Being this close to the planet's deep mineral and salt deposits, it is one of the saltiest lakes in the world. The salt content is so high (nearly ten times more concentrated than most of the world oceans) you can float effortlessly in it.

As the sun begins to set over the water, I attempt a color palette. Even at this time of day, the heat is so intense I have to work fast before the watercolors dry.

The colors of the Dead Sea at dusk are dull and don't reflect light: the muted gray sulfur of land, amber water, and the delicate muted hues of salt-encrusted rocks.

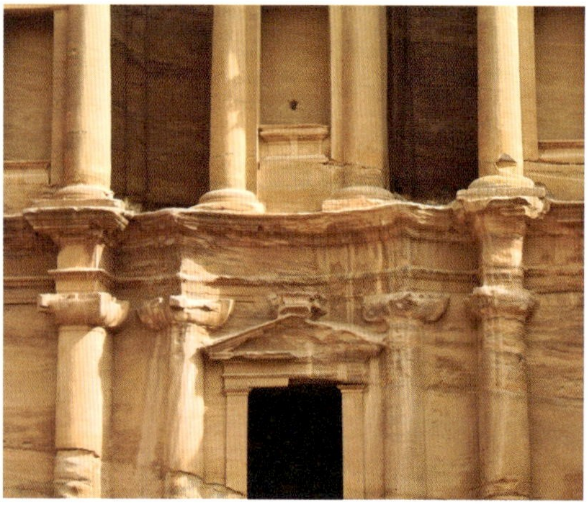

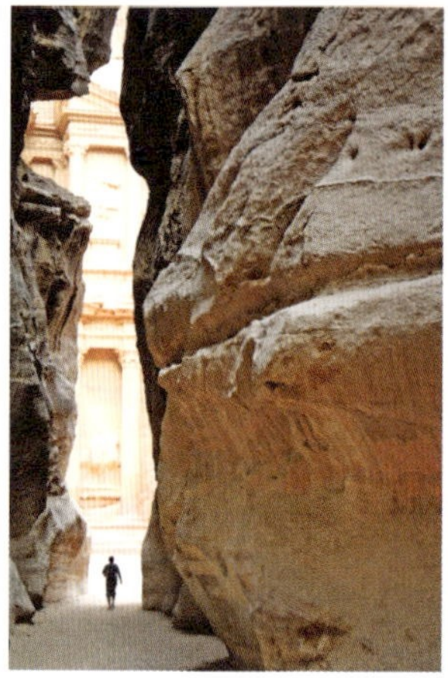

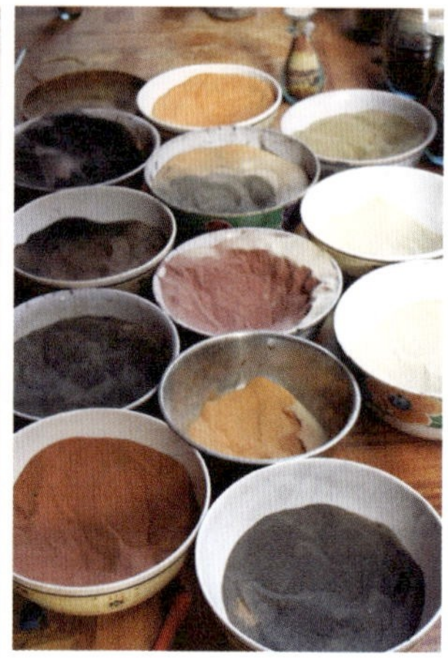

PETRA, JORDAN

Petra is perhaps the most spectacular ancient city remaining in the modern world. It gets its name from the Greek word *petros*, meaning "rock," and is carved out of sandstone cliffs that rise out of the desert.

I arrive in the predawn hours and stay until dusk, watching the colors change throughout the day. The pale yellows of early morning shift to rosy reds in the midday sun. In the early evening, as the shadows lengthen, the colors flare into purples, deep yellows, golds, and browns. At dusk, the temples, tombs, and obelisks in the area seem to hold onto the day, glowing in the lingering light.

My Petra paint box represents the sands of time, with colors of fine sand ranging from off-white to dusty red, and from ochre to violet.

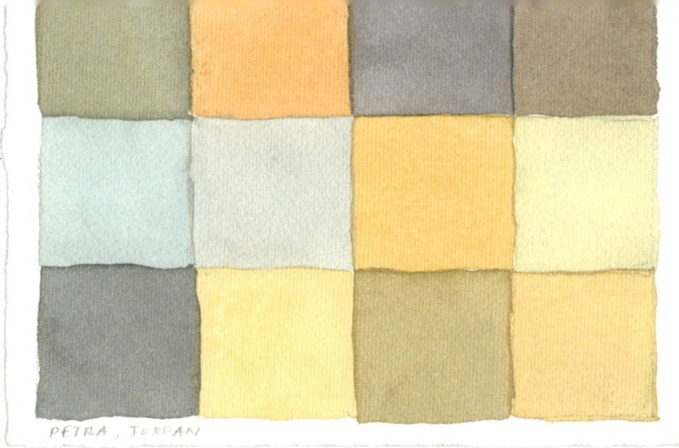

morning

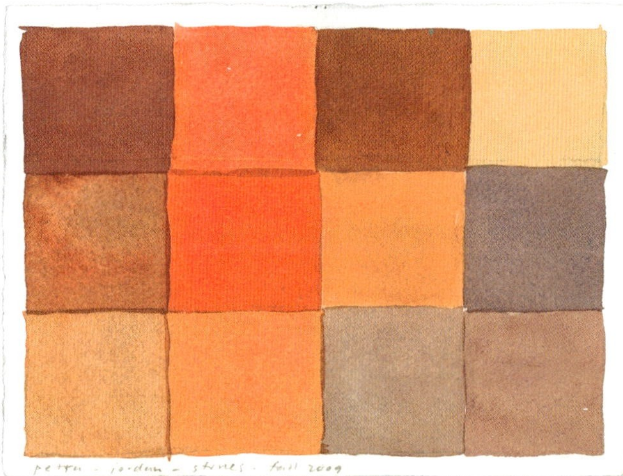

afternoon

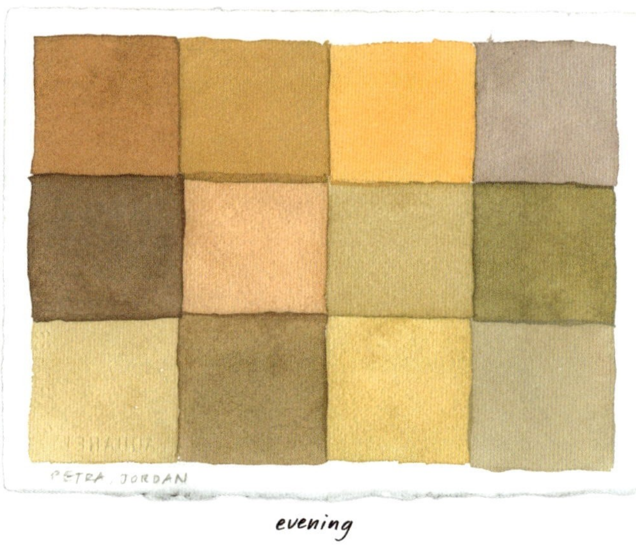

evening

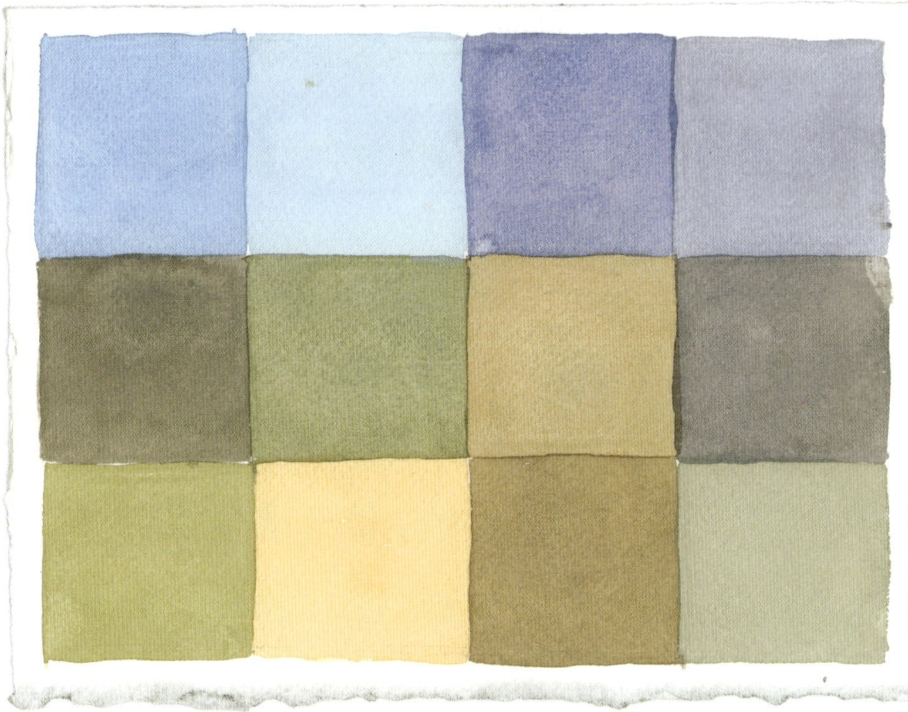

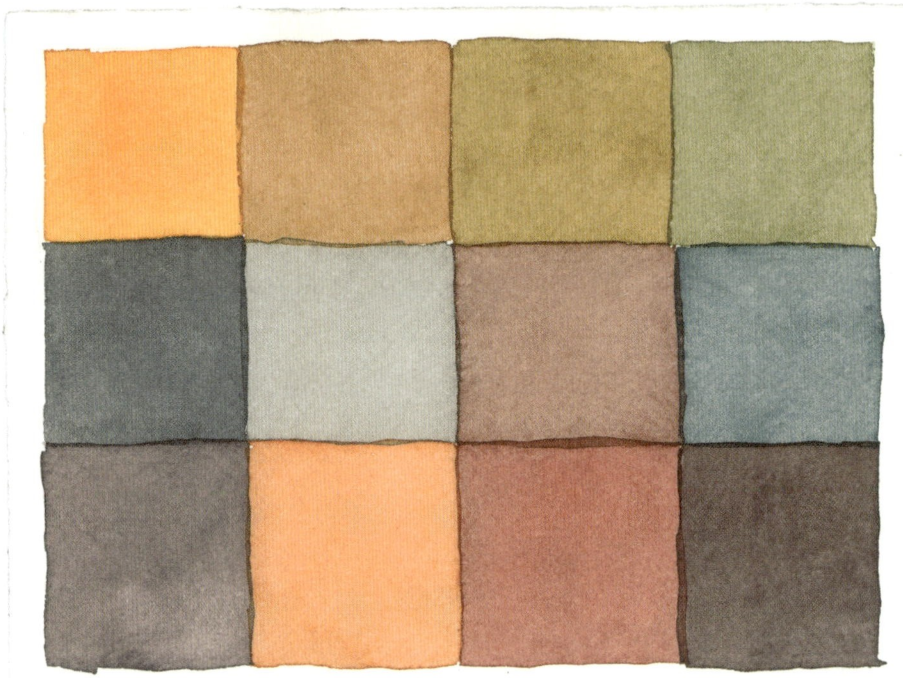

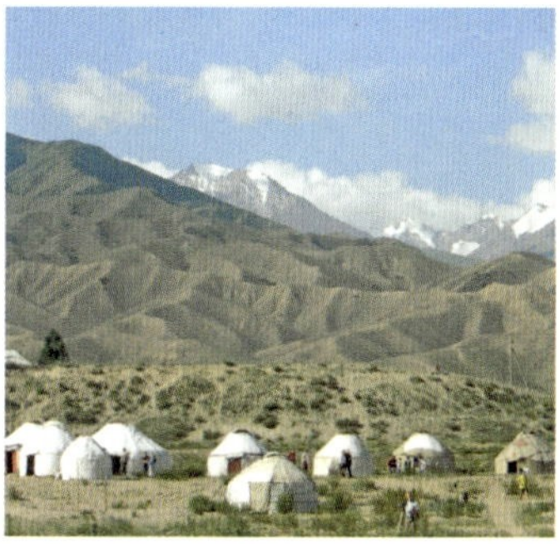

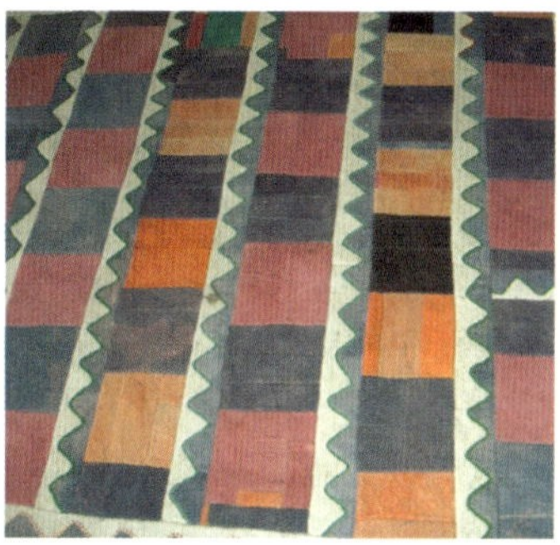

LAKE ISSYK-KUL, KYRGYZSTAN

Kyrgyzstan, in Central Asia, has been well known since the times of the legendary Silk Road. It's a land of monumental scale, characterized by the deep blues and purples of distant mountains, snow-capped peaks, and the vast sand-colored horizon. Looking at the mountain heights and endless steppes, I understand how the immensity of this land has forged the Kyrgyz nomadic character and spirit and influenced their art and culture.

On the shores of Lake Issyk-Kul, at the base of the Tien Shan Mountains, I spend the night at a yurt encampment set up temporarily for the summer months and marvel at the starry night sky.

Artisans in Kyrgyzstan are famous for their felt-making traditions. Sitting in a yurt one afternoon, I spend time with the women as they make *shyrdak* (patchwork) rugs—singing, laughing, and sewing together. The colorful felt creations are a harmonious blend of rich, warm reds, oranges, and purples with accents of magenta, colors that reflect the Kyrgyz culture and their everyday world.

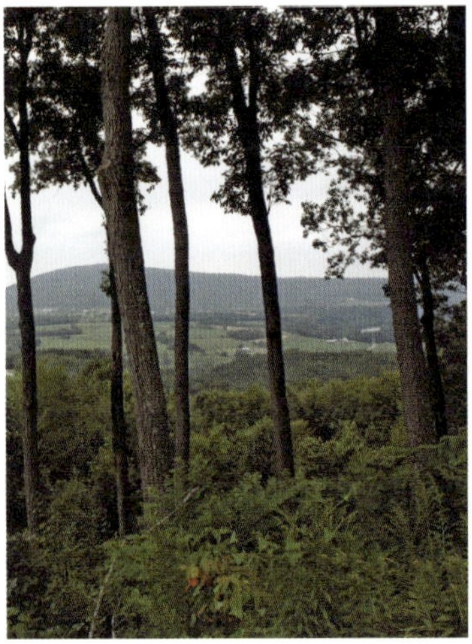 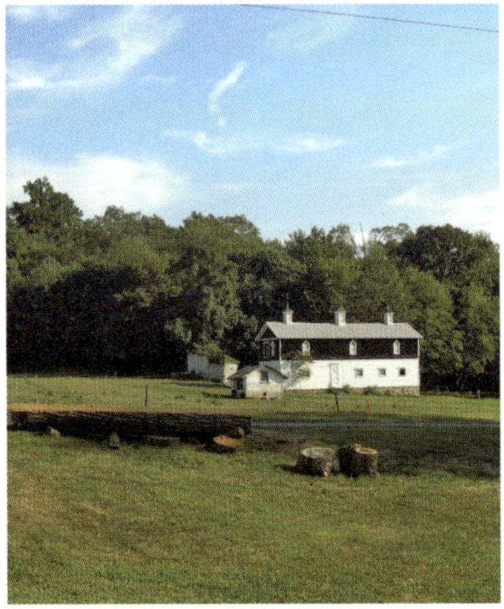 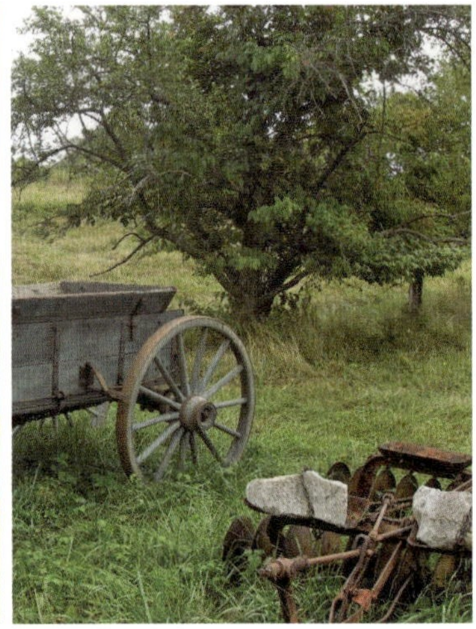

NEWPORT, PENNSYLVANIA

I have vivid memories of my grandmother's farm in central Pennsylvania—summer days lush with green vegetation and humid summer heat. There, as a child, I spent time with my family in "Sharon's Orchard," which was planted during the Depression, first as an apple orchard and then later with peaches. Sitting on the front porch with my grandmother, mother, and aunts, I helped prepare applesauce and peach preserves for the winter months ahead. Elberta, Hale Haven, and Belle of Georgia peaches were some of my grandmother's favorite varieties, along with Cortland and Jonathan apples.

Now, on cold and snowy nights, I can pull out a container of peach preserves and drift through memories of long, green summer days; images of ripe orange, red, pink, and yellow peaches; old farm baskets and crates to measure out a bushel, half a bushel, or a peck; and walks through the orchard's craggy trees, heavy with ripe peaches, set against the green, brown, and tan Pennsylvania land.

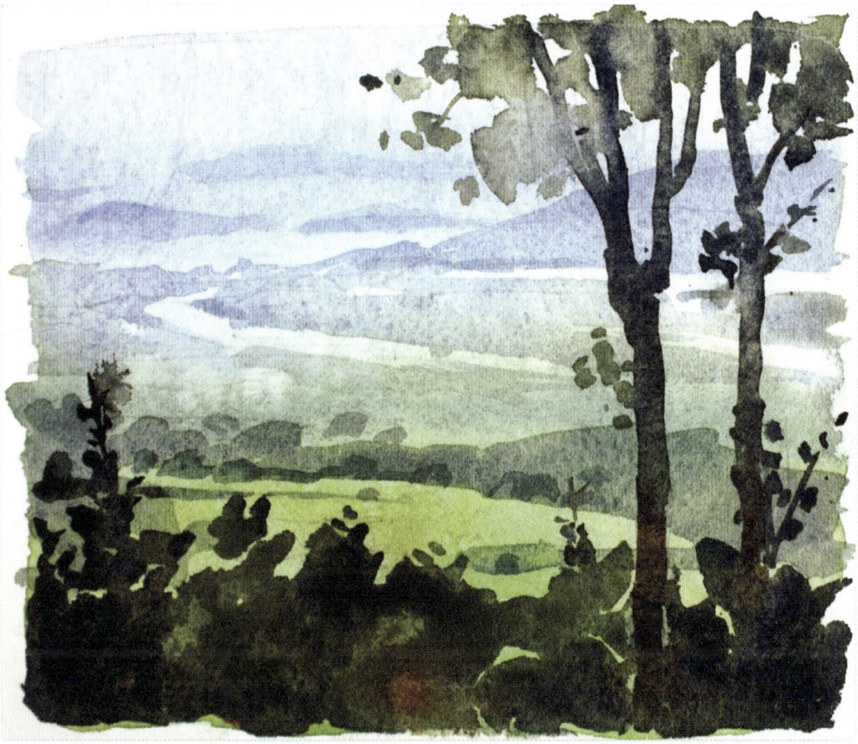

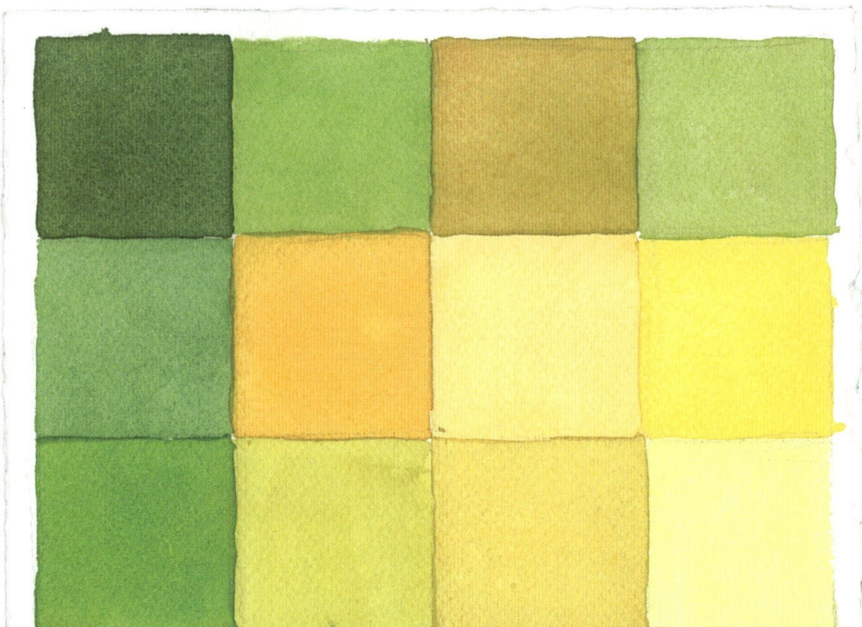
Pennsylvania, the farm, view from the ridge

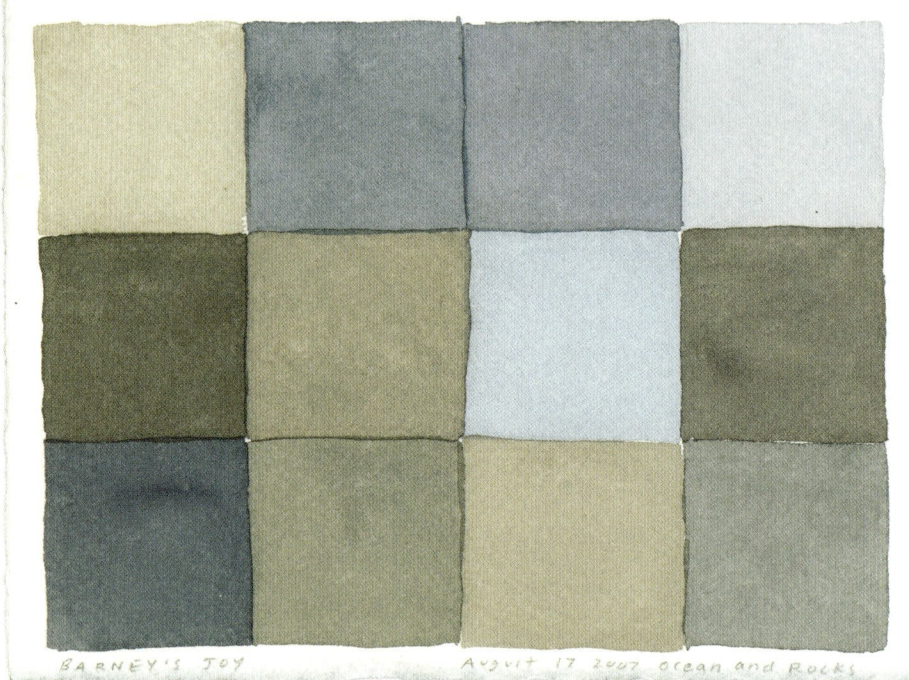
BARNEY'S JOY
August 17 2007 ocean and Rocks

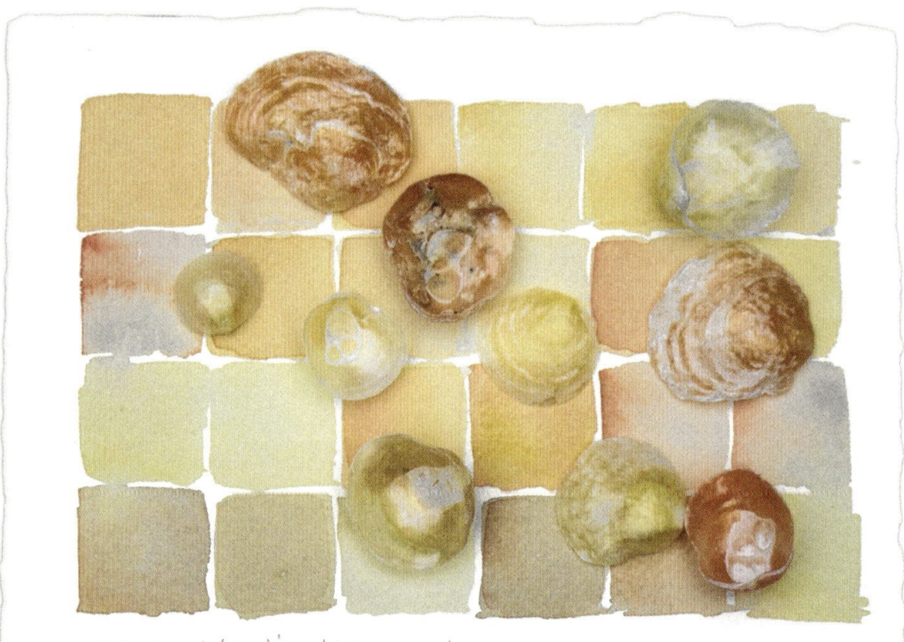
mermaids jingles, westport ma

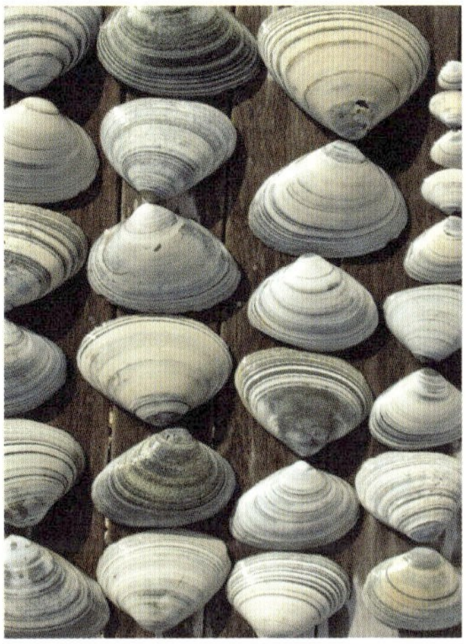

BARNEY'S JOY, MASSACHUSETTS

In South Dartmouth, a small coastal town in southeastern New England, a stretch of land called Barney's Joy sits along a cove on Buzzards Bay. The landscape includes salt marsh, coastal beach, sandplain grassland, and coastal heath. Where the ocean meets the sky, it is blue with warm tones of granite gray, like stones weathered by the sea.

On the beach, one finds quahog shells, jingle shells (affectionately called mermaid's toenails by pirates), mussel shells, and horseshoe crabs, all with their beautiful notes of colors. I love to make color palettes of the endless variations of shells, each one different and unique. I am especially inspired by the blue quahog shells of the Atlantic and all of their shades of indigo.

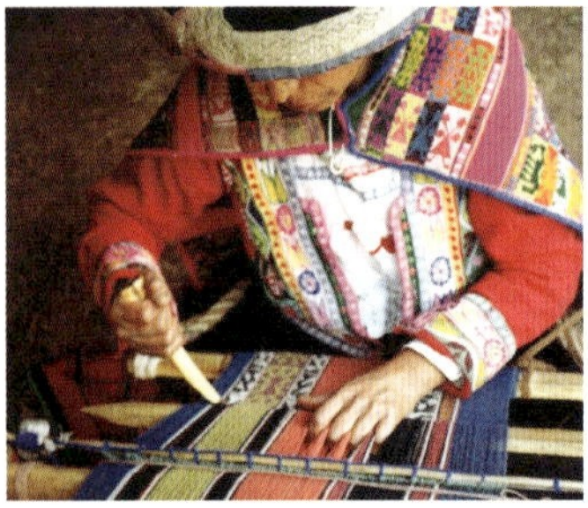

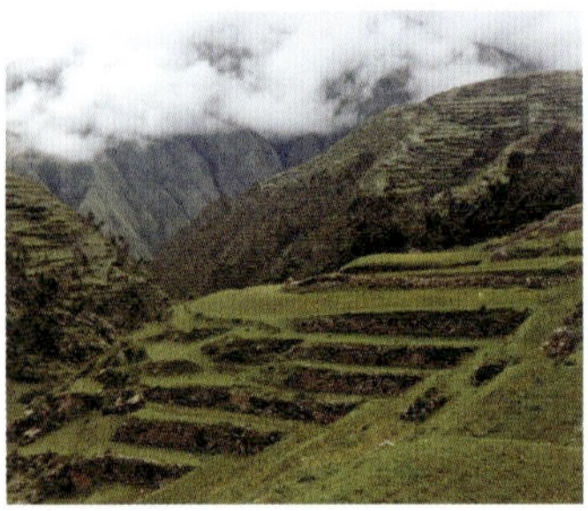

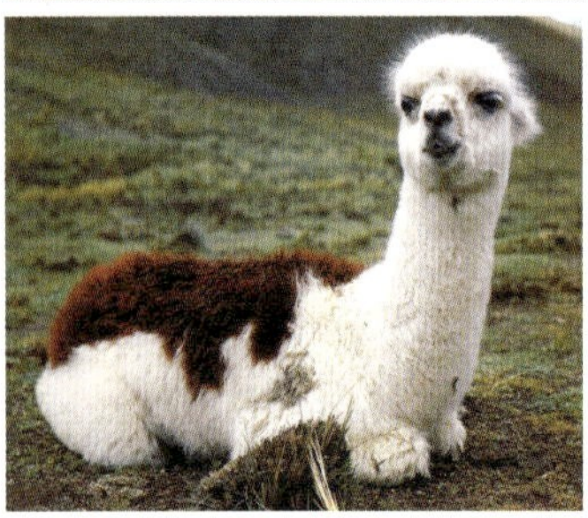

SACRED VALLEY, PERU

Located in the Andes Mountains, the Urubamba Valley is also known as the Sacred Valley of the Incas. Ancient ruins are situated throughout the gentle mountain slopes and scattered farming towns. The Incas favored this place for its specific geography and climate, which are perfectly suited to agriculture.

In early spring, as the ground begins to thaw, new colors of the season emerge throughout the region. The Urubamba landscape ranges from brownish ochre on the granite cliffs to lush green grass in the hills. The distant blue of snow-capped mountains lends a sense of mystery to this ancient place. Here I can feel the deep connection that the indigenous people have to their land. It is reflected in the construction of their homes, the fabrics they weave, the clothes they wear, and the food they eat.

Llamas and alpacas roam through the terraced terrain, their coats ranging in shades of browns, creams, and whites that blend perfectly with the natural environment.

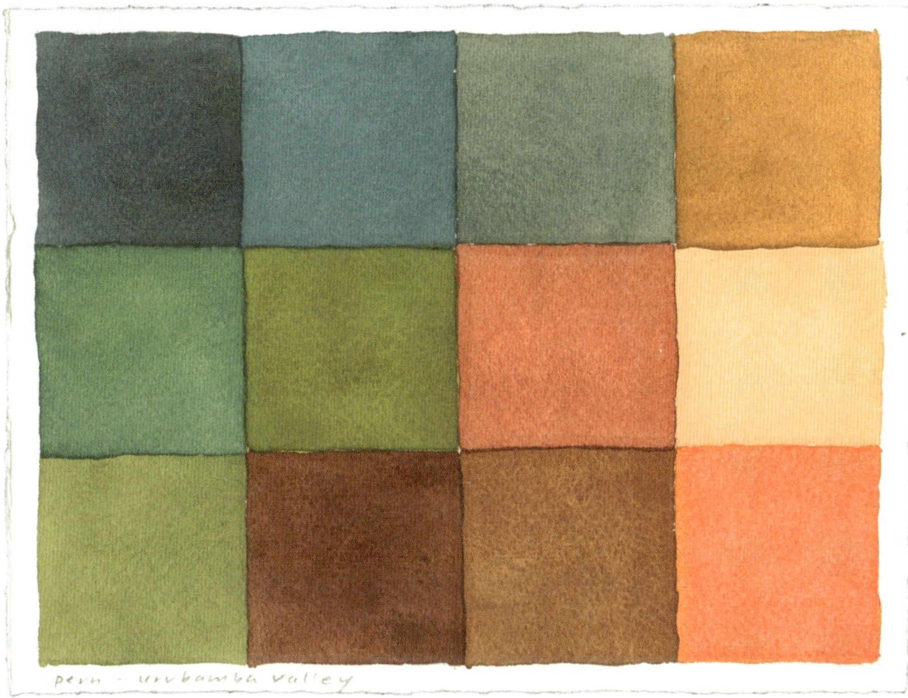
peru - urubamba valley

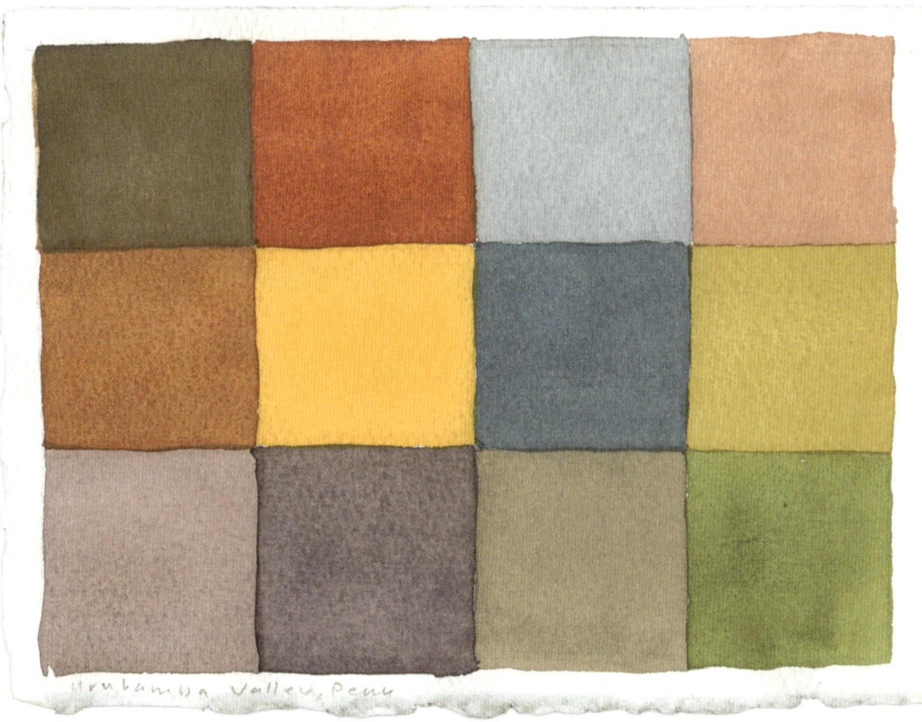
Urubamba Valley, Peru

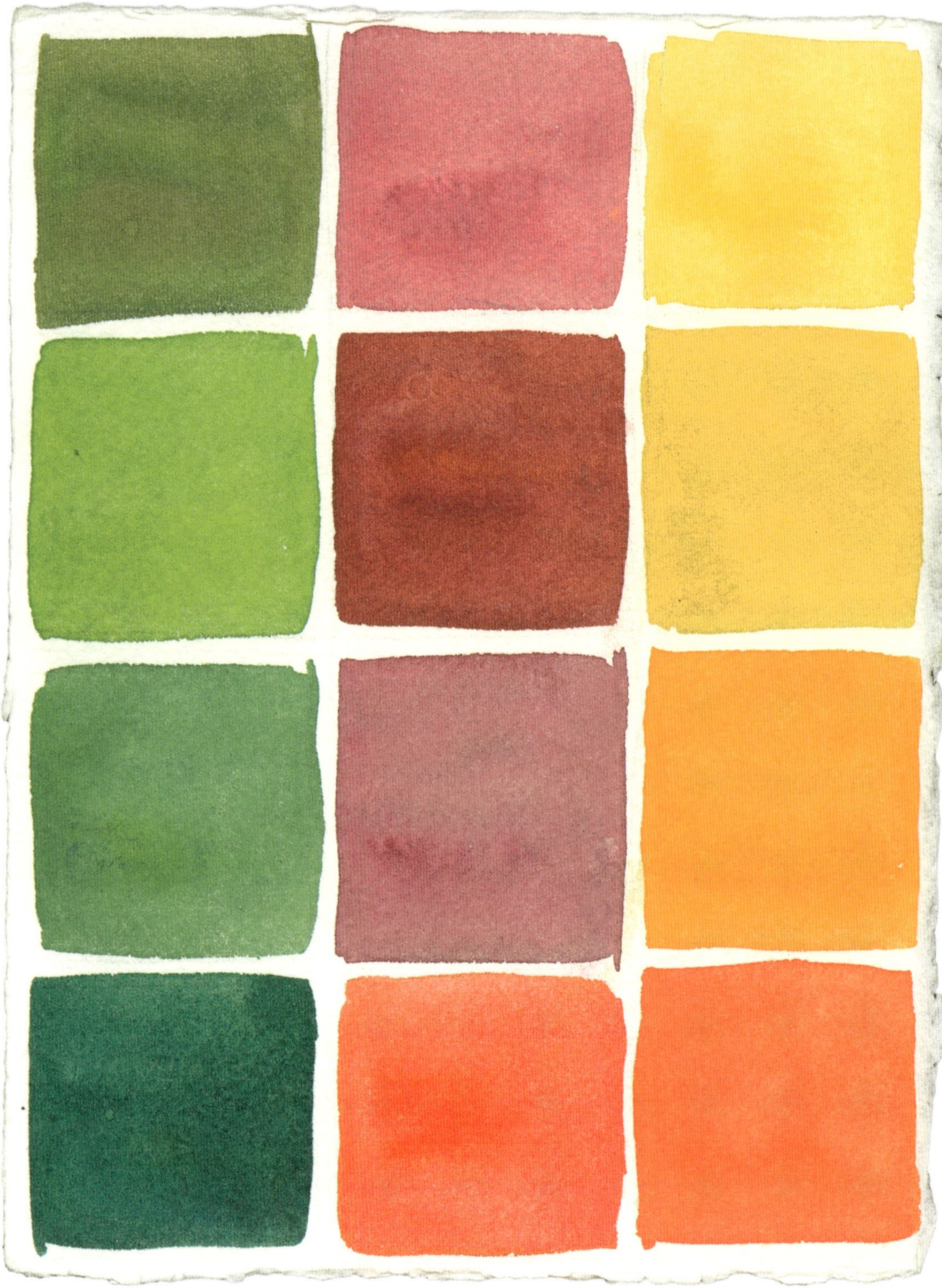

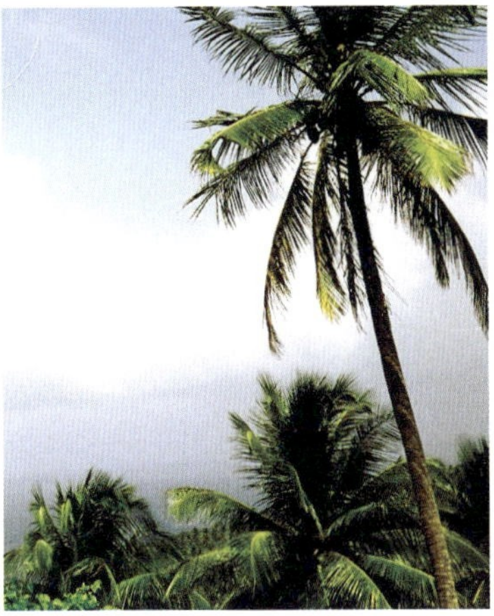
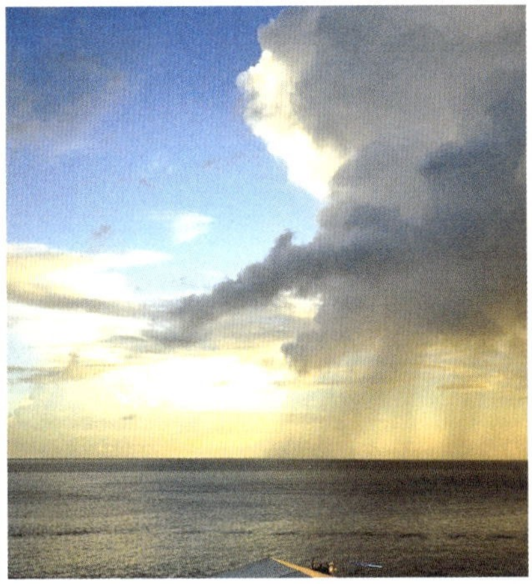
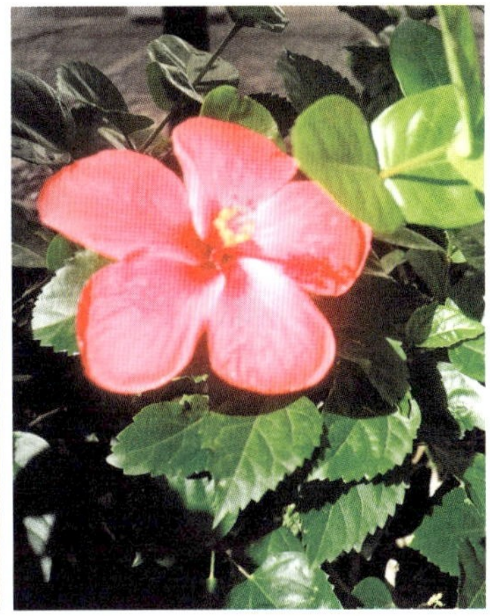

DOMINICA, WEST INDIES

Dominica, officially known as the Commonwealth of Dominica, is a small island nation at the northern end of the Windward Islands of the Lesser Antilles region of the Caribbean Sea. A paradise known for its unspoiled natural beauty, the island of Dominica features volcanic peaks; dense, primordial rainforest; waterfalls and lakes; and numerous rivers. It is home to many rare plant, animal, and bird species.

Dominica gets an extraordinary amount of rain. A Dominican rainstorm is like being in the middle of a painting, drenched in water and color. Clouds mix with sky as they merge and dance across the horizon, soaking up water from the many rivers and hovering around the highest peaks, obscuring views and shrouding the island in a luminescent mist.

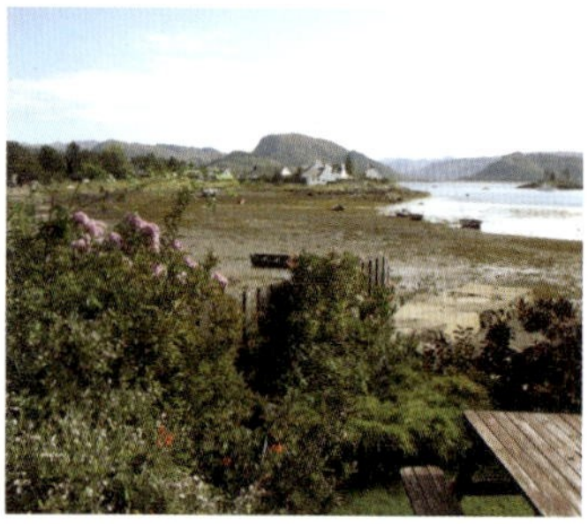

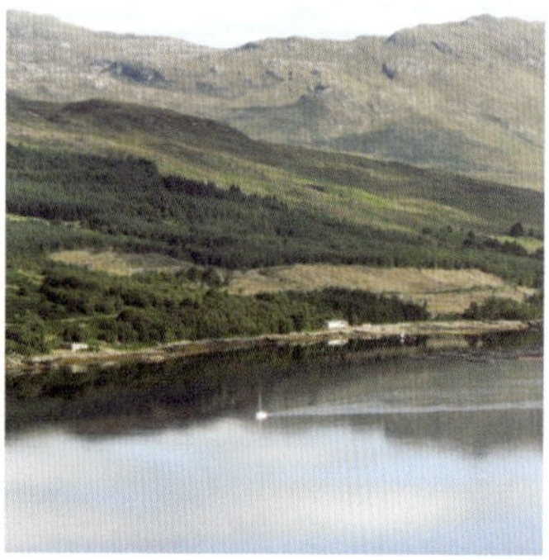

ISLE OF SKYE, SCOTLAND

The Isle of Skye, also known as the Eilean a' Cheo (Gaelic for "island of mist"), lies off the west coast of Scotland. At the base of the Cullin Hills, a craggy mountain range that dominates the landscape of the small harbor of Portree, I sit for a while and take in the quality of light and color. Bright light sparkles off the blazing blues of the curved harbor. The tide stretches back into the choppy water of the sea, laying bare a long and rocky stretch of sand. In this fresh August morning in the northern latitudes beneath this blend of cool mist and warm sun, I feel somehow closer to the sky.

The Isle of Skye is a mixture of azure blue sky, white and violet clouds, and silver mist over the greens and browns of heather.

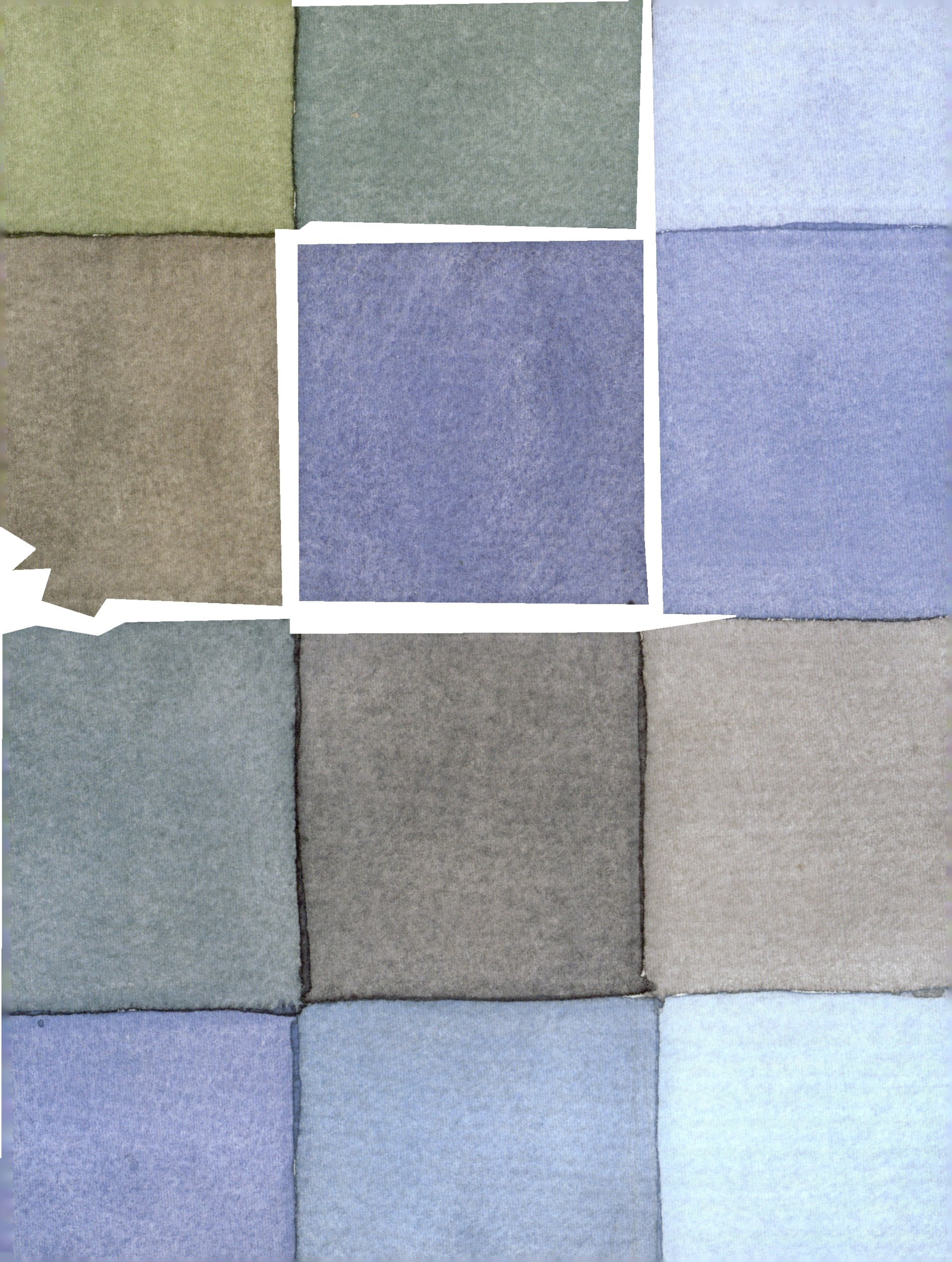

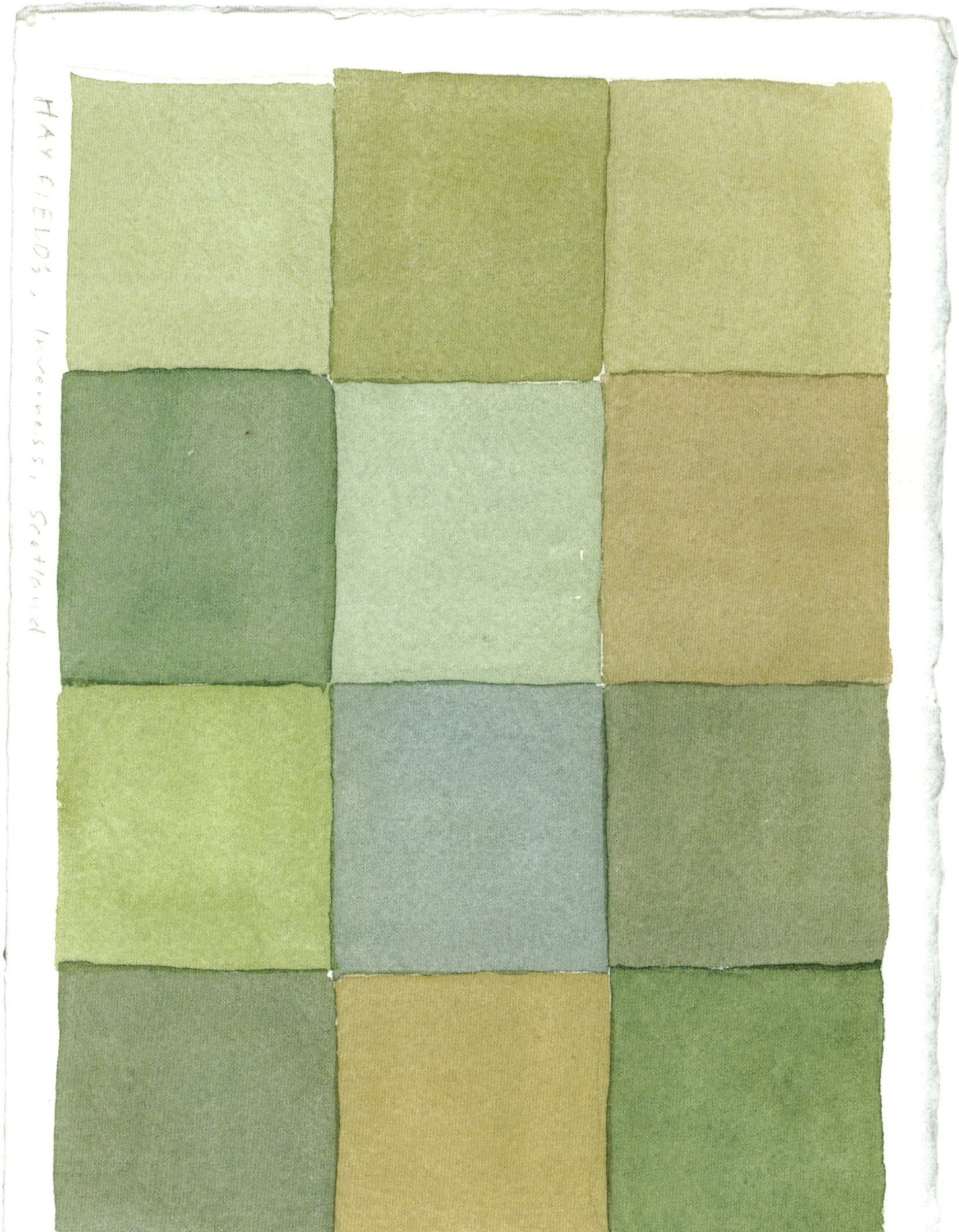
HAY FIELDS, Inverness, Scotland

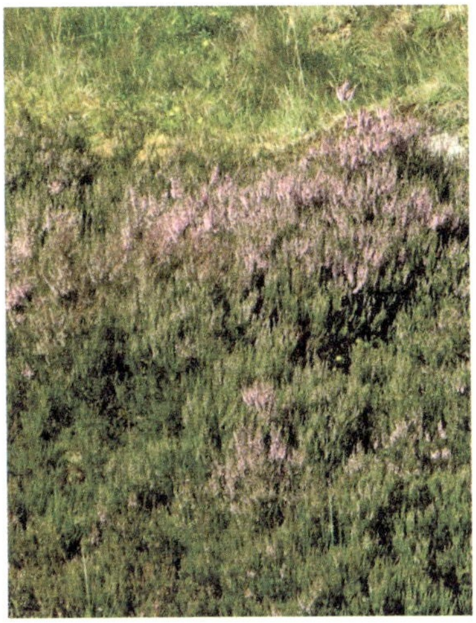
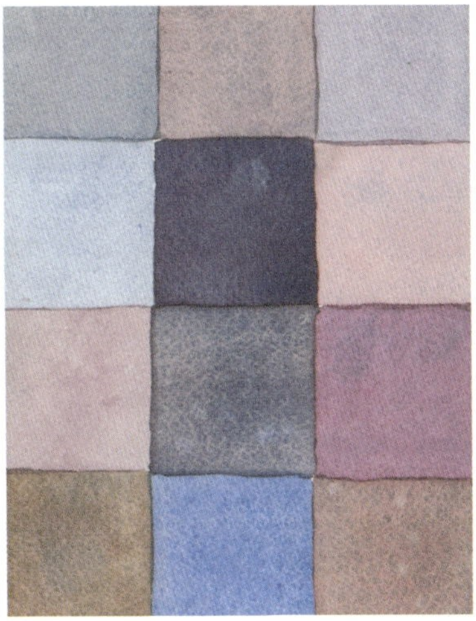
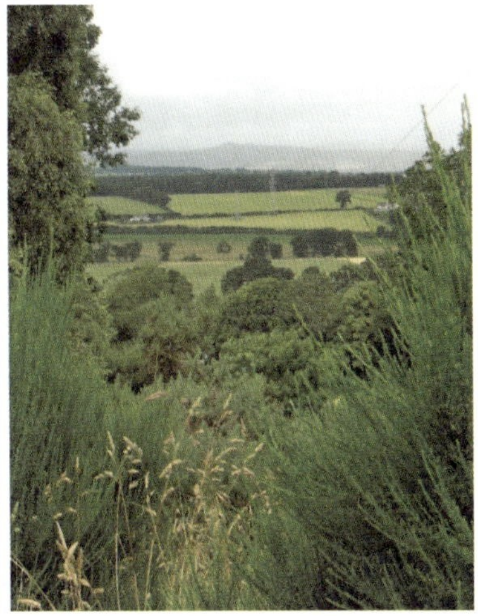

INVERNESS, SCOTLAND

Scotland has a rich agricultural and farming legacy, which is evident everywhere in the hedgerows and stone walls that divide the landscape and reveal the history of the land.

During a late summer afternoon, sitting in a freshly mowed hay field, I see infinite shades of green, giving a warm tint to the meadows. Heath blooms throughout the summer months and clusters around rocky outcroppings, framing the landscape in shades of pink and purple against dark greens.

Observing a place in this way, through color, can reveal surprising details that might otherwise go overlooked. I can't believe all that goes on in a meadow.

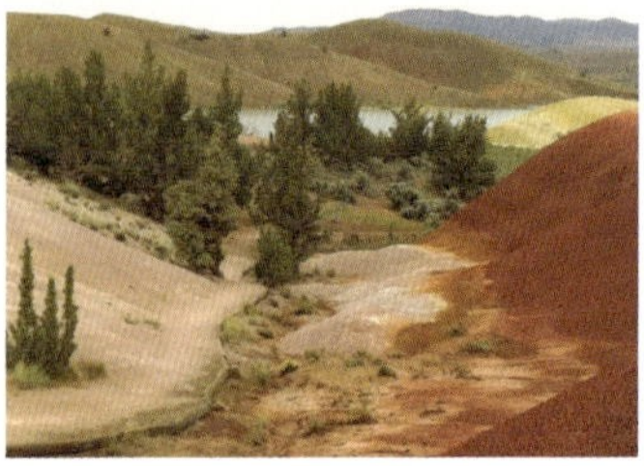

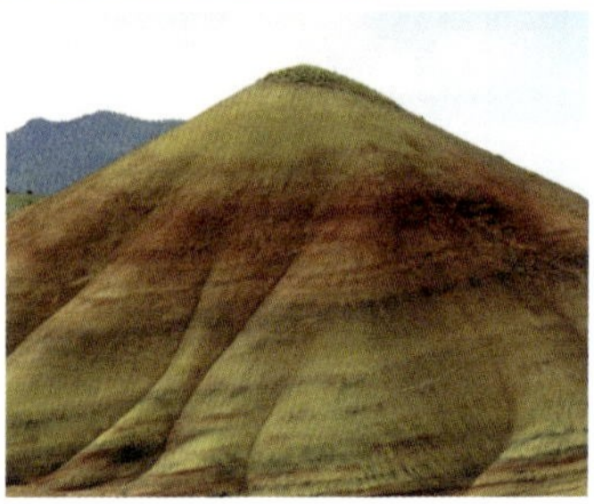

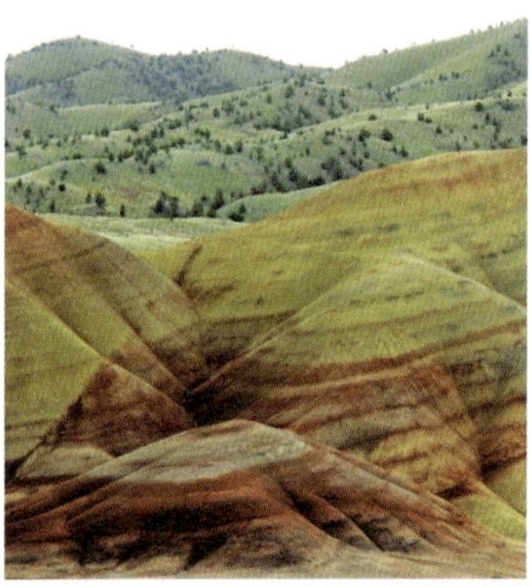

MITCHELL, OREGON

The Painted Hills in central Oregon show you the colors of ancient time. These layers of striped sediment were laid down more than thirty-five million years ago, when the Cascade Volcanoes spewed layers of volcanic ash over a series of eruptions across hundreds of miles, stretching across parts of British Columbia, Washington, Oregon, and Northern California. Over time, the lava and ash mixed with plants, minerals, and groundwater, to leave the distinct marks of each period of this distant time.

Differences in weathering and mineral content display themselves in a striking show of colorful stripes. Vivid reds, yellow, pale gold, and green are laced with streaks of black magnesium. Blue hills fade to purple under the vast sky. Sagebrush dots the landscape and perfumes the air. A cloud forms overhead, and the colors soften. Caught in a light rain, the colors become more saturated and intense as clay soil absorbs the moisture.

The trails within the Painted Hills, part of John Day Fossil Beds National Monument, wind around and through the soft, undulating mounds of this ochre- and sienna-colored earth. I love painting the varying stripes of color that trace the folds of the hills, plateaus, and basin. For me, this simple act of recording colors in a sketchpad is the best way to really see a place, be present with it, and make it my own.

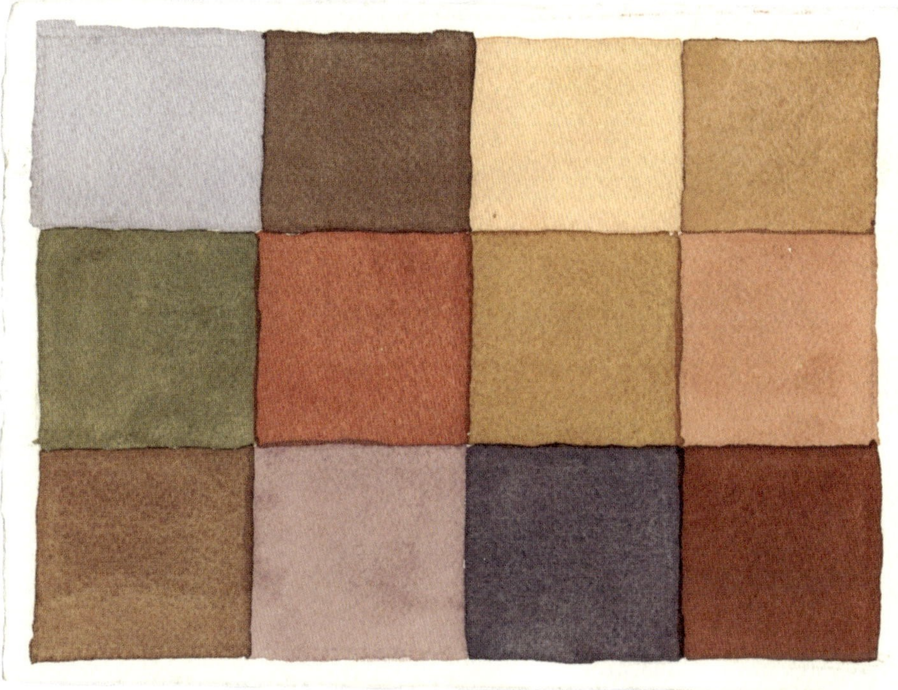

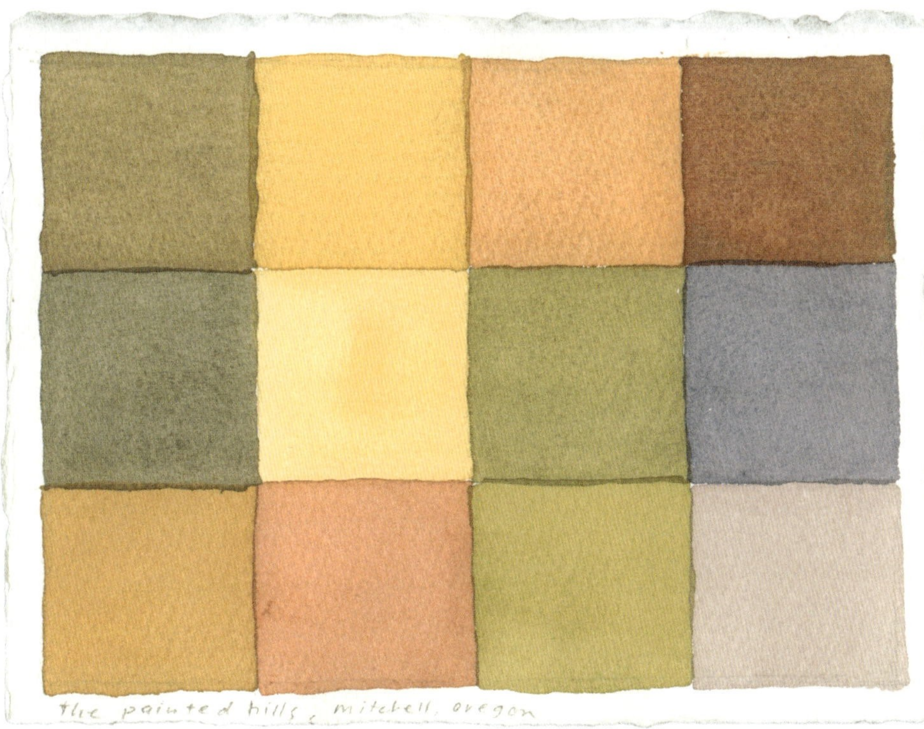
the painted hills, mitchell, oregon

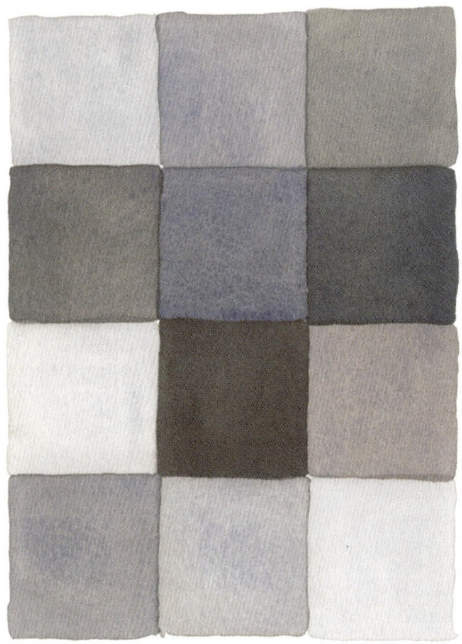

CHELSEA NYC palette no. 4

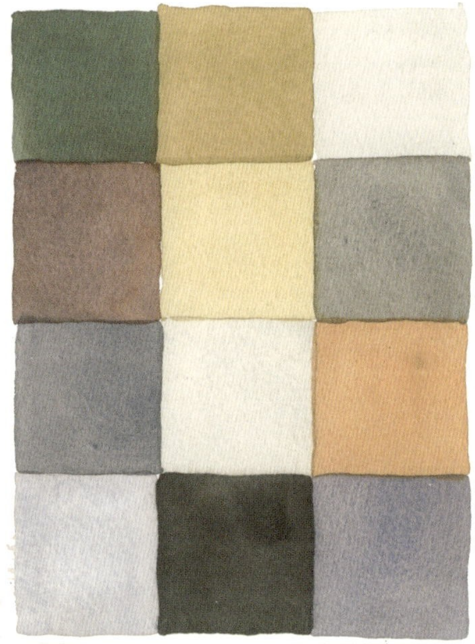

HUDSON RIVER NYC palette no. 6

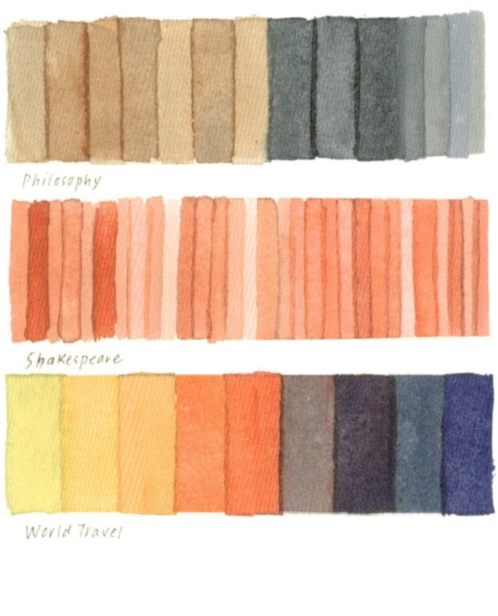

NY PUBLIC LIBRARY NYC palette no. 5

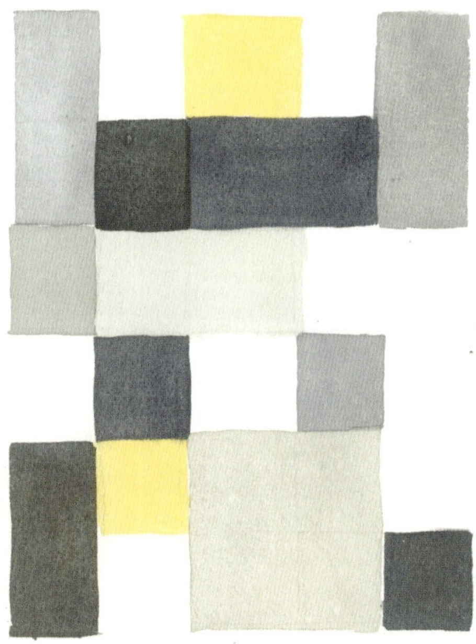

MIDTOWN NYC palette no. 3
five shades of slush and a yellow taxi

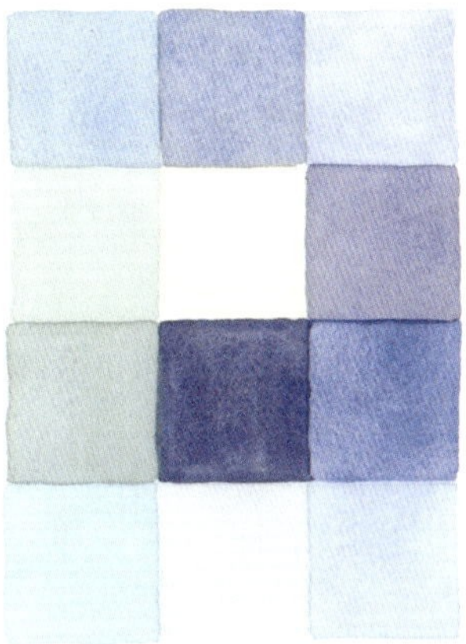

CENTRAL PARK NYC palette no. 1

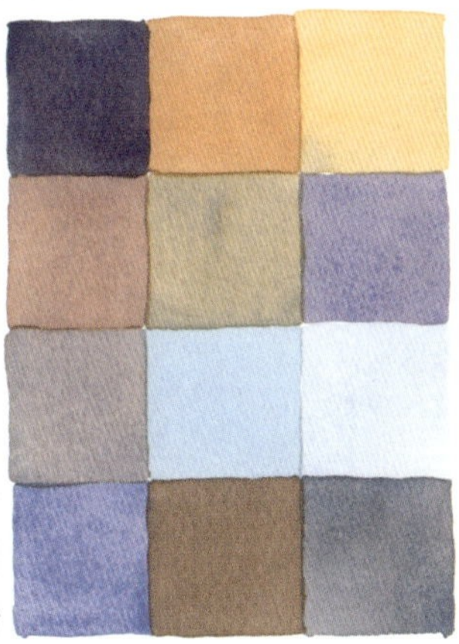

TIMES SQUARE NYC palette no. 2

NEW YORK, NEW YORK

From a distance, New York City can appear as a black-and-white film with subtle colors: glittering asphalt sidewalks, walls of reflective glass and steel, silver skyscrapers, purple skylines, elegant shades of gray, black, brown, and brick red, and the colors of grit, soot, and steam. It is up close on the street, however, that it explodes with splashes of vibrant, unpredictable color: bright metal food carts, precarious piles of bananas, plastic turquoise bangles, and bouquets of flowers sold in corner stores. Neon street signs, yellow taxis, and the people all add to the local color.

New York City is a large collection of small places, each with its own personality, mood, and distinctive colors, conveniently arranged in a grid. It is also a pulsing metropolis—a constant flow of moving people, dramatic light and shadow, energy, rhythm, and tempo.

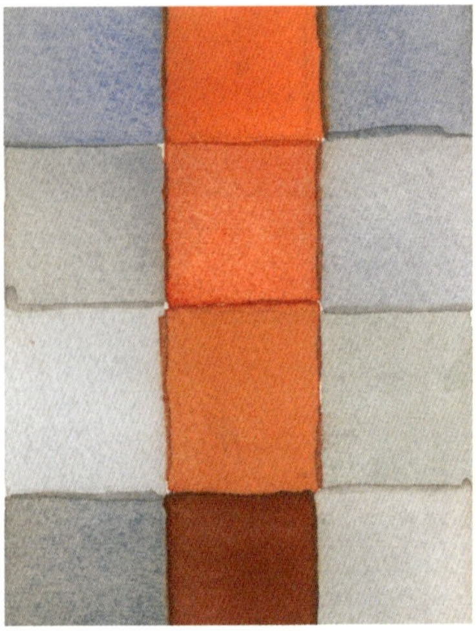

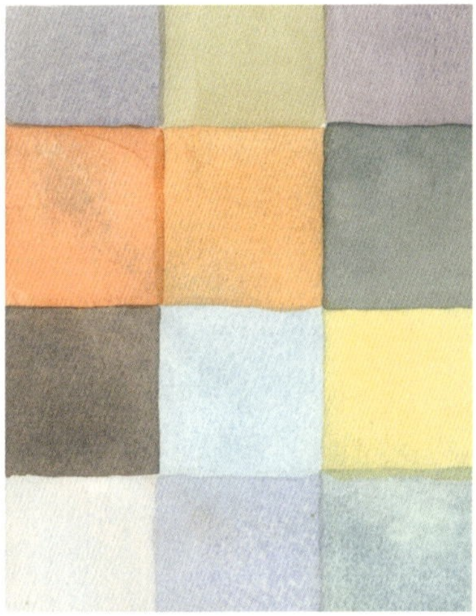

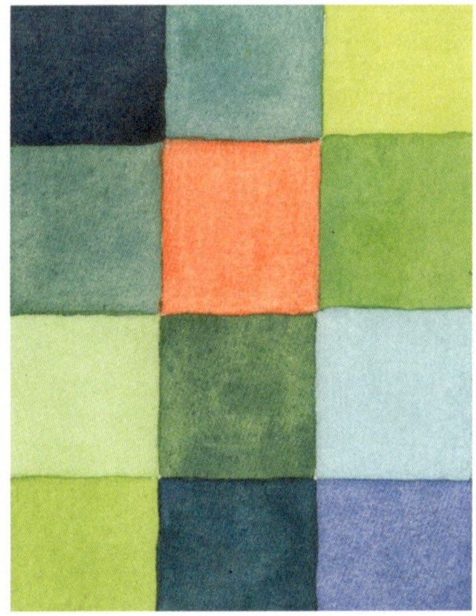

SAN FRANCISCO, CALIFORNIA

San Francisco is a city of hills. Approaching it from the Golden Gate Bridge, I see the brightness of the city and the way the light glimmers and shimmers. There are long views from every hill. Sea spray and salt crystals from the coast mingle with the light to cast a glow over the scene. From the steep hills I can catch views of San Francisco Bay. The teal blue of the Pacific is always beyond.

One of the first things I notice about San Francisco is that it is a tropical paradise: giant ferns and palm trees mix with Monterey pines. Some of the most beautiful plants I have ever seen grow here in sidewalk cracks.

Wild parrots fly through the trees on Telegraph Hill, blurred glimpses of scarlet and green in the sky. Stairways zig and zag through the shade of dark green sword ferns amidst patches of cerulean blue sky and pink bougainvillea. Small cottages, seemingly on top of one another, stack up along the hill, creating a mixture of pastel grays, whites, yellows, and terra-cotta.

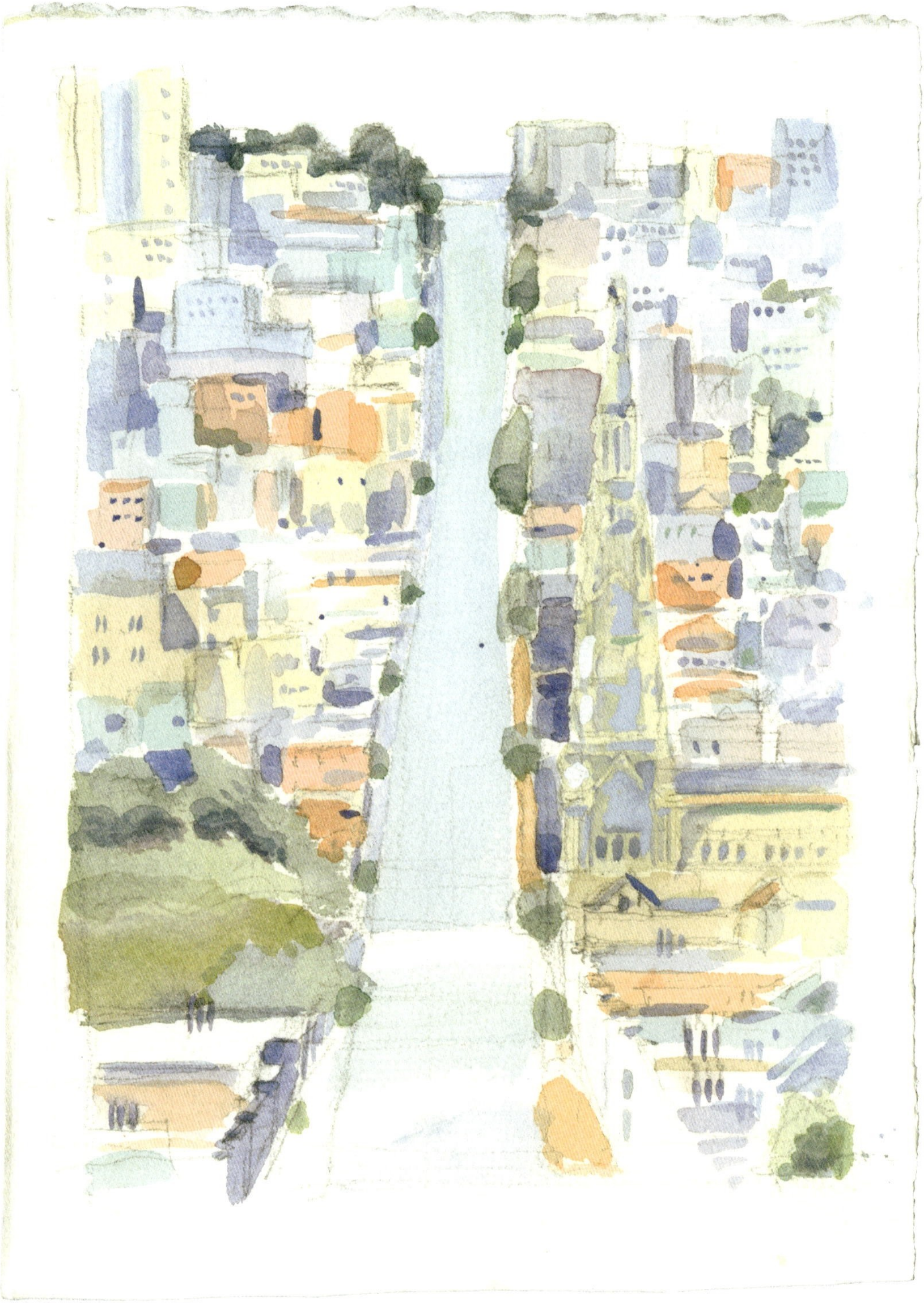

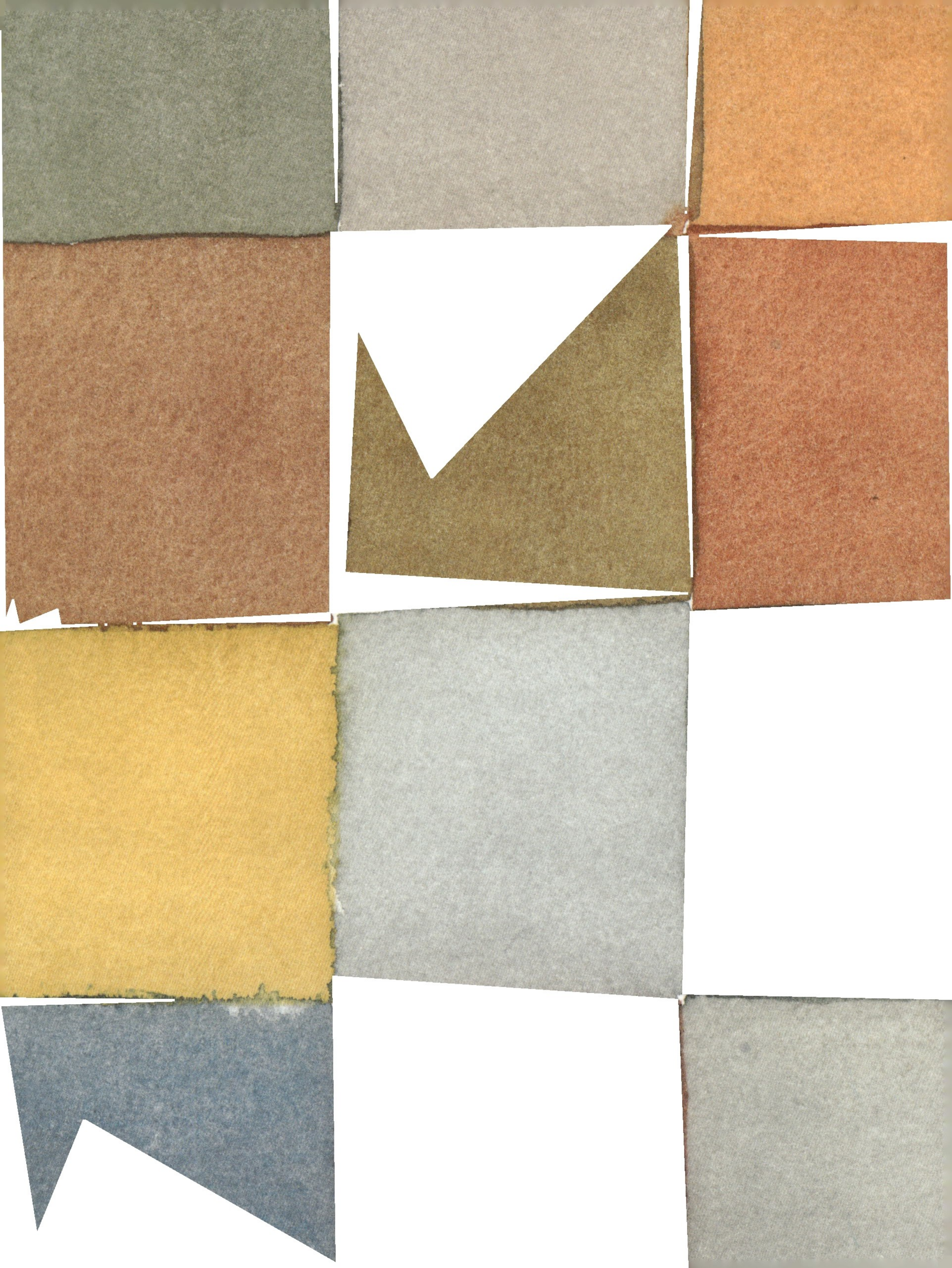

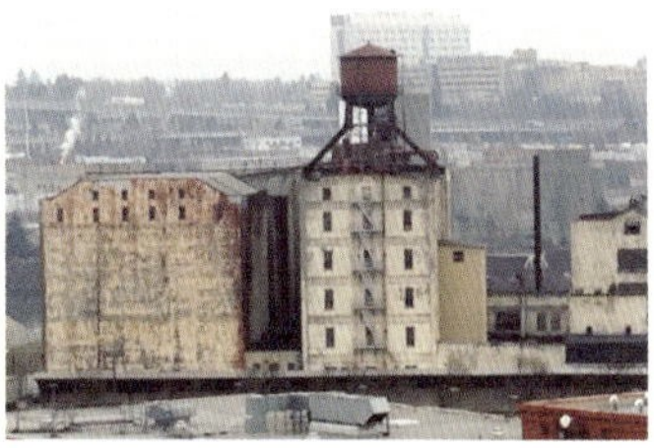

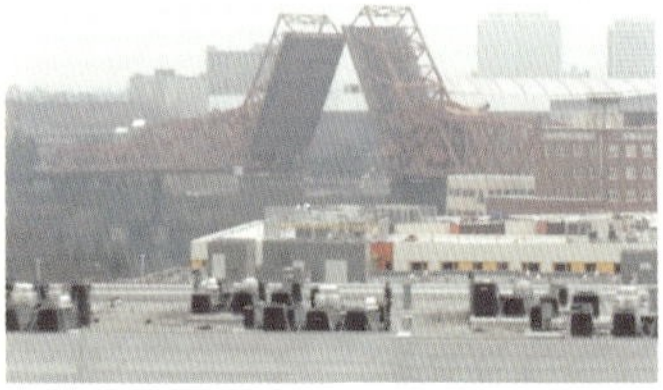

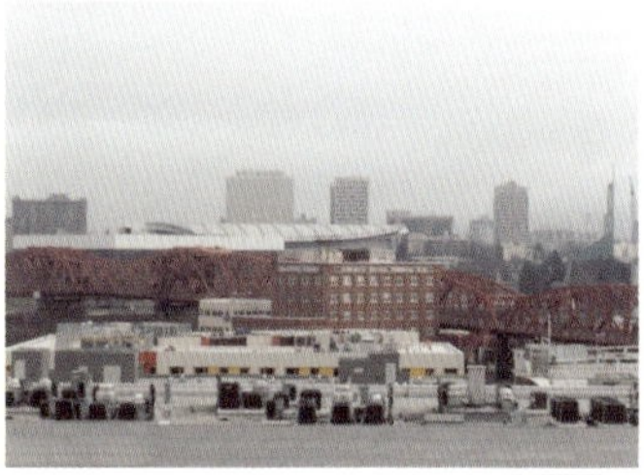

PORTLAND, OREGON

Portland, Oregon, sits along the Willamette River, its bridges raising up to let the boat traffic through. Gliding by, the river traffic resembles a modern painting—streaks of blue and red boats, black-and-white barges, and tugboats accented with international orange.

Small city blocks give Portland an intimate feel, and its old brick industrial buildings, some still bearing faded advertisements, give it a rugged beauty and a sense of history.

I see pearl gray colors in the rainy sky. Waiting for spring takes patience. In this corner of the Pacific Northwest, the Cascade Mountains trap rain in their peaks, keeping the weather cloudy. February is a gray month. The colors are saturated by the rain: mosses soaked with hues of electric green, tree bark wet with lichen, and the warehouse brick its deepest red. But when the sun does come out, watch out. The brilliance is breathtaking.

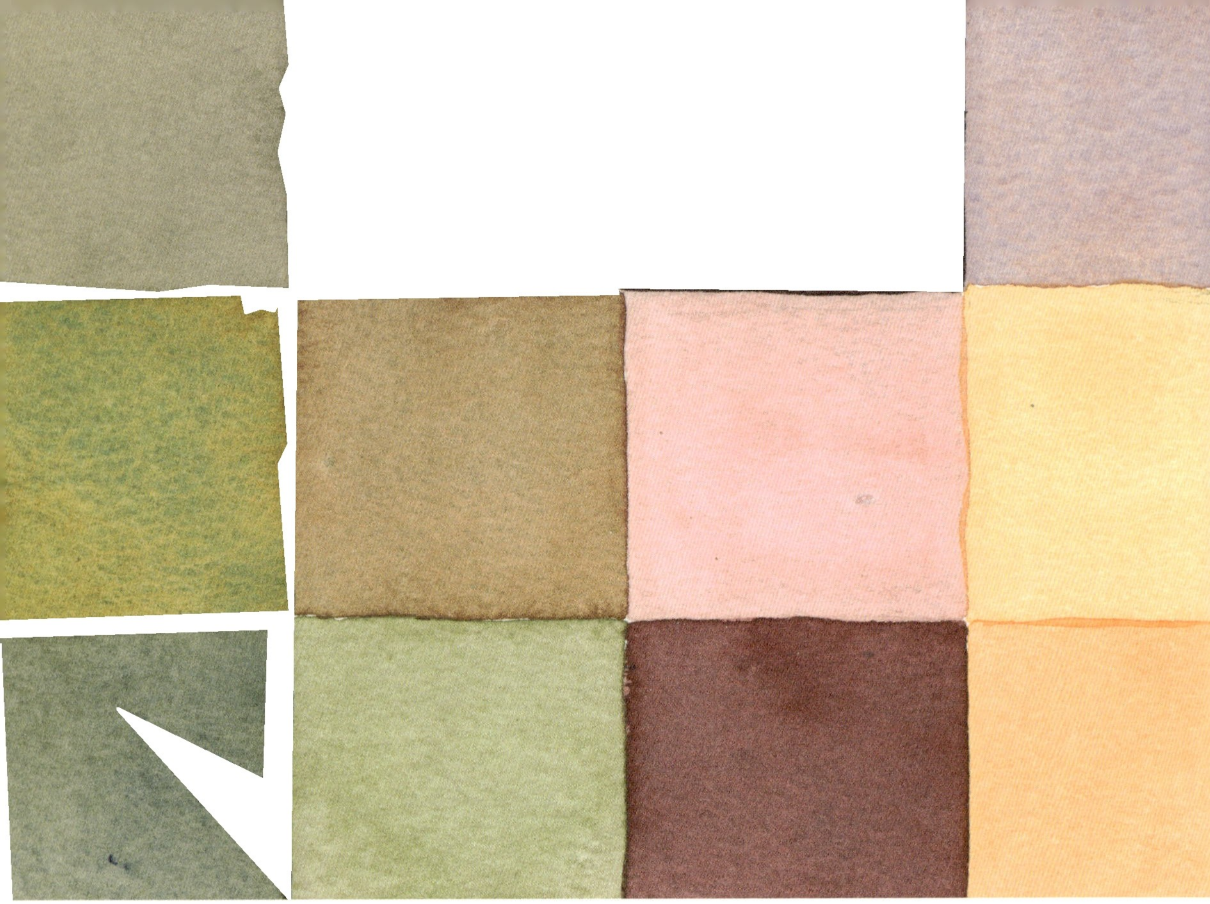

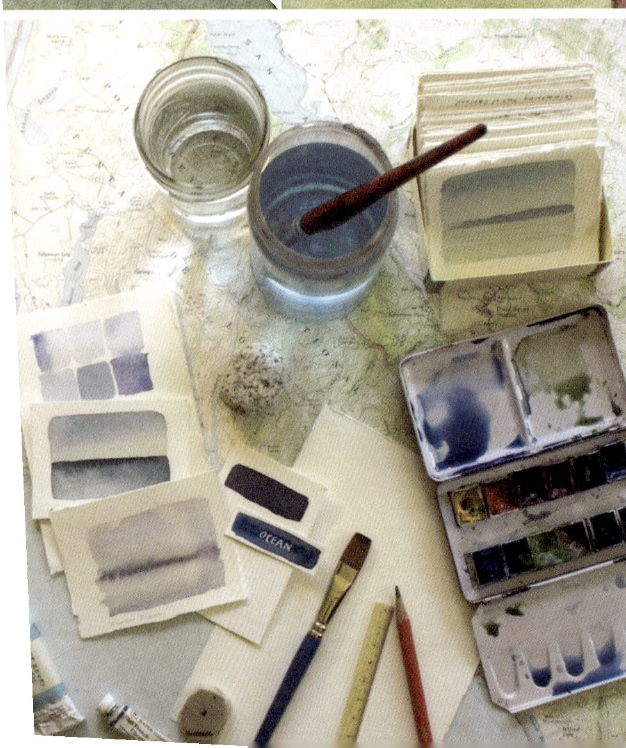
OCEAN

CHAPTER FIVE

Wherever You Go: Field Studies

It's fun to go out into the world and look at color. The more ways you look, the more you'll see. Looking at the different components of the environment or landscape brings out the variety of colors. Each of the practices in this chapter is a starting point, a different door to an experience of color. Feel free to create other practices for yourself along the way. You are developing your own personal color sense.

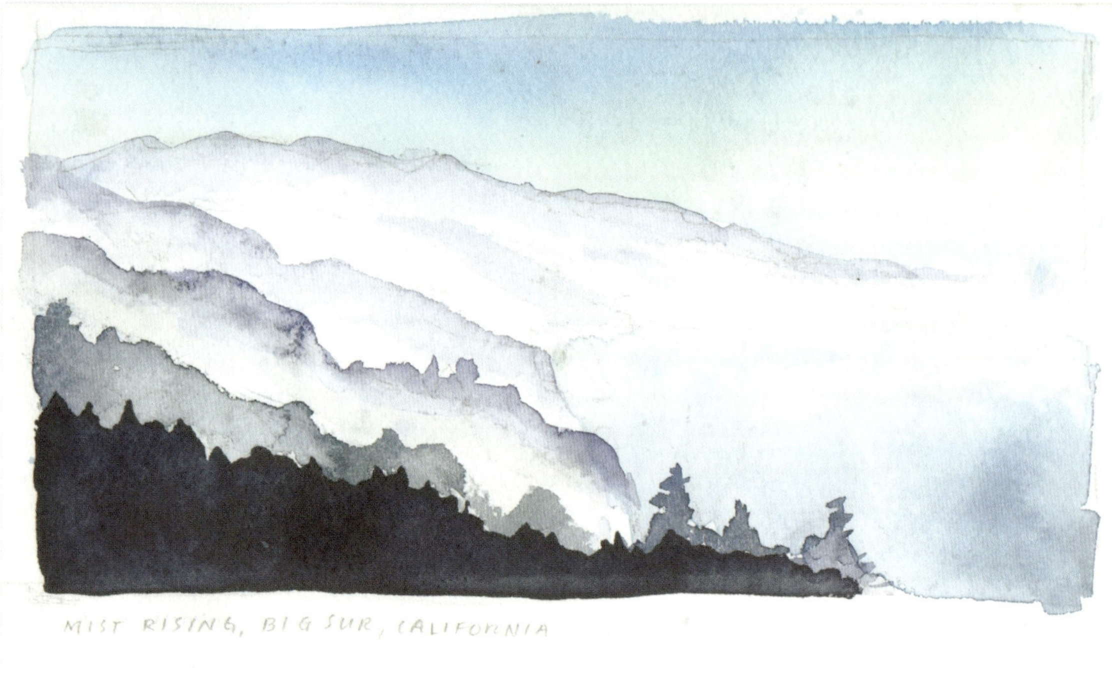

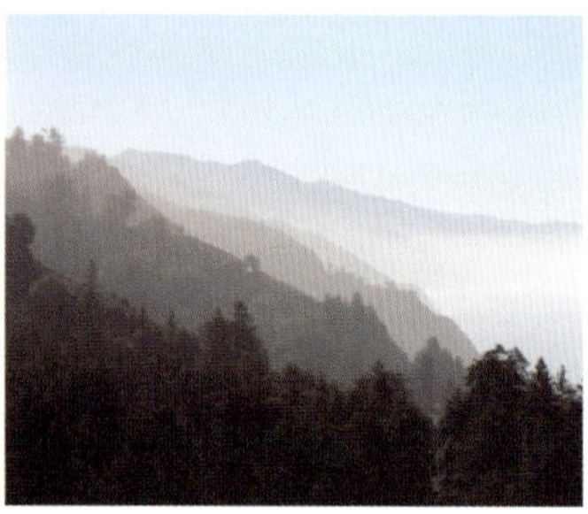

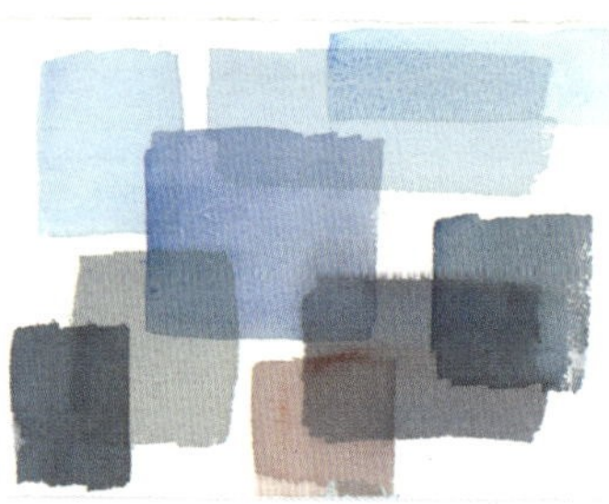

BIG PICTURE

Find a big view. It could be an urban or a rural vista. Before you focus on details, look across the full range of it for how the colors and forms come together to give you a feeling of the place. Distance creates perspective, in the same way that stepping back from your work allows you to see how the piece is coming together.

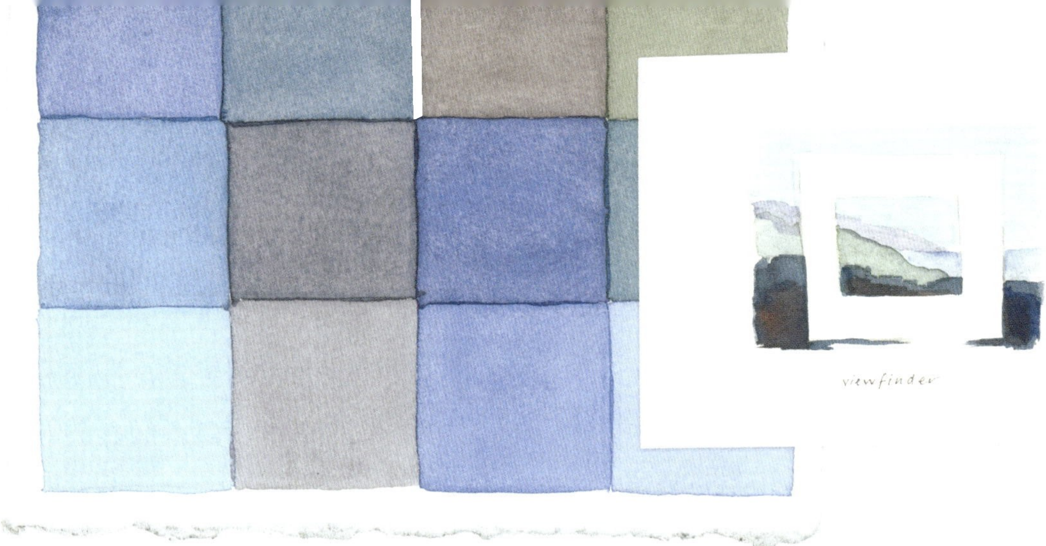

PRACTICE

- Look at the landscape as a whole. Pick out something that interests you and put down that first color, trying to match its value as best you can. Focus on the main elements and simplify; tuning out details will allow you to concentrate on the big notes of color that you first see.
- Look for big shapes of color, as if the scene before you was a puzzle. Paint the proportions of color—for example, is it 75 percent blue with purple accents? Divide up your paper to reflect the proportions you see in front of you.
- Observe the layers of color; break the vista into foreground, middle ground, and background. The area closest to you typically has the strongest colors, shifting to midtones as you move back in space, often ending in a muted blue gray in the distance.
- Sometimes the view is just too big to focus on. A simple viewfinder helps our brains make sense of the chaos. I use a 3" x 3" square and a 2" x 4" rectangle made of heavyweight paper. Hold the viewfinder at arm's length to find a composition of colors that you want to paint.
- Capture ephemeral events. While I was painting a palette of a view one day, a bluebird swooped in. I quickly added his intense blue against the lime-green grasses into my palette. It provided a welcome accent of an opposite color and made the palette more interesting.
- Create a series of three palettes from the same view. If it's big, break it into sections and do a palette for each section, then look at them side by side.

DETAIL

Inspecting small things invites you to look carefully and slowly. Get specific: a color is often not just one color but many shades and gradations. Note the way color changes as it wraps around a form. An apple might have a highlight of yellow shifting toward orange red, then cool violet as it approaches the curved edge, transitioning to a warm purple shadow. There are many shades of gray in a rock, or pinks in a cherry blossom sprig. In every season, there are many wonderful, small moments to enjoy in the natural world.

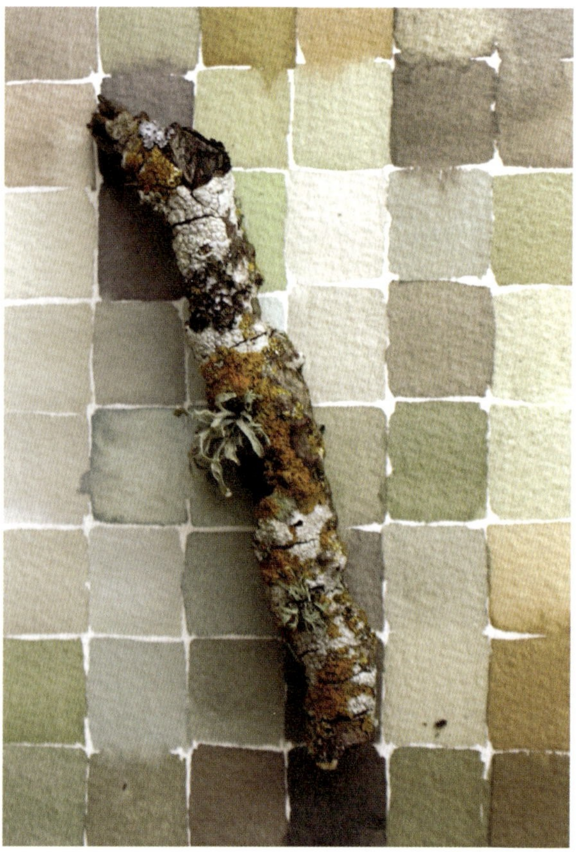

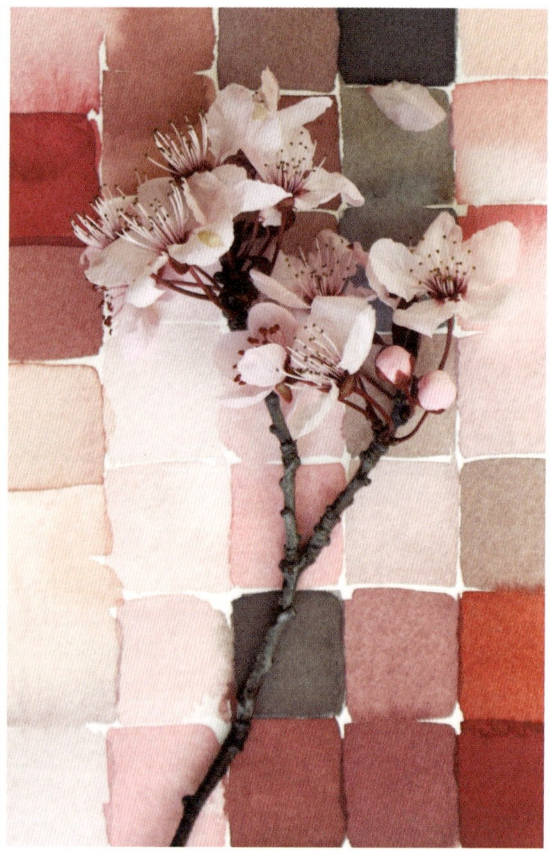

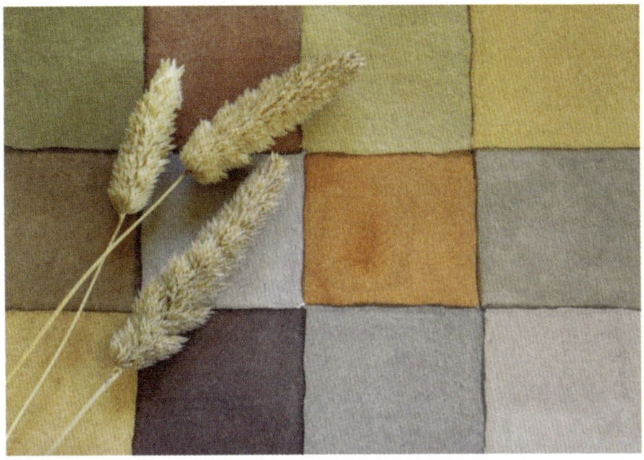

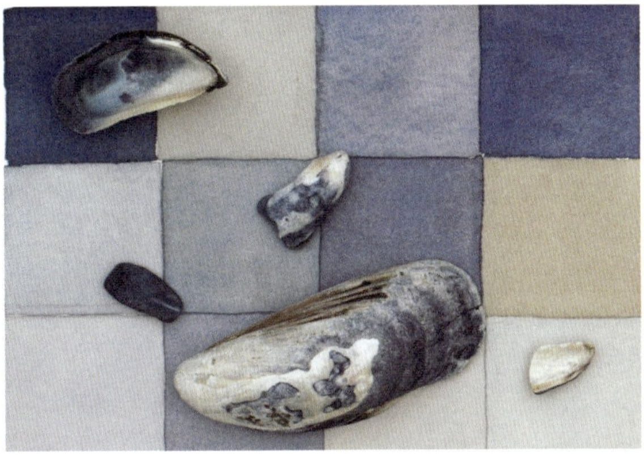

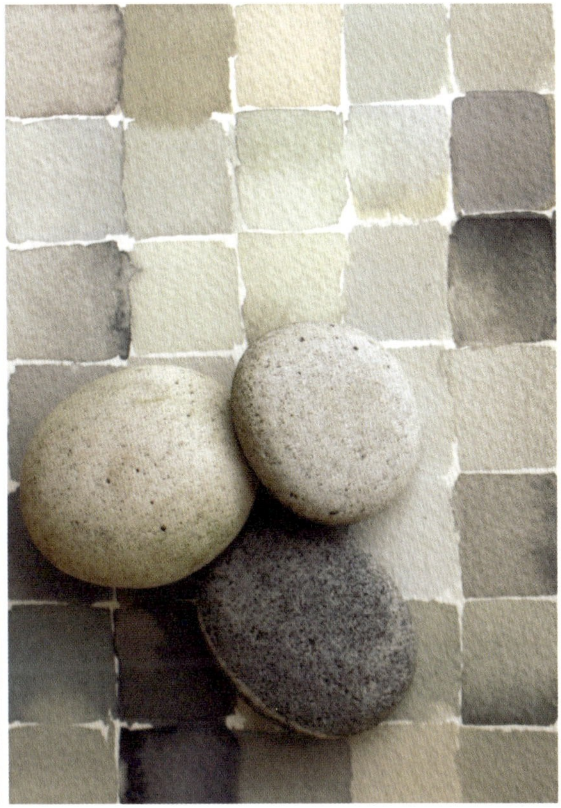

PRACTICE

- Find a small object and explore all the notes of color. From these, create a value study. What are the lightest lights, the darkest darks, and all the hues in between? Keep mixing and trying out the paints until you think you have it right. To create a more detailed palette, try using just one brush width for each note of color.
- While you're working, keep your brush loose and your body relaxed. From time to time, step back from your work and get some perspective on it. Walk away and then come back. Turn the paper upside down. You may see things in a new light.

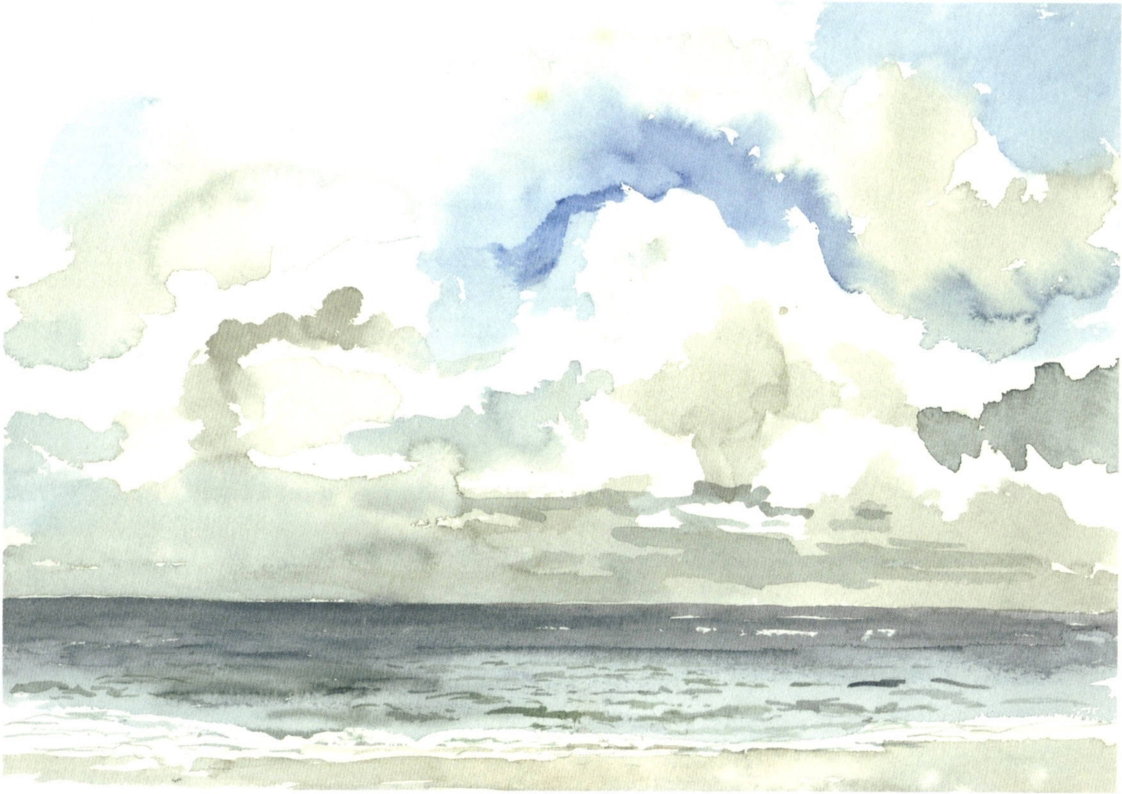

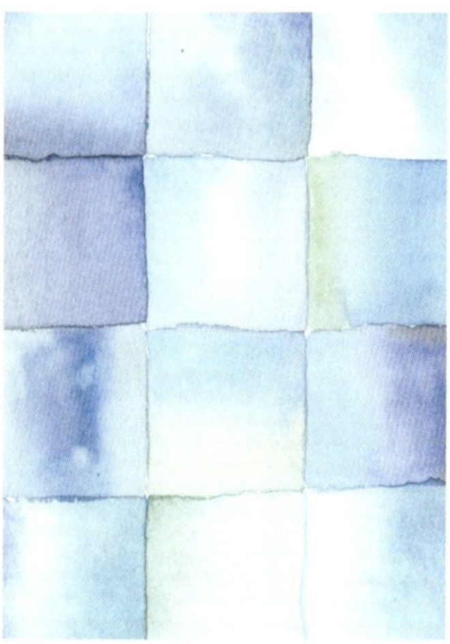

SKY PATCH

Let your eyes rest in the vastness of the sky and notice how the colors change from dawn to dusk. It's wonderful to lie on your back and look up at the sky, whether it's a starry night or the blue of a summer day.

Painters throughout history have painted the sky. John Constable, through a lifetime of observation and practice, turned the sky into a world all its own—and came to know it for all its shapes, colors, and moods. Constable's skies have a lot to teach us about how our landscapes are endlessly changing, always interesting, and what the practice of observing them carefully can give us.

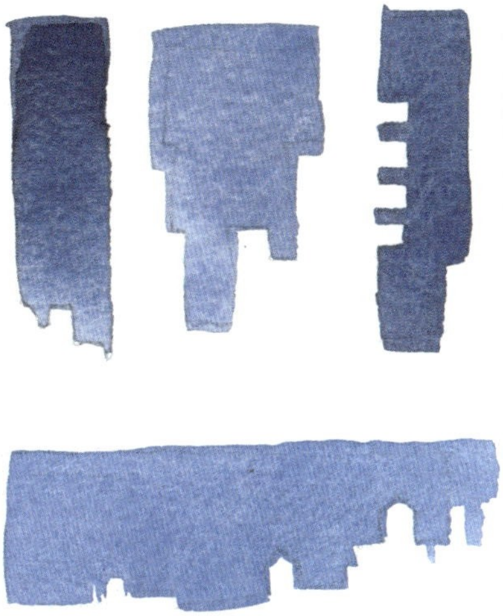

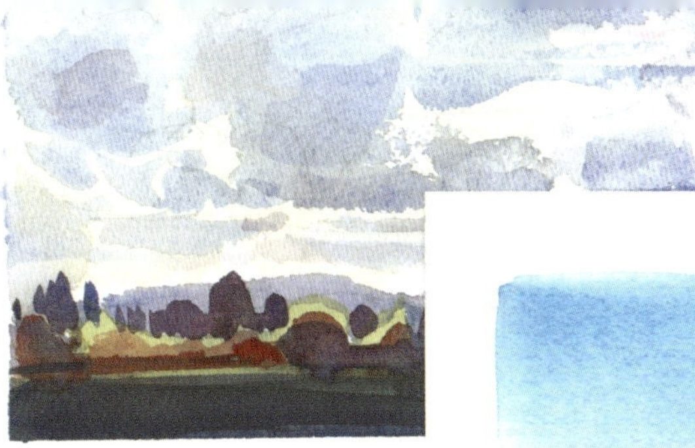

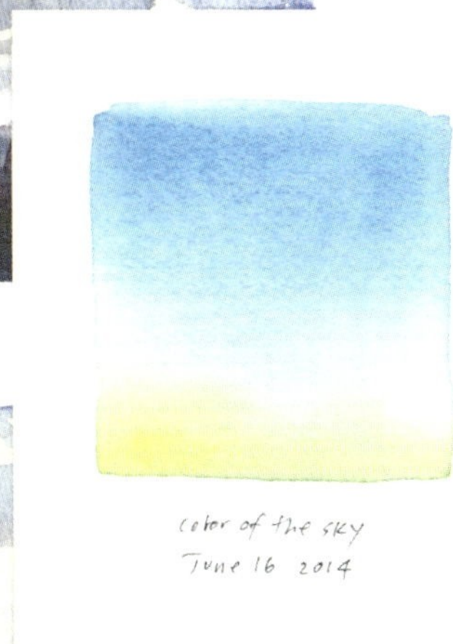

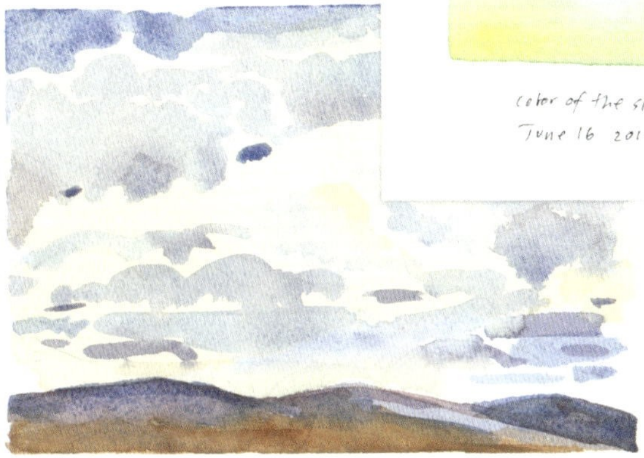

PRACTICE

- Do a color palette of the clouds in the sky. If the clouds have shadows, paint those, too. The mist in the clouds is often pearl gray with hints of pale yellow and subtle grays, and the shadows are often purple. See if you can feel their lightness, or their heaviness if a storm is coming, and reflect that in your palette.
- Focus on the negative space and look for patches of sky.
- In a city, what colors do you see in between the buildings? In a park, what colors do you see through the branches or between the trees?
- Paint the sky at different times of day and at different times of the year: dawn, twilight, sunset, the end of a summer day, a winter sky, a spring rainstorm.
- Note on the back of your sky studies the prevailing weather conditions, direction of light, and time of day.

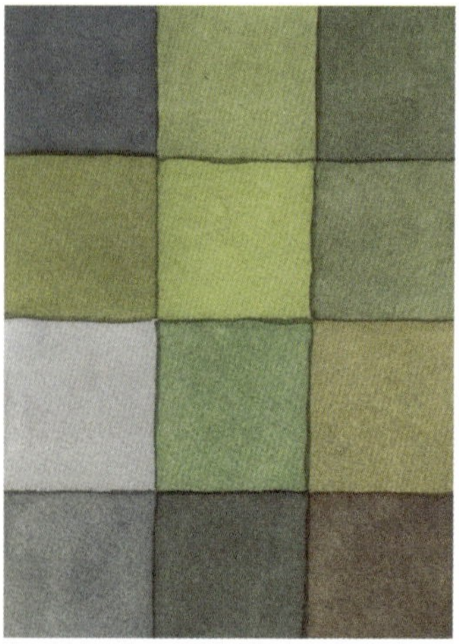

TERRAIN

Terrain (which can include the elevation, topography, and vegetation of a place) is one aspect of habitat. Desert, jungle, beach, mountain, city, and countryside are all types of terrain. The face of a mountain will have different colors than a boggy swamp. The dusty gray-green cactus colors in the high-altitude deserts are far different from the dark-green pine of a Maine forest at sea level.

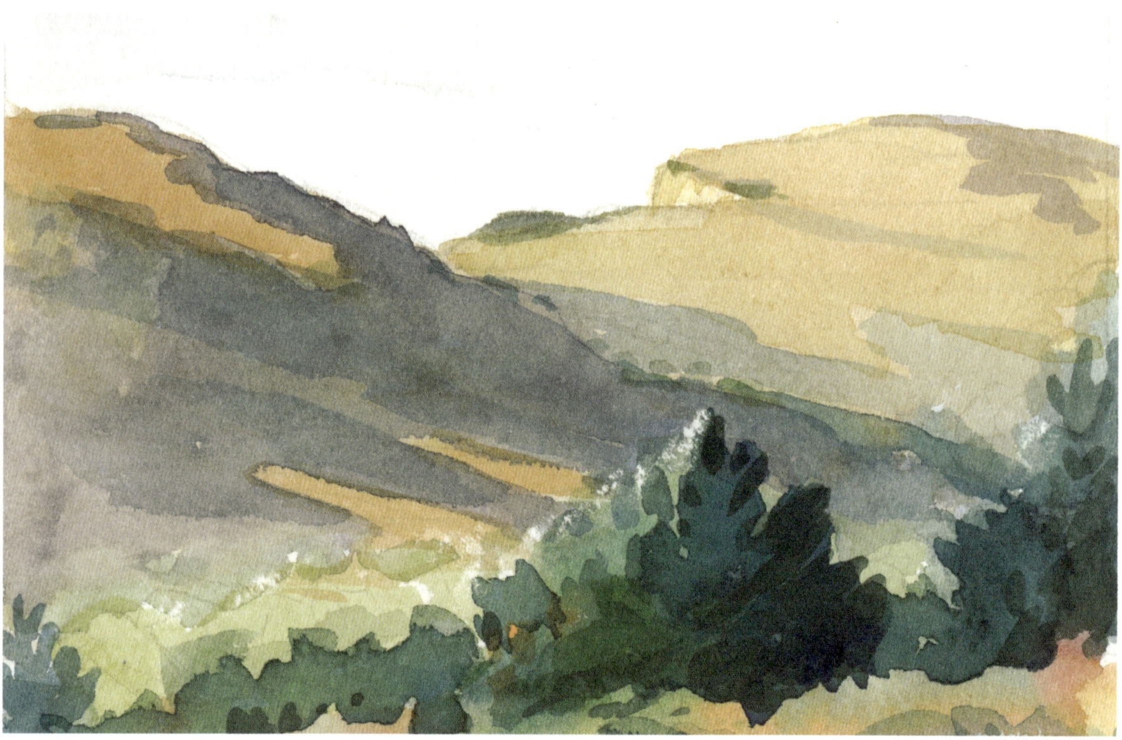

Walking in the foothills of the Sierra Nevada Mountains, I feel a sense of the hillside topography as colors fade to blue and then purple in the distance.

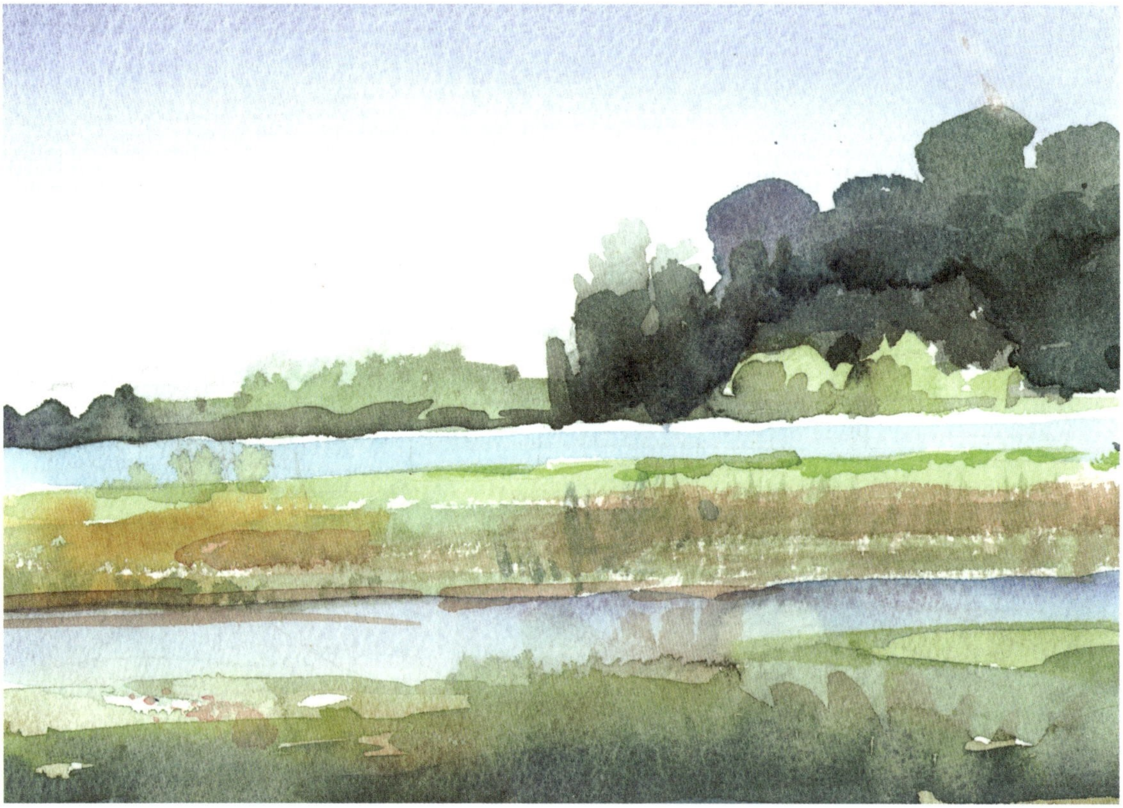

One of my favorite types of terrain is salt marsh—an ever-changing zone between land and open salt water. The rhythm of the tides brings a variety of color palettes: water reflecting the sky when the tide is in, mud in primordial shades of rich browns and greens when the tide is out, and grasses in green and yellow.

PRACTICE

- **Wherever you are, notice the elevation. Are you at sea level, on a mountain, in a desert or jungle? What is the terrain like? Is it flat, hilly, rocky? How does it feel under your feet? Is it gravel, cobblestone, asphalt, sand?**
- **Paint the colors of these features. Try to adapt your technique to the specific terrain. A watery terrain, for example, invites a wet-on-wet technique and soft edges, whereas a hillside with a pattern of trees or a streetscape might call for layering colors that have defined edges.**

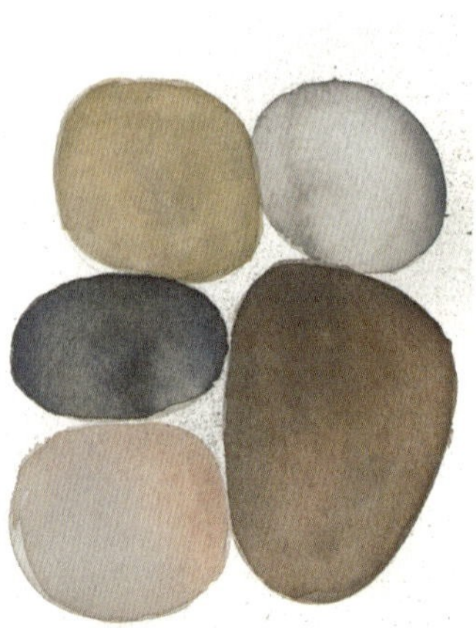

ROCKS

Rocks speak of an Earth that is 4.5 billion years old. I love to hold a smooth rock in my hand—a touchstone through time and place.

Rocks—round, flat, egg-shaped, moonstones, heart-shaped, with rings around them, striped, speckled—embody what happens to color through the ages in response to such things as temperature, wind, rain, or erosion. To paint the colors of rocks, you need to hone your senses to the subtleties of the colors they contain. It's a great way to practice mixing colors. You won't get the color of rocks right out of a tube.

Built environments, too, tell the color of place: brownstones in Manhattan, gray-yellow volcanic stone in Rome, terra-cotta bricks in Portland, Oregon, and Boston.

Not only are there colors in rocks, but rocks are colors. The origin of paint pigments started out as rocks in particular places: burnt sienna originally came from a certain soil in Italy, red ochre from a mine in the aboriginal lands of Australia, ultramarine from semiprecious stone in northeastern Afghanistan.

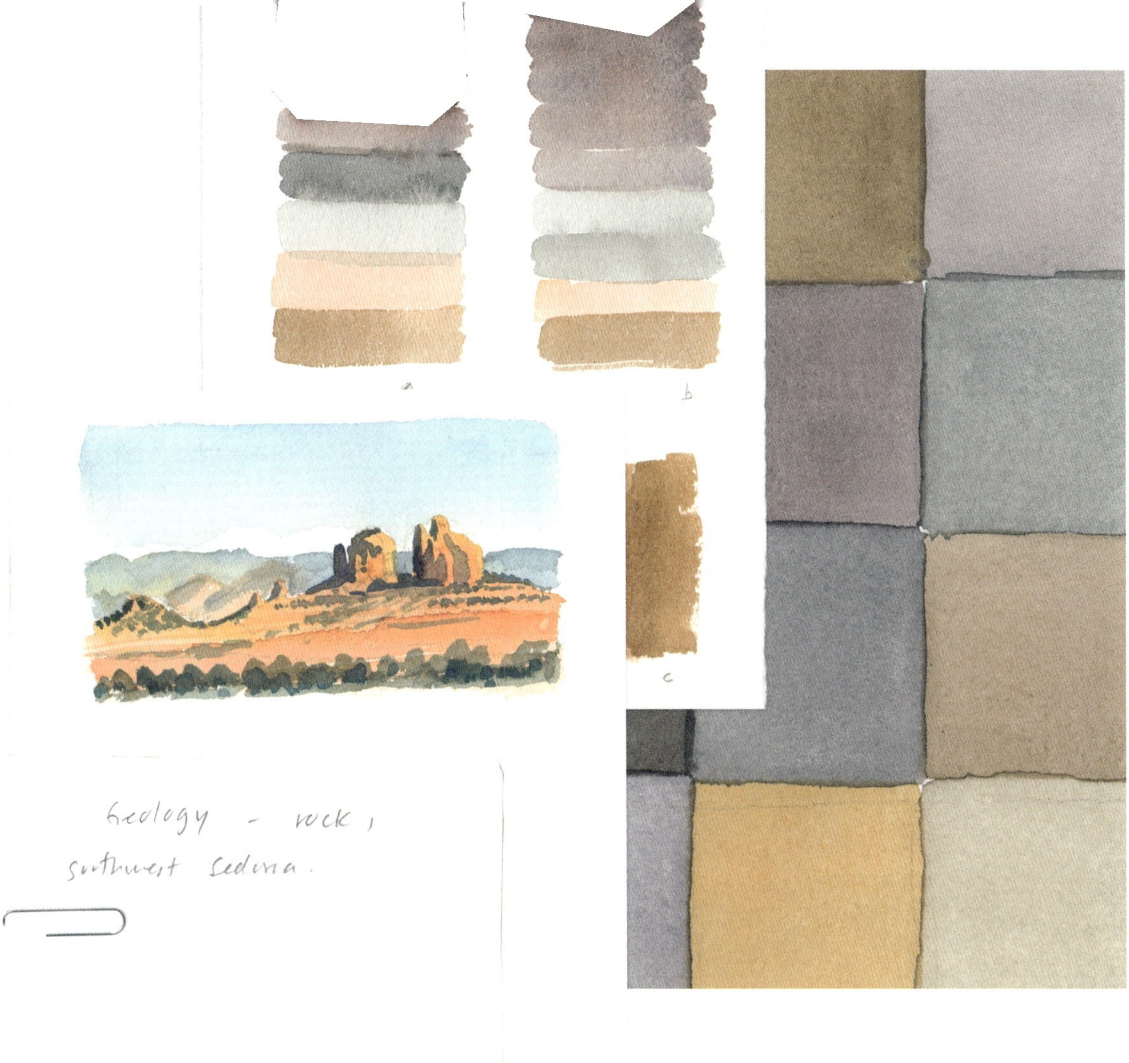

PRACTICE

- Pick up any kind of rock—from ones found while hiking in the forest or desert to pebbles found on the street. Note the different colors and striations and paint a palette of the colors you see.
- Paint a palette of rocks at the beach. Notice the differences in colors when they are wet versus dry.
- Paint the subtle colors you see in a stone wall or an old brick wall. How do these palettes differ?

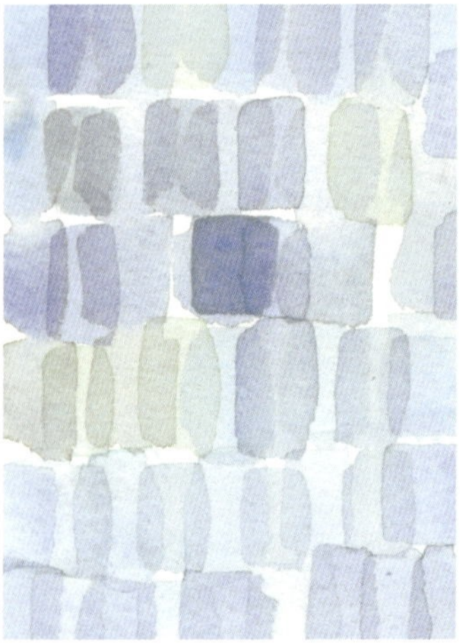

WATER

Water invites us to quiet our minds. Whether it be an ocean, river, fountain, or pond, water can be mesmerizing. Notice how many forms water takes, from streams to rivers, ocean to mist, fog to rain. Capturing the endless color variations can keep an artist busy for a lifetime.

Watercolors are a natural medium for painting water. They speak for themselves: pigment suspended in water. Use big brushes and lots of water and move color and water across the page.

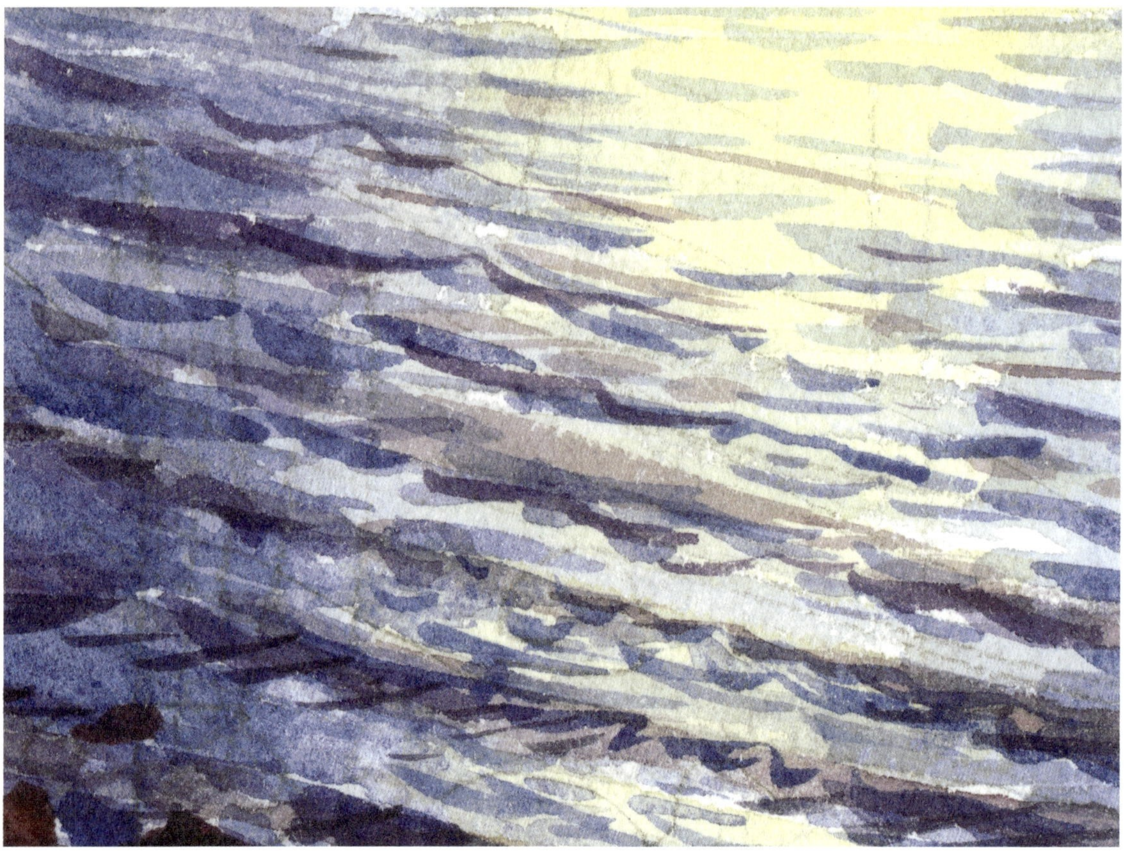

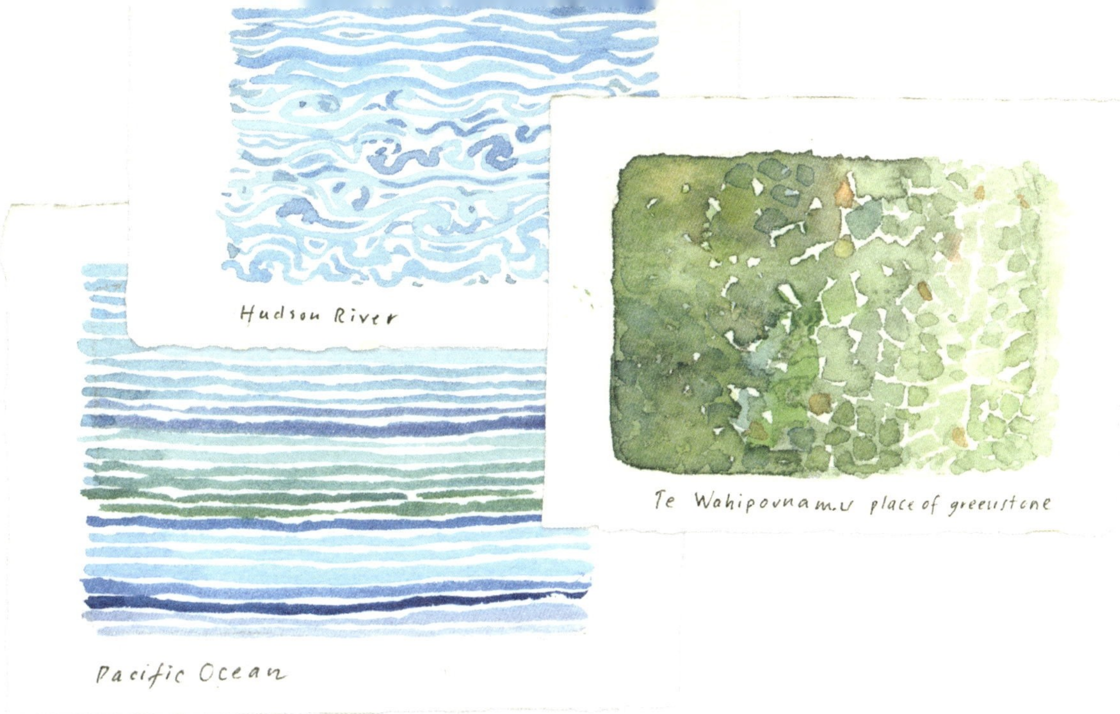

Try using bands of color to give the feeling of the shape of waves.

PRACTICE

- Sit next to some water, or look at the rain, a pond, a puddle, a glass of water, a drop of dew. What colors do you see? Lay down one band of color, let it set for a moment, then add another color. Or work wet on wet.

- Note the big color relationships between water and sky. Try making two brushstrokes that capture the sky and water. On a foggy day the horizon and the water merge. In late afternoon the horizon line might be a dark band of ultramarine blue.

- Look at the colors in a pond or a puddle. What's in it, around it, reflected in it, including the sky?

- Try painting the colors of waves, exploring rhythm and movement. Water always moves, and so should your brush. Create some play between fast and slow strokes. Don't worry about getting it right—let your brush move with the water. Start by mixing the colors that you see, and make lines of color that reflect the moving water. Keep your brushstrokes loose to express the quality of things that are alive, moving, and flowing.

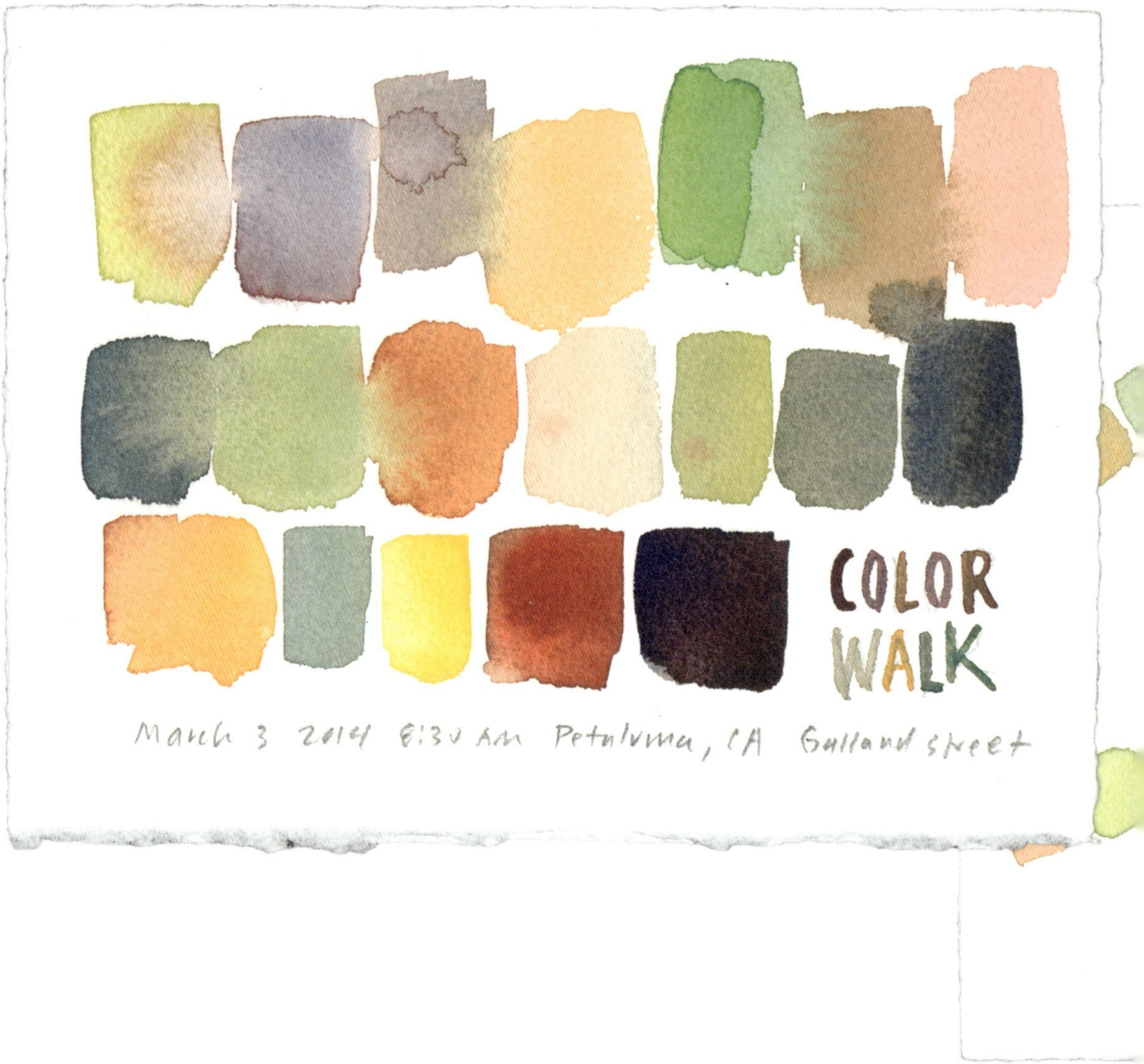

COLOR WALK

Go out with the intention of looking only at color. Clear your mind and focus only on the colors in your immediate surroundings. Soon, your walk will become a parade of color. As you move along, you become a collection of color in motion.

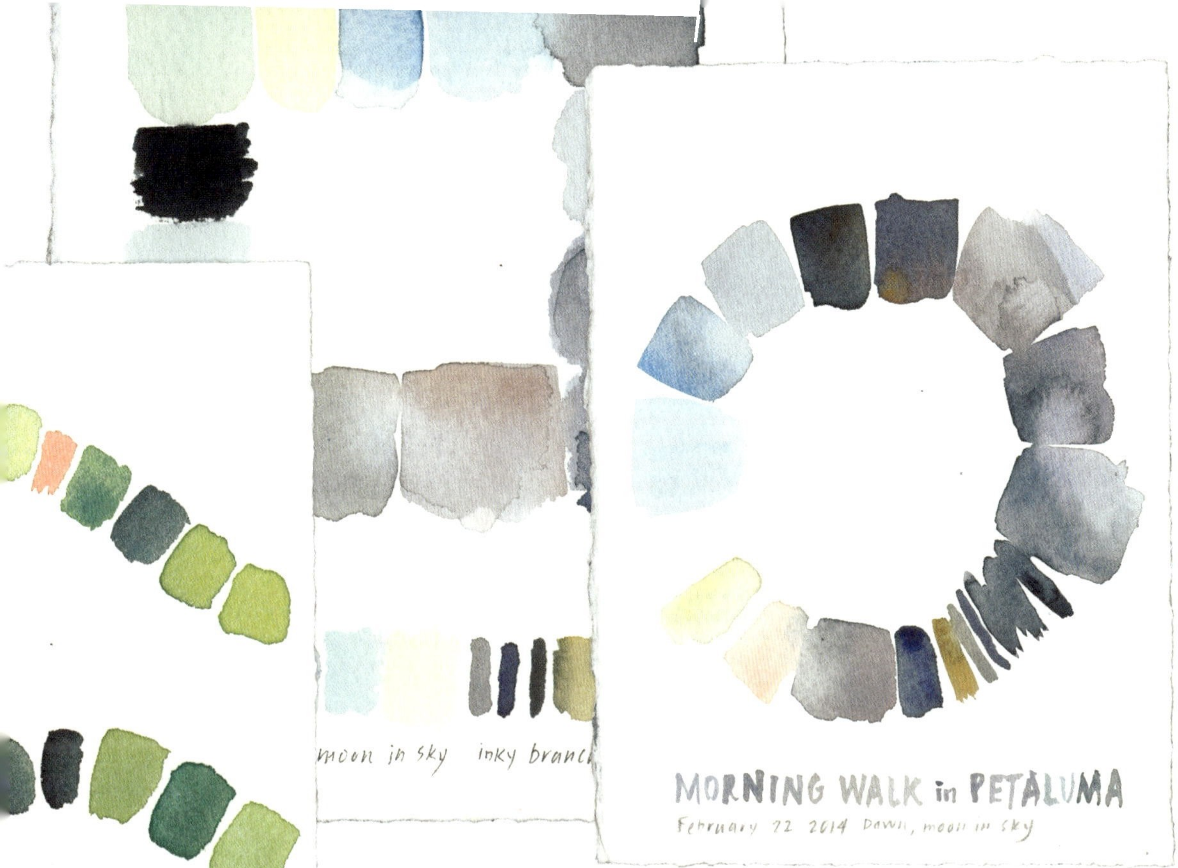

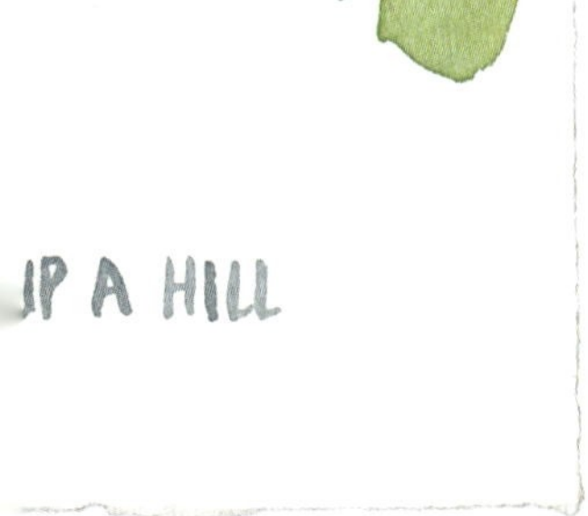

PRACTICE

- Bring a small notebook to jot down what you see along the way. Record the date, place, time, and season. Assign a word or phrase to each thing whose color you notice—you will come back to these later.
- When you return from your walk, open to the notes in your notebook, and take out your paints. Use the words as a prompt to start mixing your colors, and see what you remember.
- Your first impressions are usually the best, so go with them. For another dimension, paint the shape of your walk—around a city block, down a rambling path—as you put down the colors. From that, make a palette.
- If you do the same walk throughout the seasons, your palettes and notes will record the shift of colors altered by light and weather.

COLOR MEMORY

Artists mine their memories to inspire painting. This is time travel using colors as stepping-stones into your memory bank. To find your color memories, look within to the colors stored in your life experiences, a place between memory, dream, and presence.

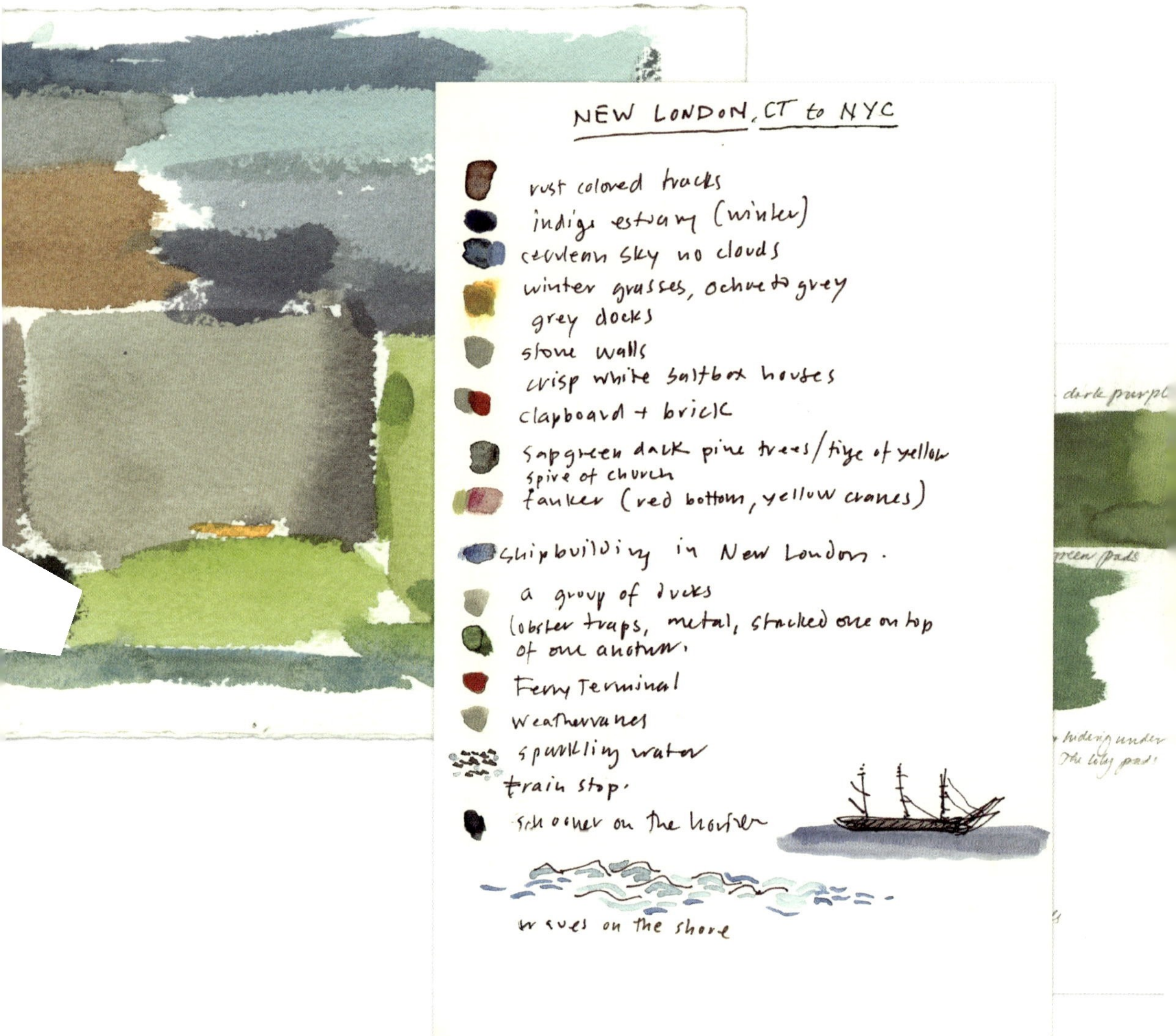

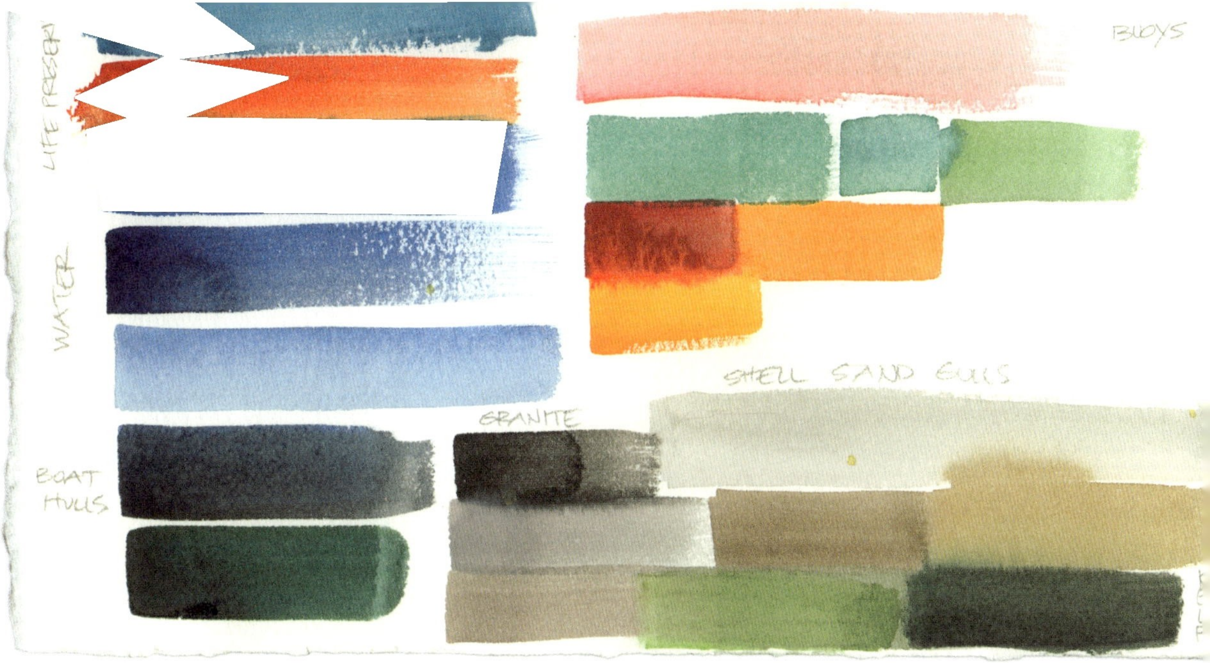

PRACTICE

For these practices, you may want to work larger, on a 11" x 15" watercolor paper, to encourage a sense of freedom. Limit yourself to twenty minutes for each memory exercise. This is a fun exercise to do with friends and compare memories.

- Close your eyes and think back to a place or object in a particular moment in your life, whether yesterday or years ago: a summer day in your childhood, the view from your bedroom window, a favorite object, a place you loved.
- Start by writing details you remember on the paper, or start with the color and add the words later. Beginning anywhere on the paper, fill the page. Be generous with the color. Mix one color you remember and let the process lead you to other colors.
- Don't worry if the colors run or overlap, and don't think about what it looks like. Take that little note of color in your memory and say to yourself, "Was that a teal green? Or was it lighter? Or greener?"
- If you feel stuck, invite in all of your senses to ignite your memory. The more you do this exercise, the more your memories will flow, so try doing more than one.

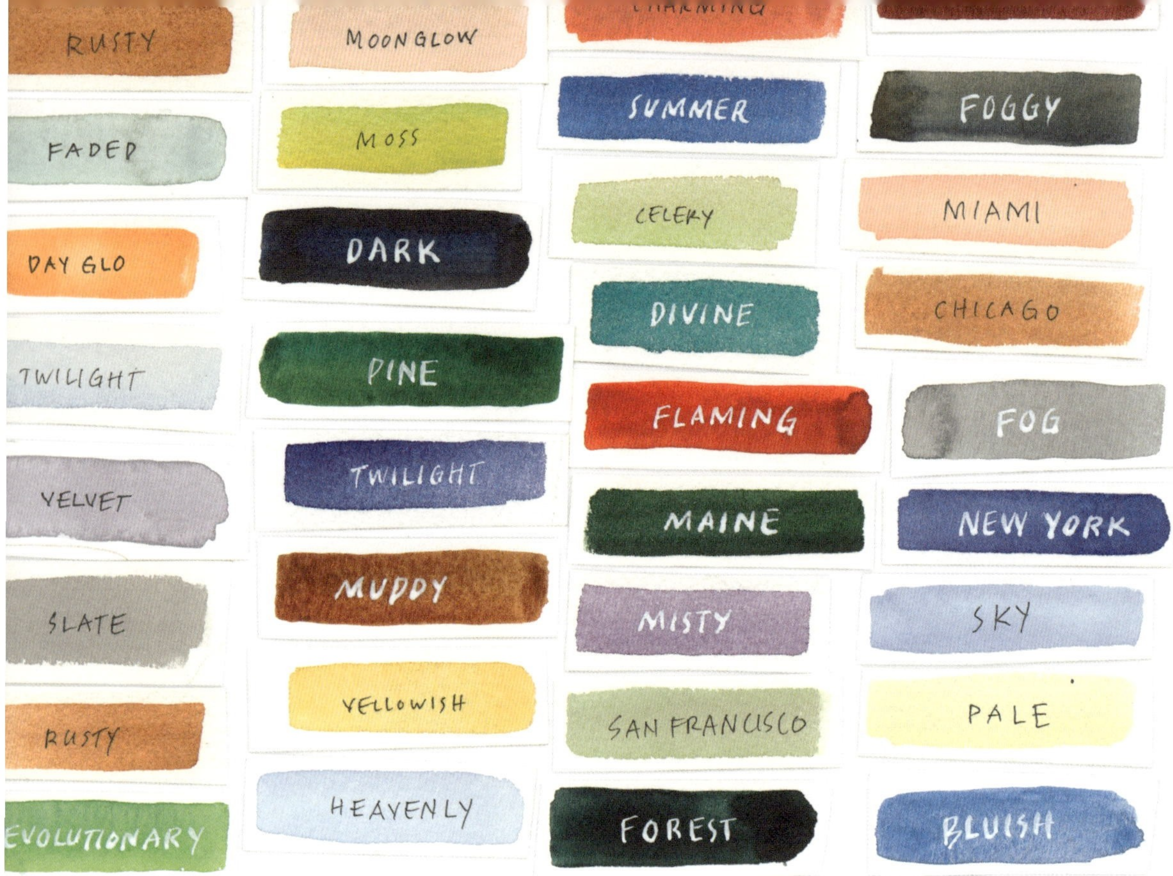

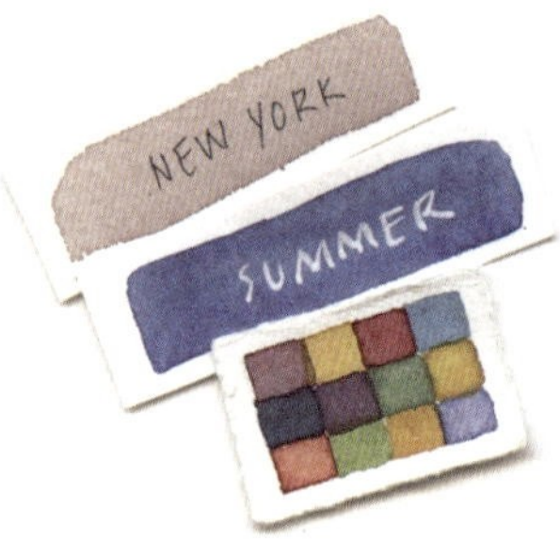

NAMING COLORS

From the time we were coloring with crayons, colors were given names: blizzard blue, shocking pink, jungle green, cornflower, maize. Names are useful, giving us a collective language. But consider naming colors for yourself, from your own experience, and have fun developing your own personal color vocabulary. Are you painting Maine-rock gray, tree-bark gray, misty-Atlantic gray, pigeon-feather gray, sidewalk gray?

I like to rename my colors and make them more personal to me. You can also rename colors to make them more personal to you. What has more resonance—Pantone 299 or Point Reyes Pacific Blue? Each place inspires new color names. Every day can bring a new set of names.

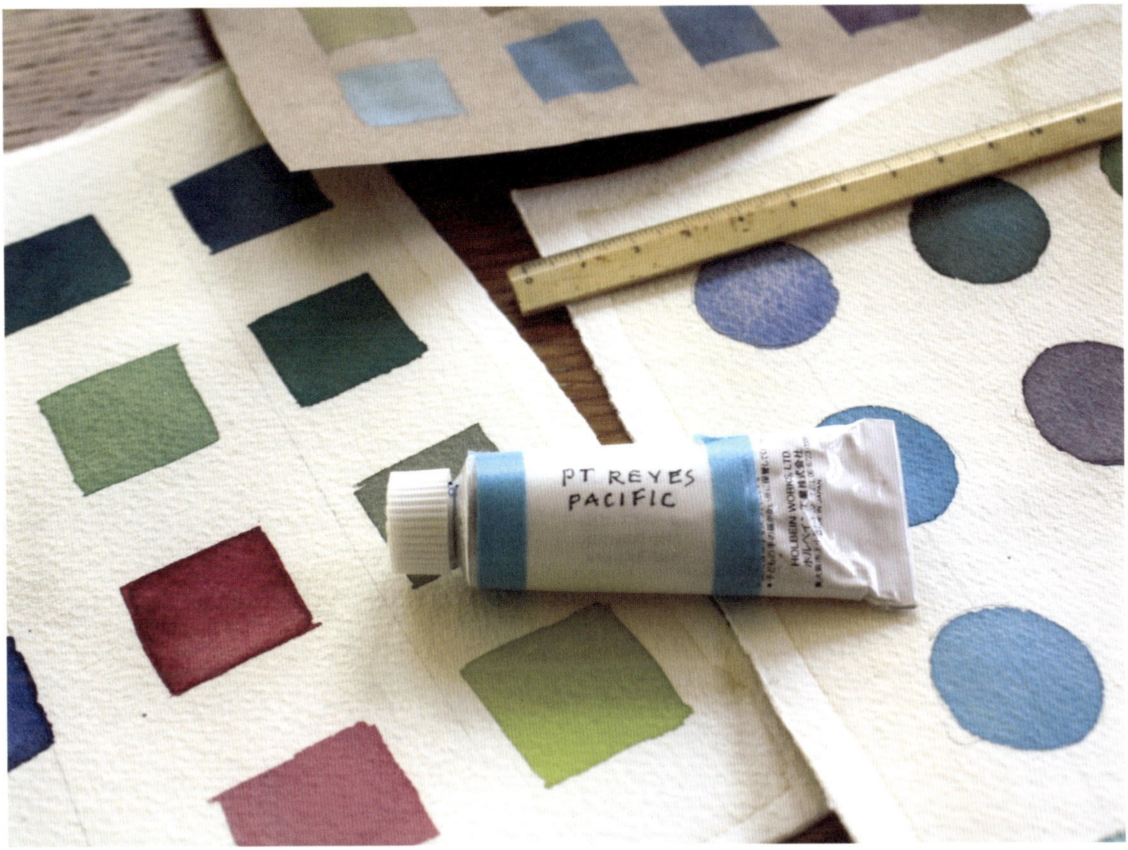

PRACTICE

- Wherever you are right now, look around. Consider everything part of the local color and part of your palette of place. What would you name the color of the tea you are drinking? The color of the wall as the sun hits it? The No. 2 Dixon Ticonderoga pencil? The colors of your friend's eyes?
- What qualities can you use to describe your color names: light, dark, deep, gentle, luminous, dull, soft, transparent, opaque? "Deep scarlet plum" has more detail than "red." Colors have their own energies and moods: happy, moody, pensive, calm, thrilling, quirky. Combine words and color and see what you come up with.

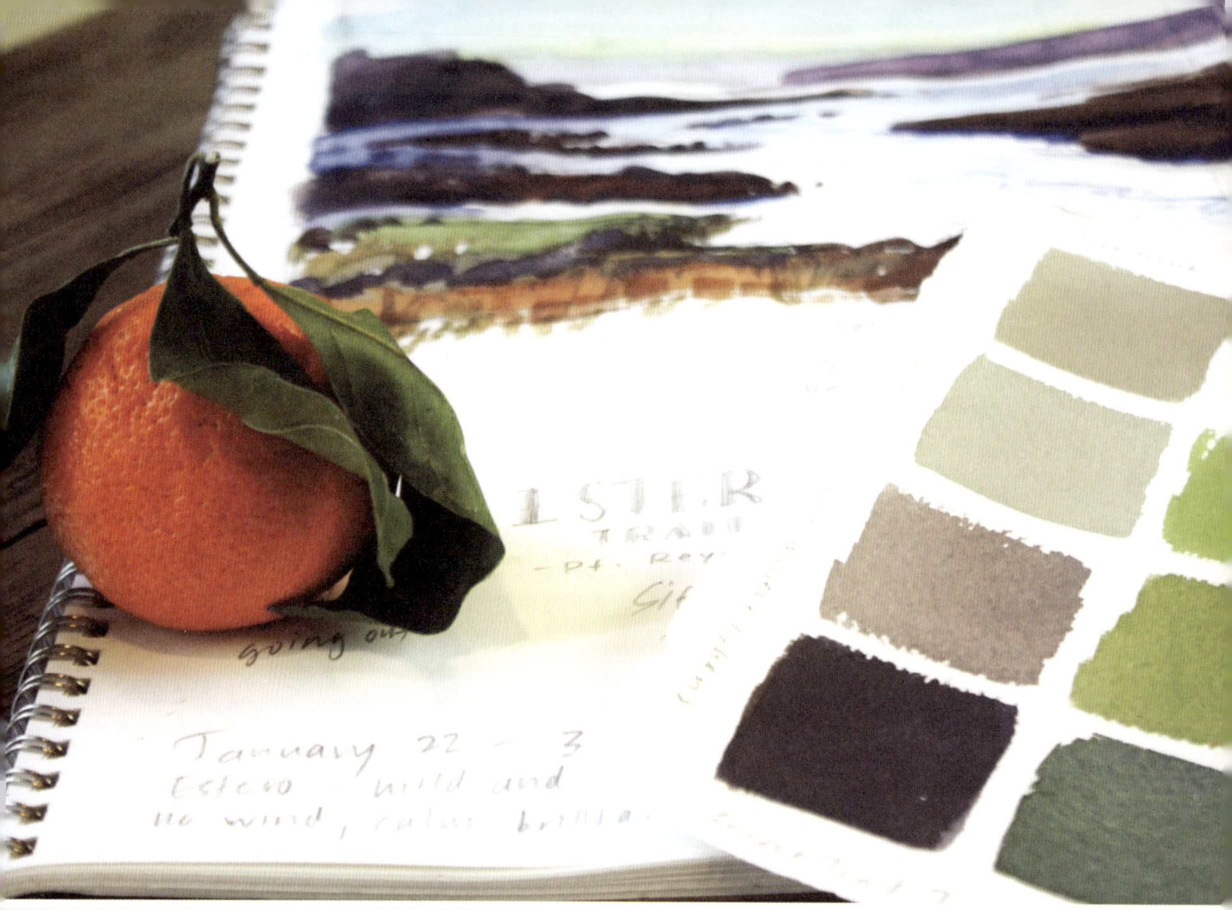
January 22 - 3

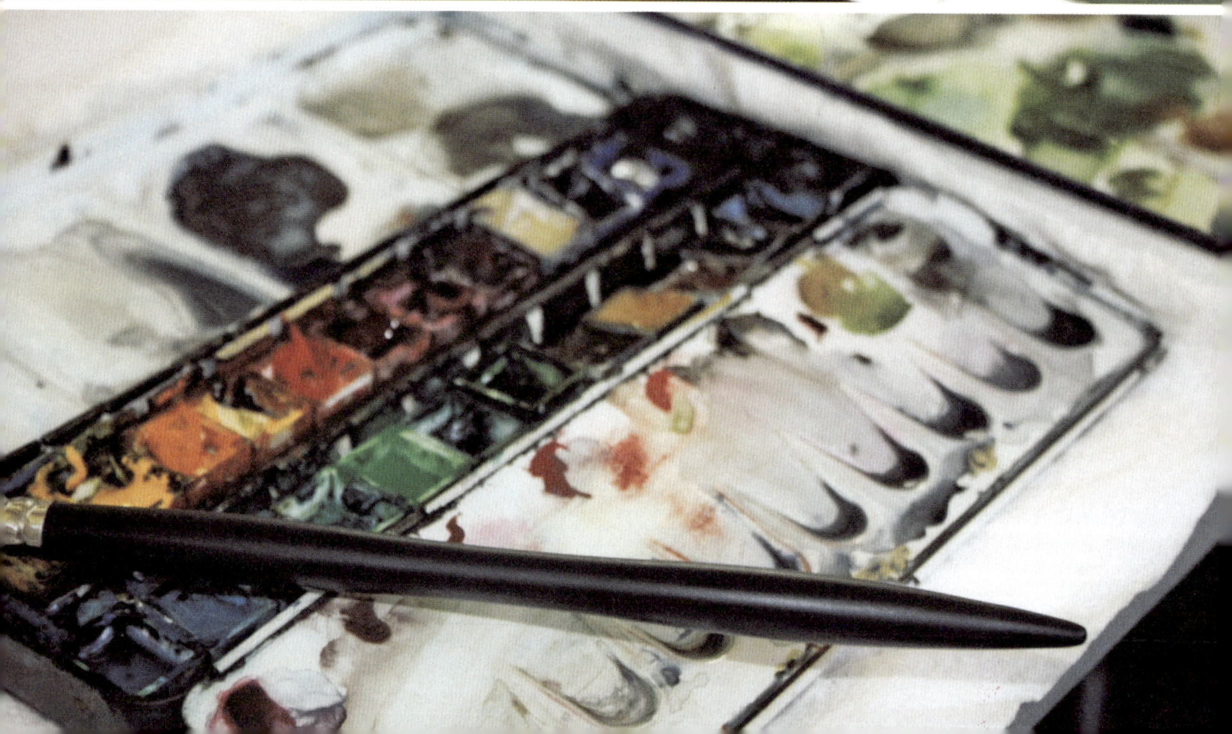

CHAPTER SIX

Palettes to Painting: Some Places

There is no perfection in painting. It is an ongoing practice that invites you to open your eyes to the world around you and cultivate your sense of curiosity and wonder.

Through creating color palettes, I look more deeply and intensely at the colors I see, then move them into a painting.

a summer day —

which one will you make yours

cobalt blue, cerulean or ultrama

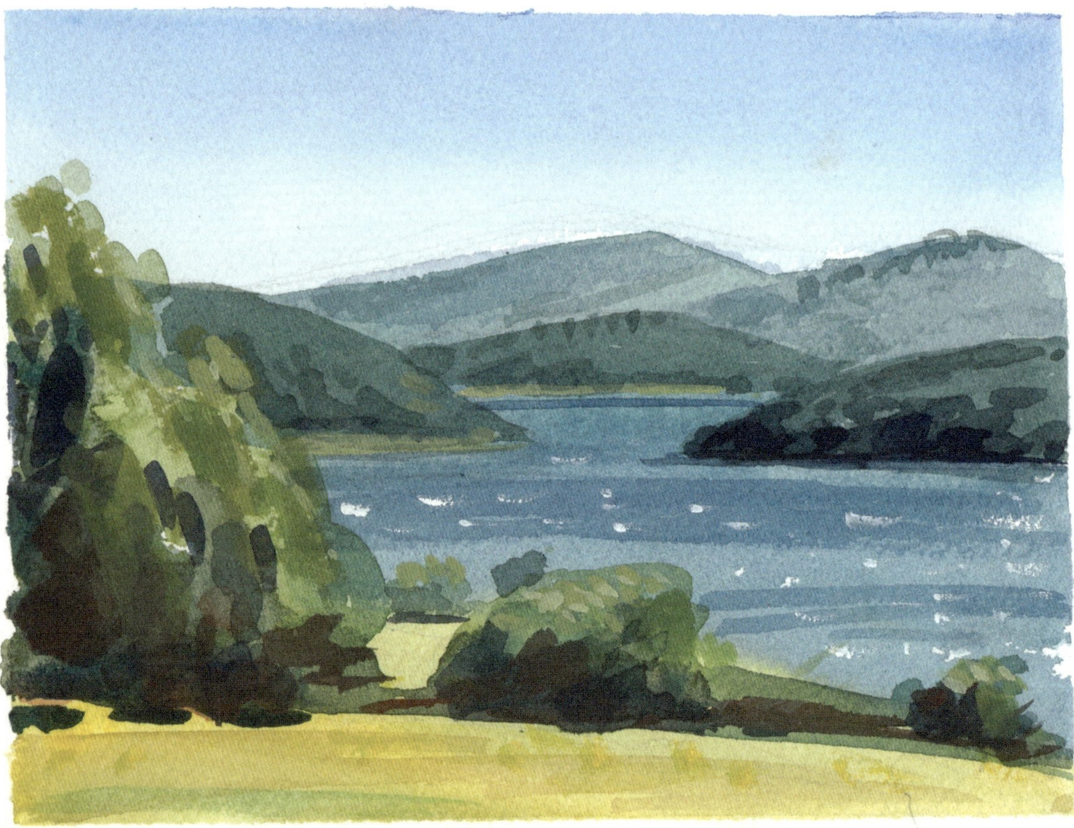

windy day

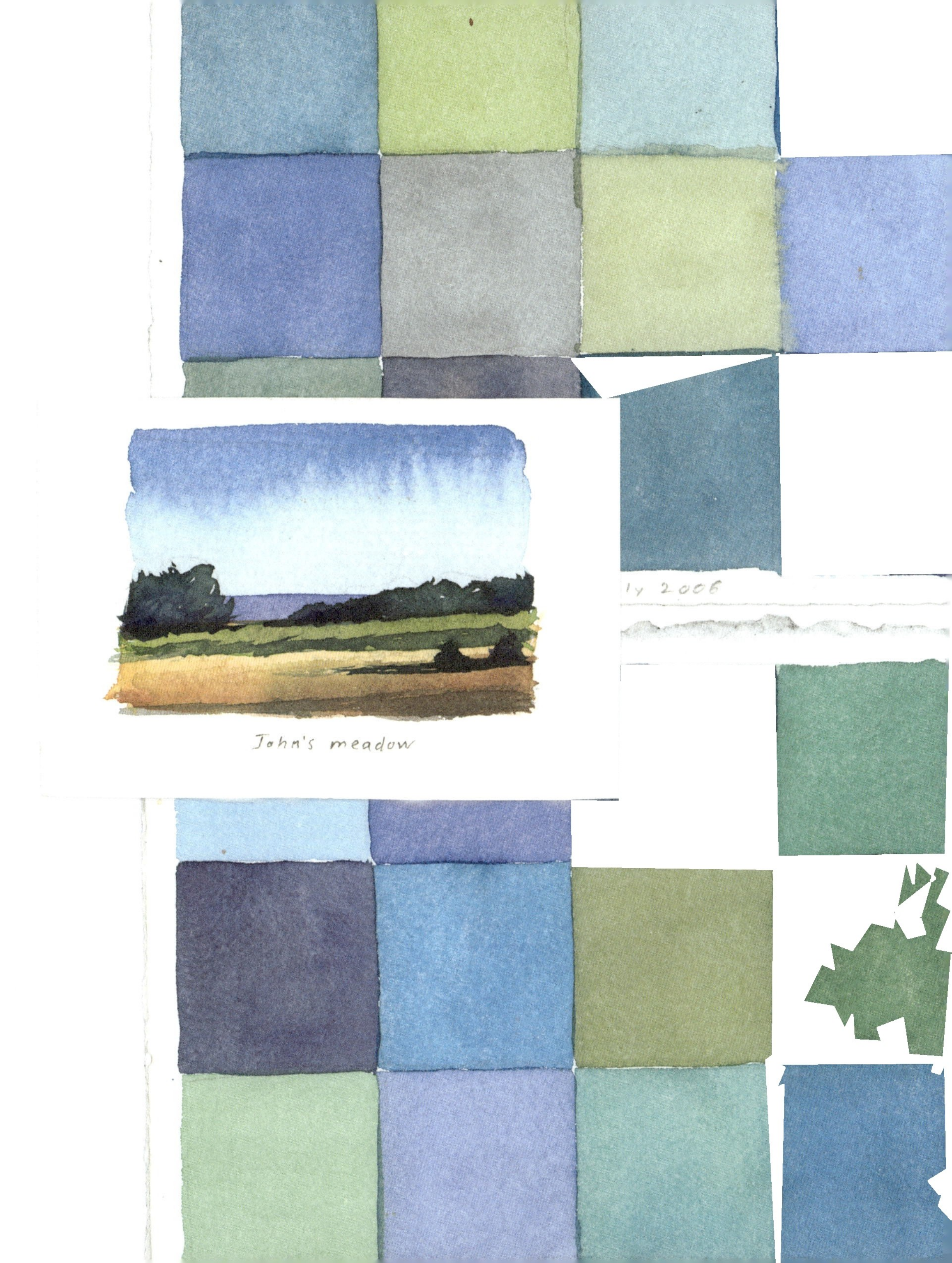
ly 2006
John's meadow

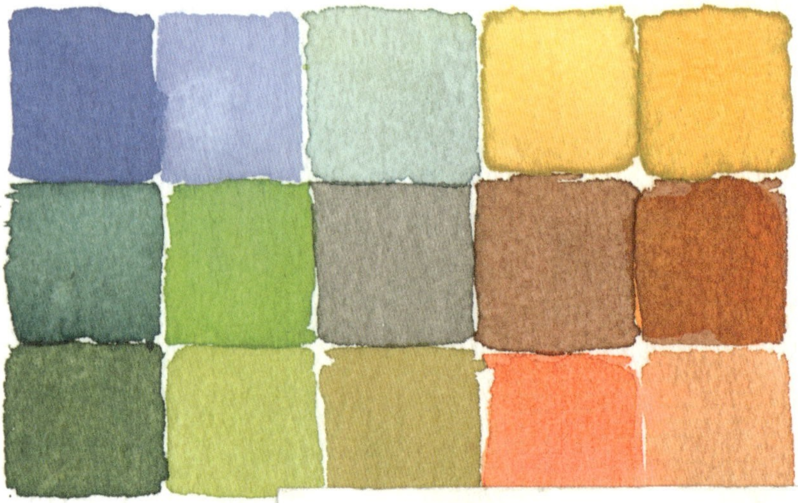

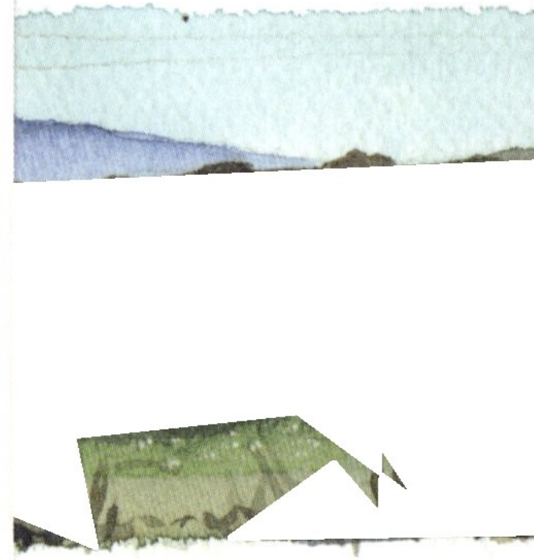

marsh

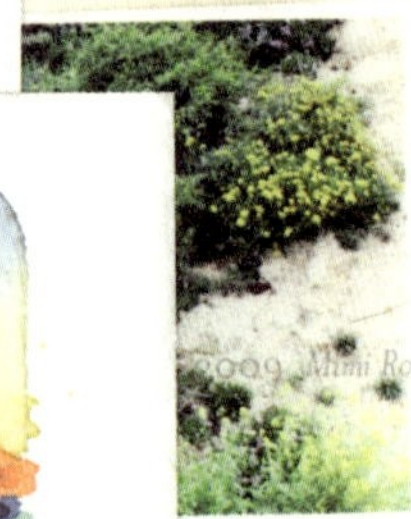

falls

50's lower 60's
5-10 mph
over 400 elephan
which are

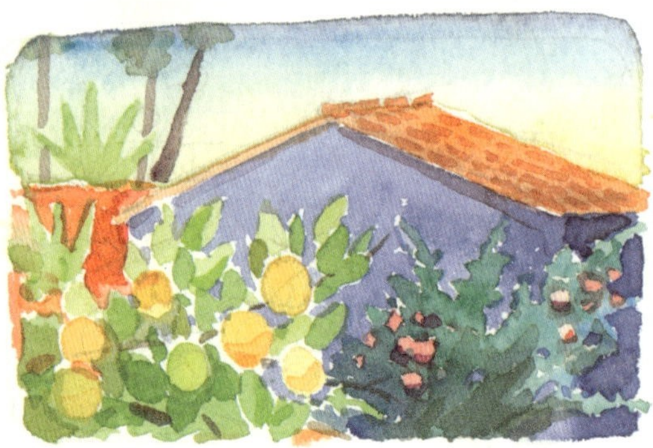

CASA AZUL Antigua Feb 2013 Guatemala

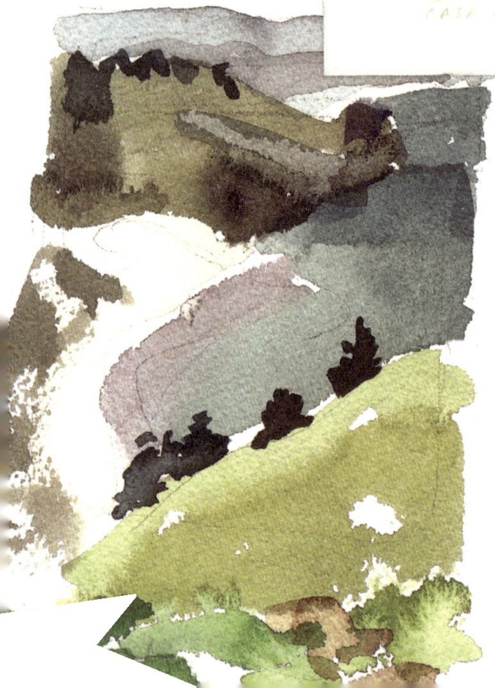

COLORS of WIND - northern wind palette

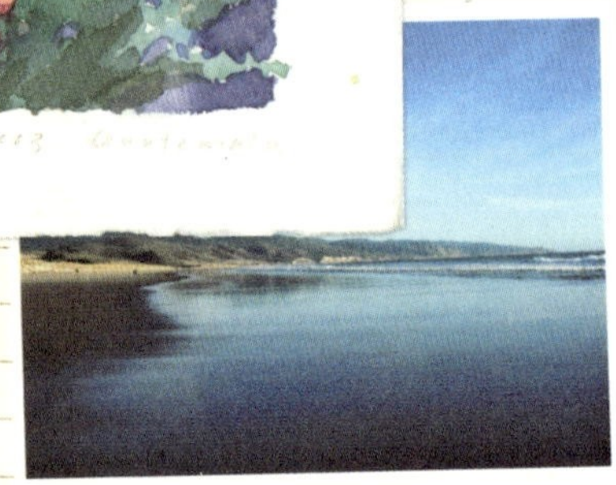

calm morning

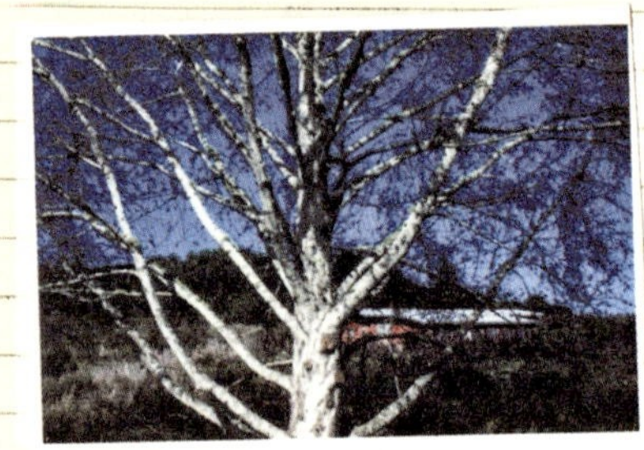

buckeye

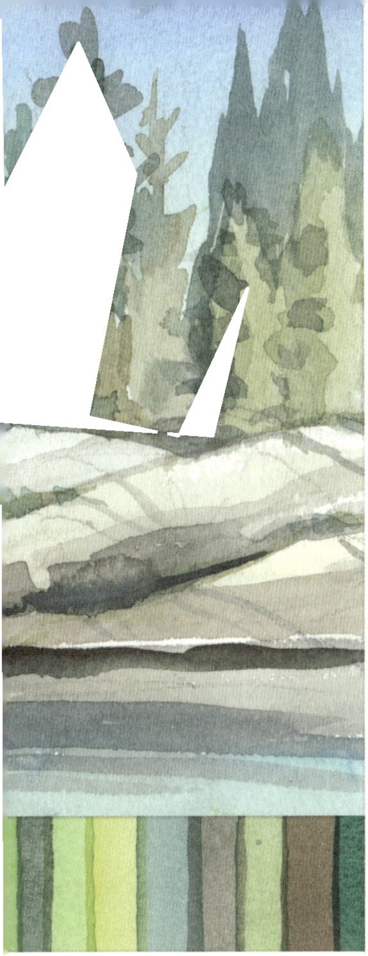

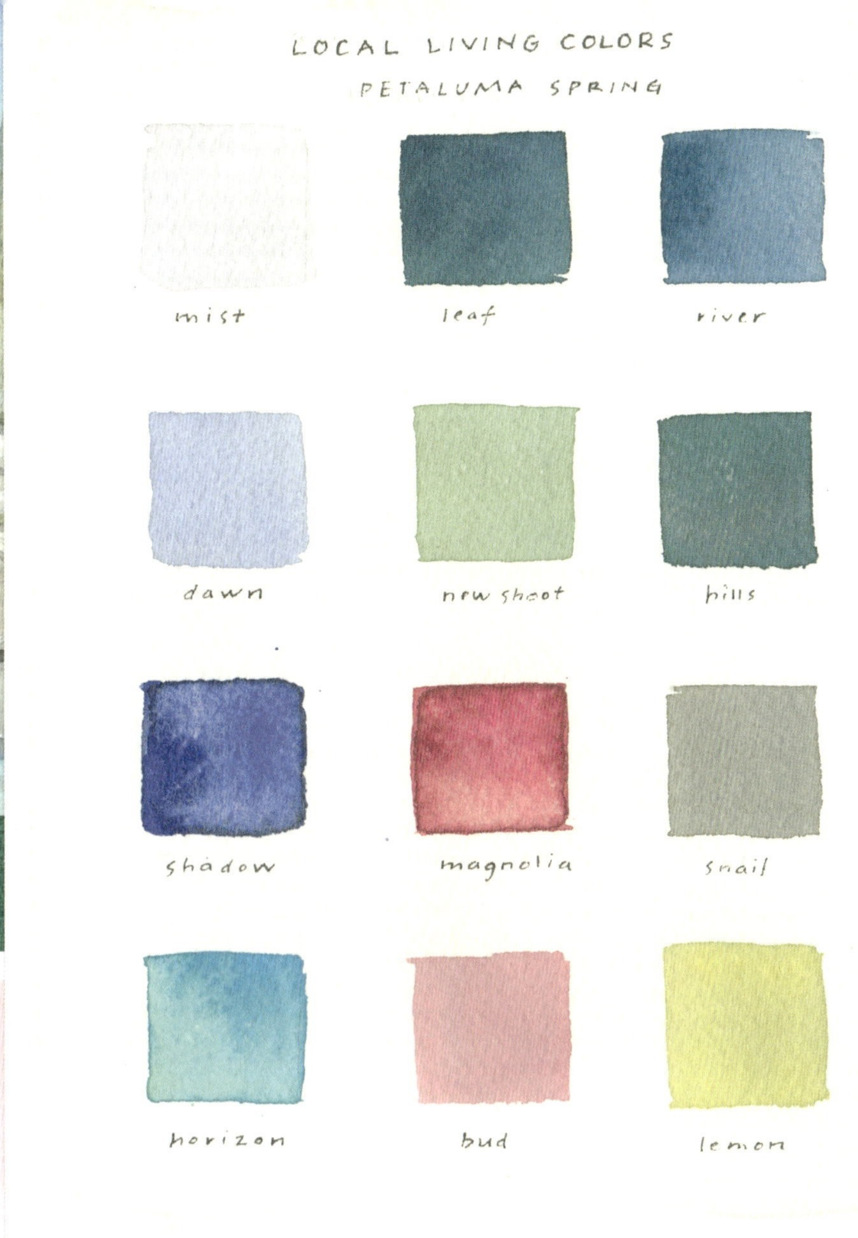
LOCAL LIVING COLORS
PETALUMA SPRING
mist
leaf
river
dawn
new shoot
hills
shadow
magnolia
snail
horizon
bud
lemon

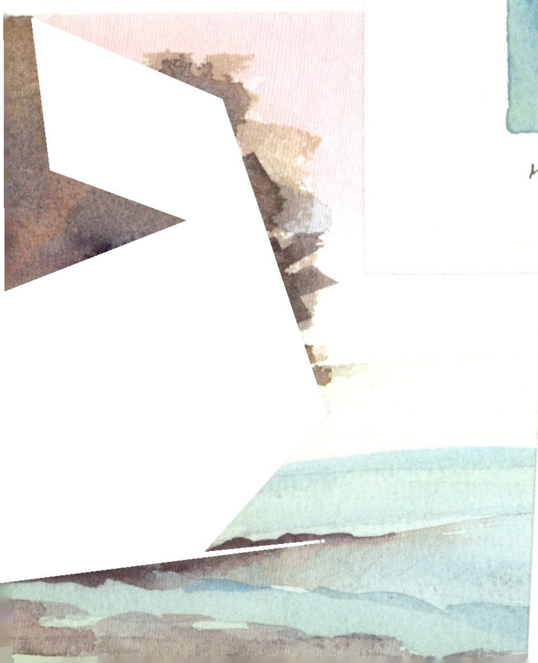

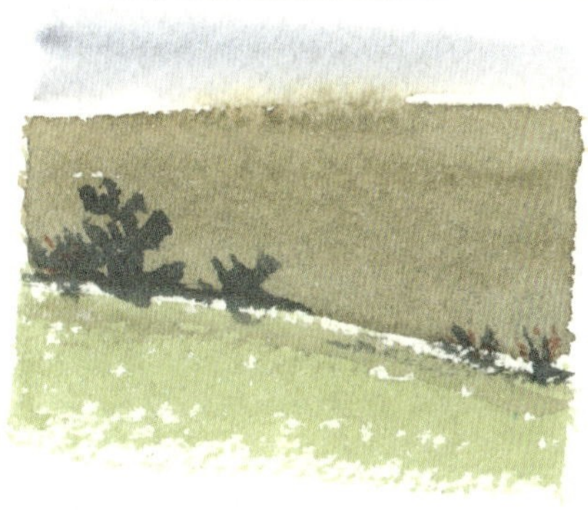

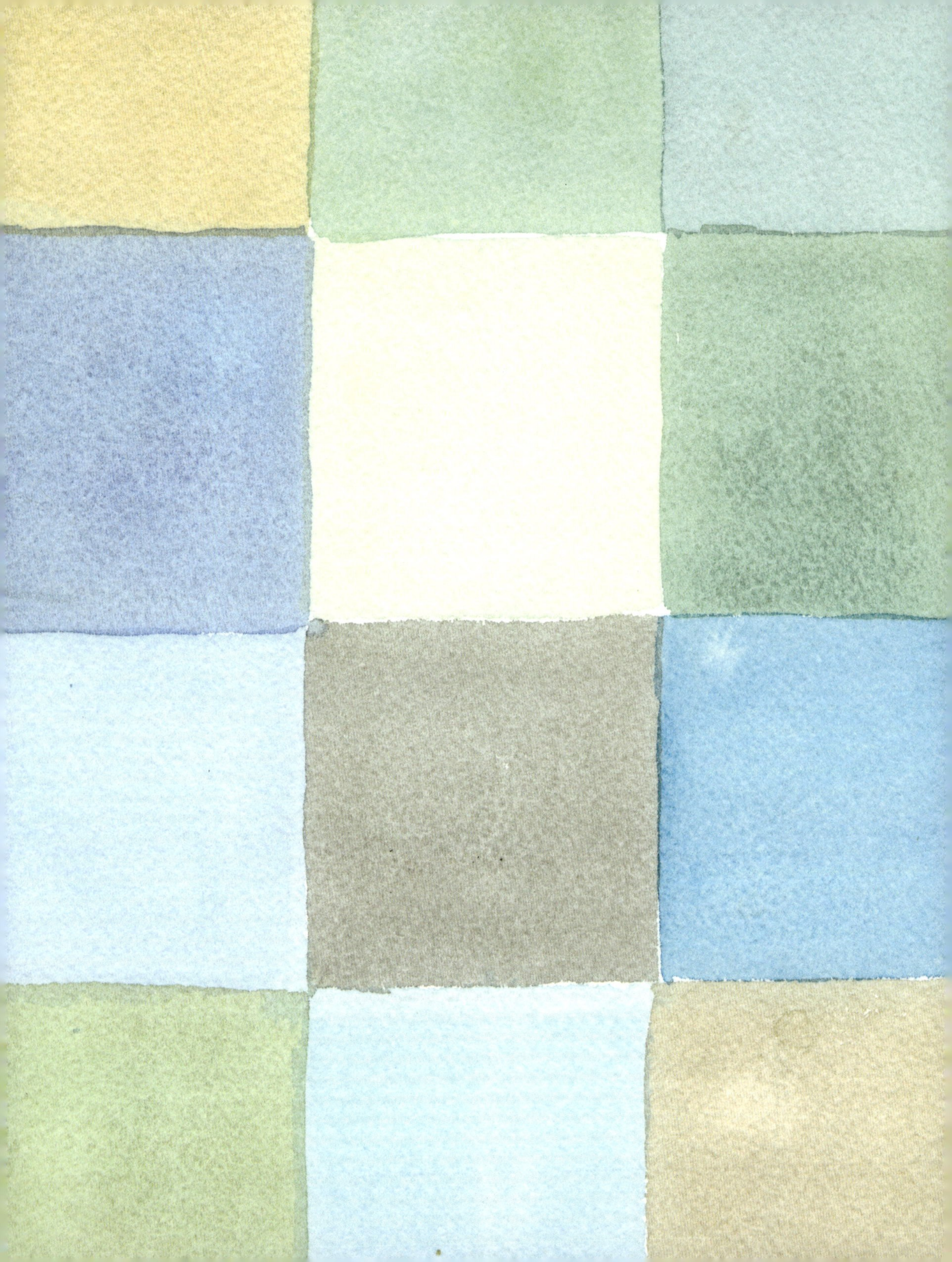

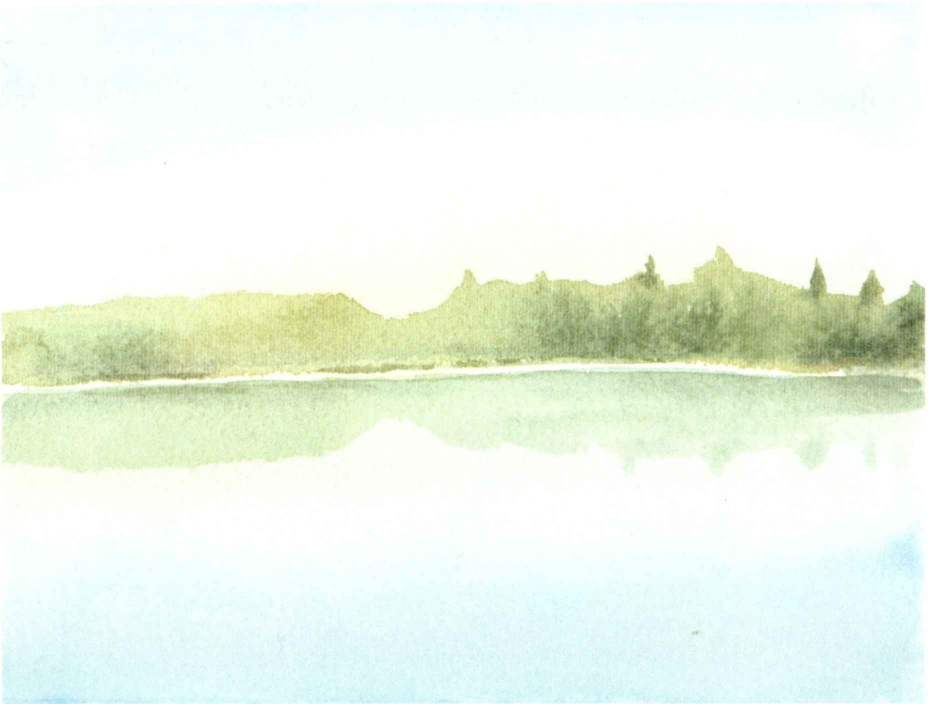

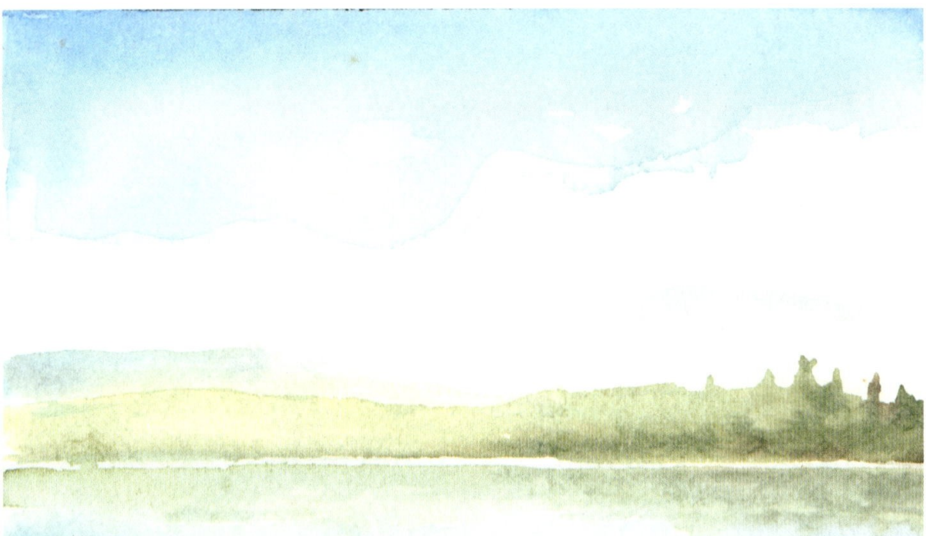

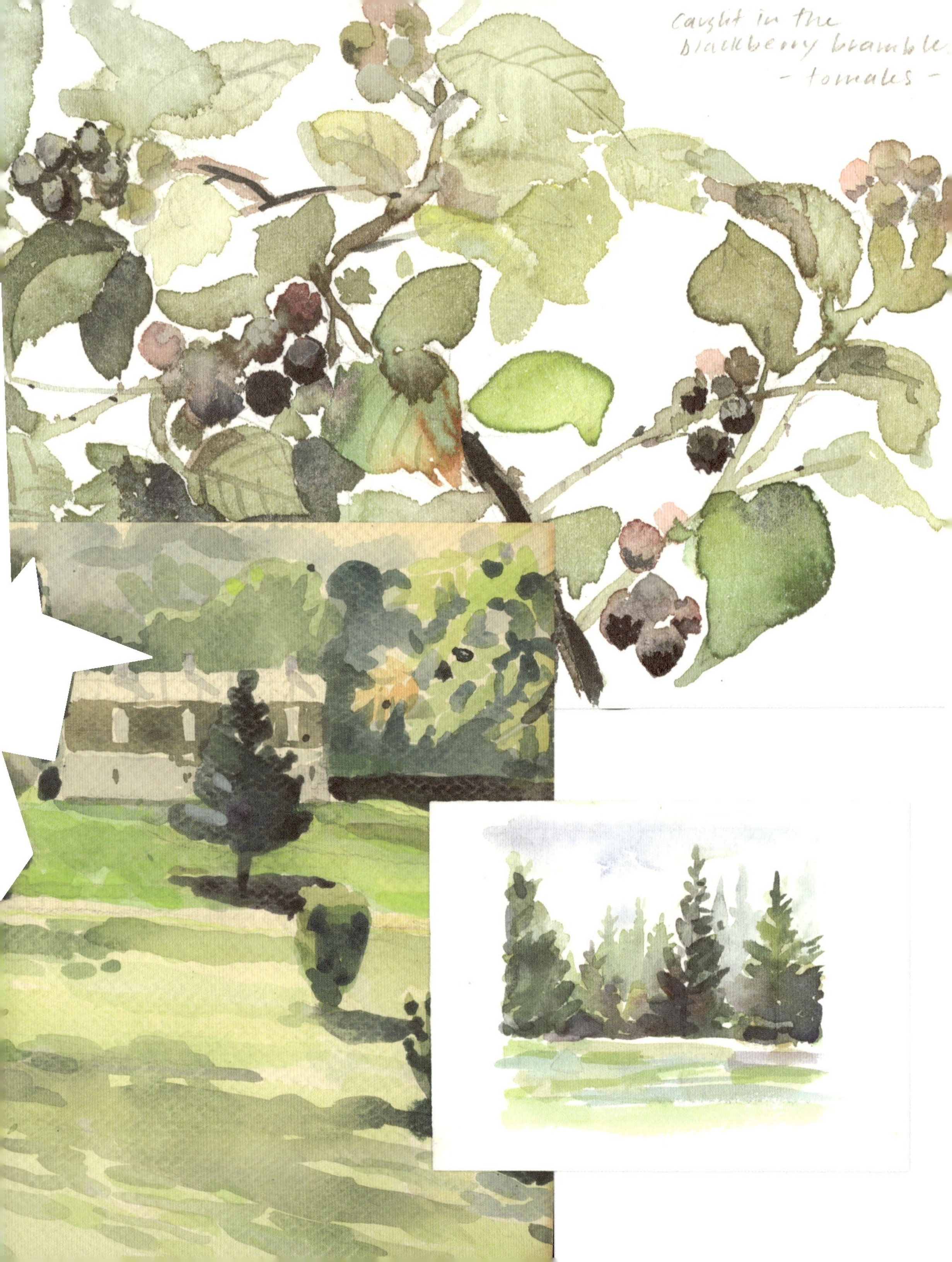
caught in the
blackberry bramble
- tomales -

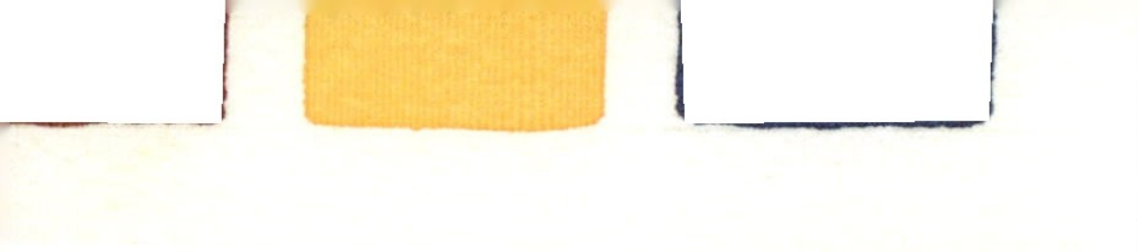

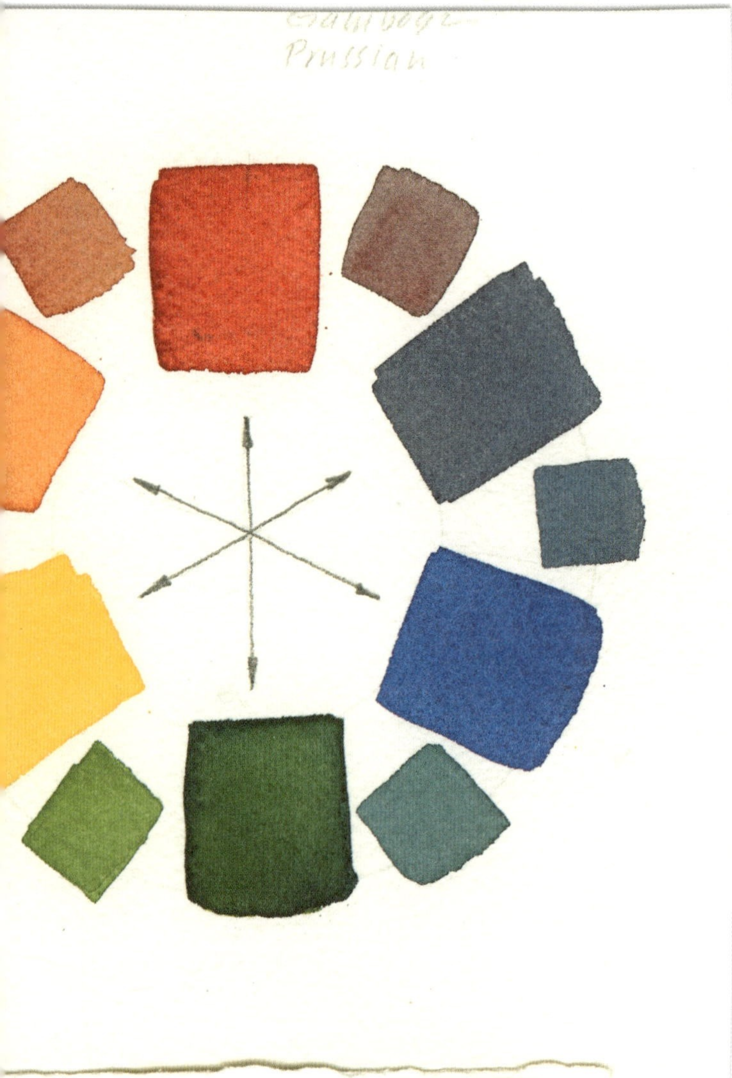
Prussian

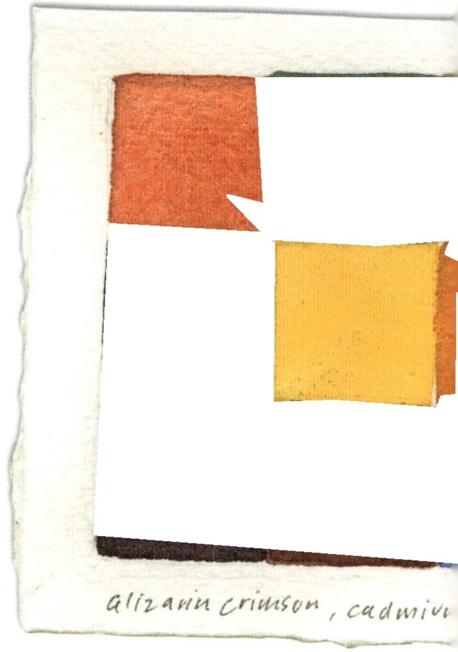
alizarin crimson, cadmium

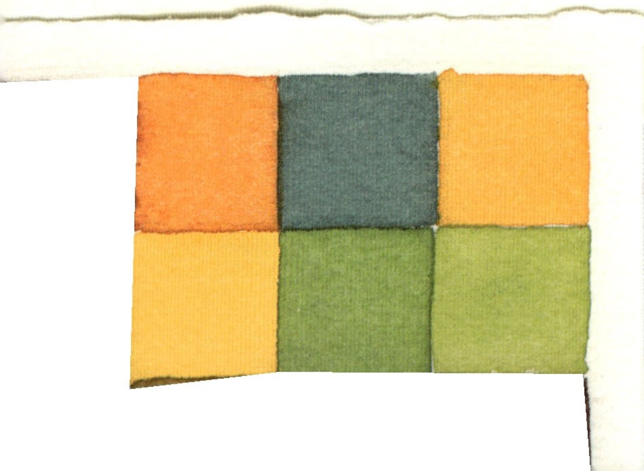

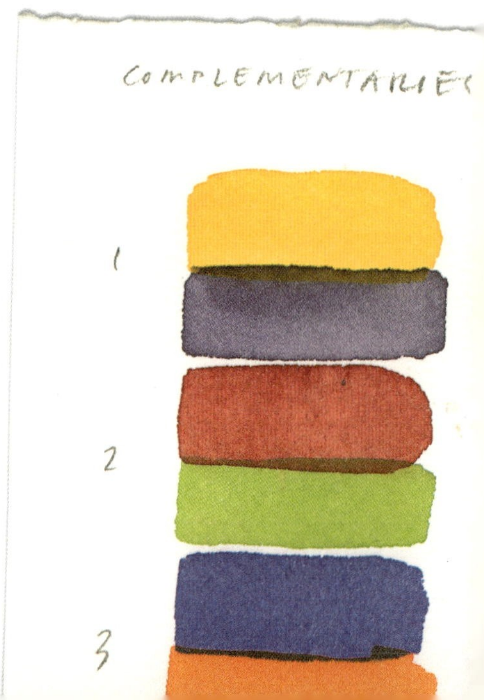
COMPLEMENTARIES
1
2
3

CHAPTER SEVEN

Color Mixing: The Basics

Color mixing is a key part of developing your color sense. You need to experiment in order to learn how colors interact when you mix them. As you do, you will develop an intimate knowledge of how your materials work together: the ratio of pigment to water, the differences between transparent and opaque pigments, cool versus warm colors, knowing your brushes, and all the nuances of color mixing. By practicing mixing colors, you'll know what to use to get the color you want when you're out in the field. Try out pigments from different manufacturers to see the properties of each.

There are no mistakes. It's about experimentation—see what happens when you put unusual colors together. Start developing recipes that you like. Take notes.

There's a world of resources, both in books and online, about color principles and paint mixing. Here are the basics.

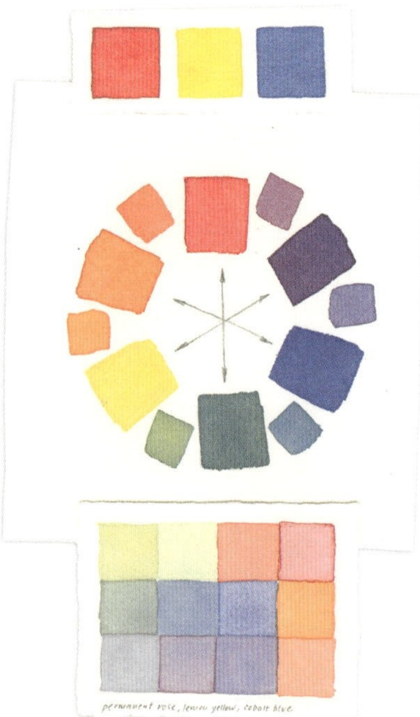

Limited palette 1 (clear and bright):
Permanent rose, lemon yellow, cobalt blue

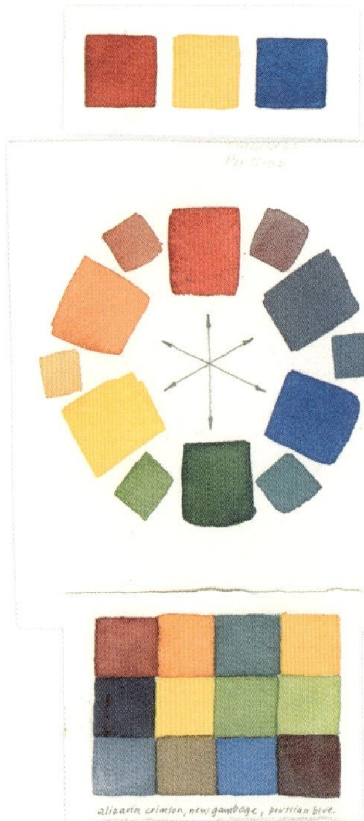

Limited palette 2 (versatile):
Permanent alizarin crimson, new gamboge, Prussian blue

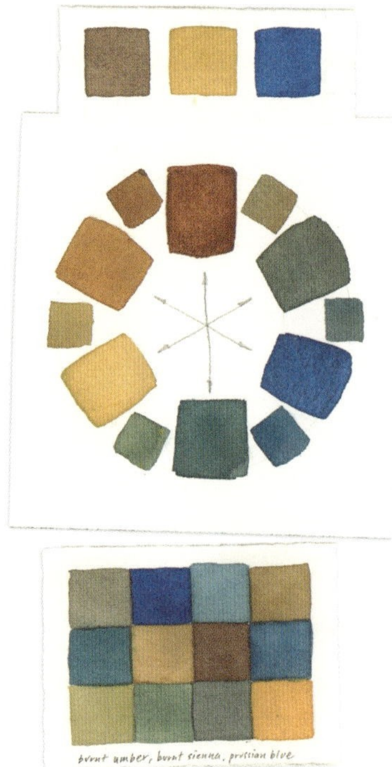

Limited palette 3 (earth-based palette):
Burnt umber, burnt sienna, Prussian blue

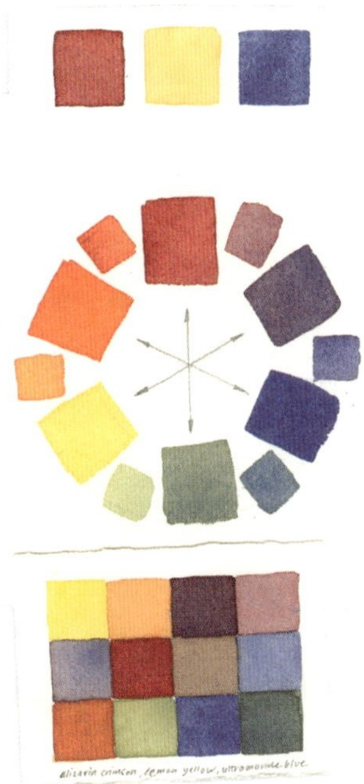

Limited palette 4 (basic and bold): **Permanent alizarin crimson, lemon yellow, ultramarine blue**

COLOR MIXING

The color wheel is a visual tool that helps us organize color in our minds. Create your own color wheels using different triads to create limited palettes. Limiting your palette to three colors will allow you to explore mixing and create harmonious relationships of color. Here are a few basic color terms.

Hue

The spectrum of colors that appear in the rainbow: red, orange, yellow, blue, green, violet.

Primary and Secondary Colors

The three primary colors are yellow, red, and blue. Secondary colors green, orange, and violet are mixed from the primary colors.

Tertiary Colors

The colors formed by mixing adjacent primary and secondary colors: yellow orange, red orange, red purple, blue purple, blue green, and yellow green.

Analogous Colors

Colors that sit next to one another on the color wheel, such as yellow, red, and orange.

Complementary Colors

Colors that sit opposite one another on the color wheel, such as yellow and purple or red and green. Complementary colors accentuate one another; mixing complements together mutes or grays the color.

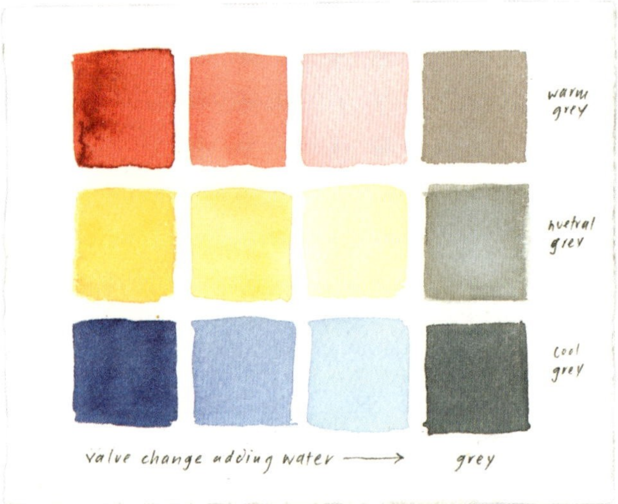

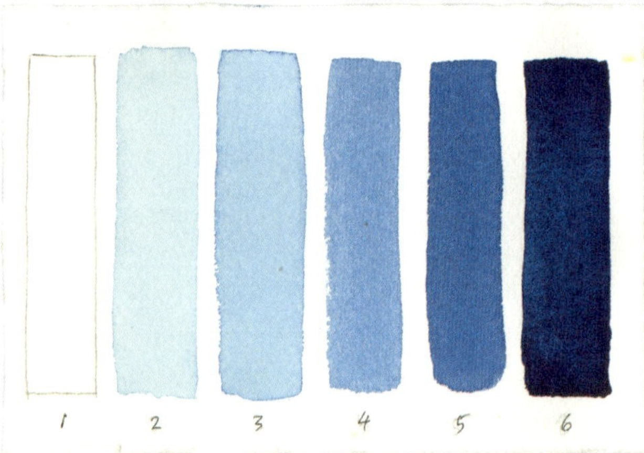

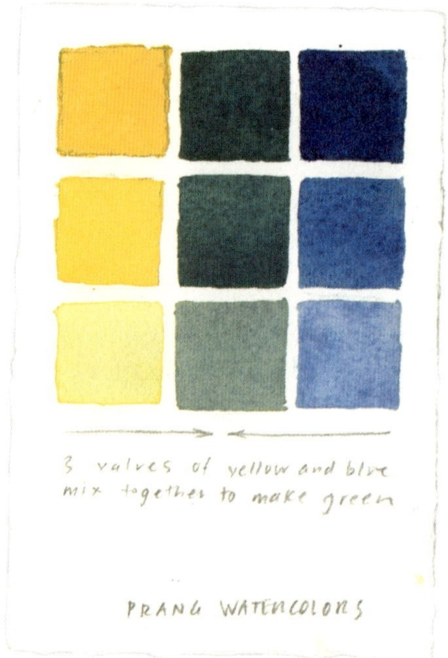

Value or Tone

The relative lightness or darkness of a color. Having different color values adds rhythm and depth to any painting through contrast and gradation of tones. Breaking down color values helps to simplify a complicated scene.

You can look at any subject or view and simplify it into three distinct values: the lightest, darkest, and medium tones. To add depth of tone, I sometimes work with a range of five values, including the white of the paper.

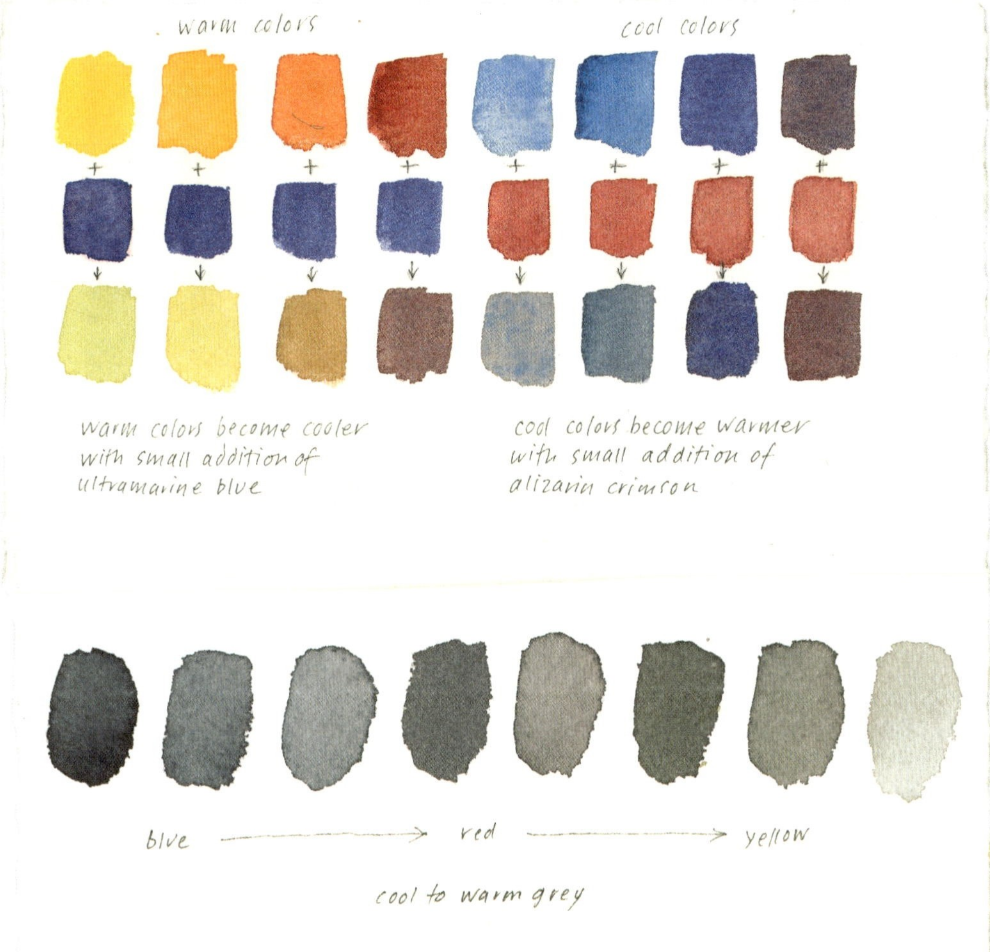

Color Temperature

All colors have a temperature, warm or cool, that can create moods. When you put two complementary colors together, each appears more intense, and their relationship is pleasing to the eye. You can shift any color toward warm, cool, or neutral: to make blue warmer, add a small touch of red; to make a yellow cooler, add a touch of blue; to make a vivid orange more gray, add a touch of purple, which will neutralize it. I sometimes adjust the temperature of two colors next to each other to create cool against warm.

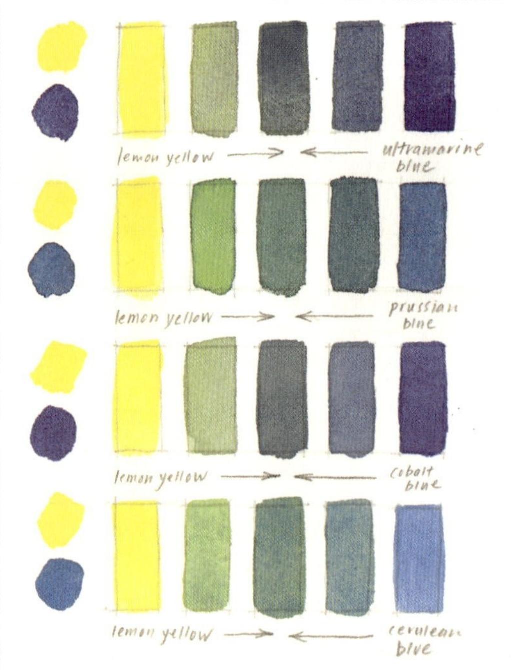

1. GREEN MIXTURES

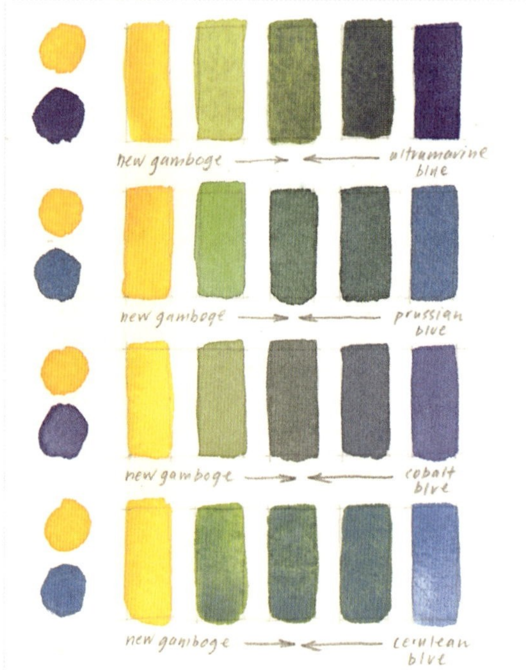

2. GREEN MIXTURES

HOW MANY GREENS ARE THERE?

Unless you live in Antarctica, you likely see greens everywhere. Greens challenge a painter: how do you represent all the tones, values, intensities? Green is abundant in nature, on the ground, in the leaves, reflected in the water: emerald green, aqua, lime green, dull green.

Different seasons have different greens. Bright soft yellow greens of spring shift to dense dark green foliage in the heat of summer. Mixing your own greens will give you a variety of vibrant and subtle colors that work for different seasons, light conditions, and places.

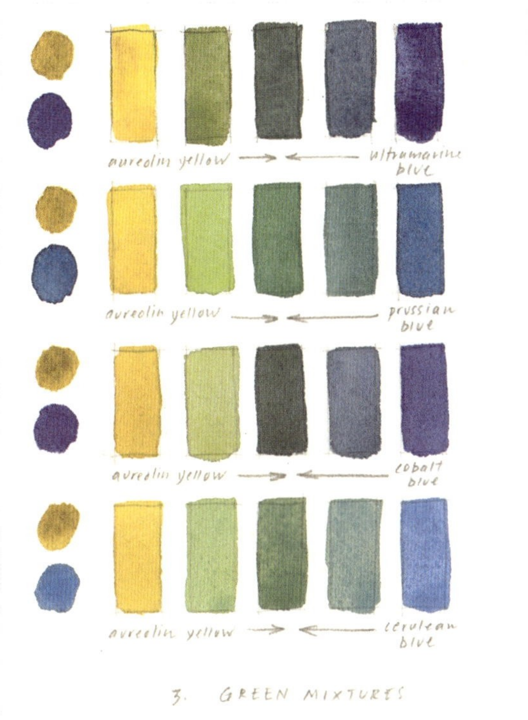

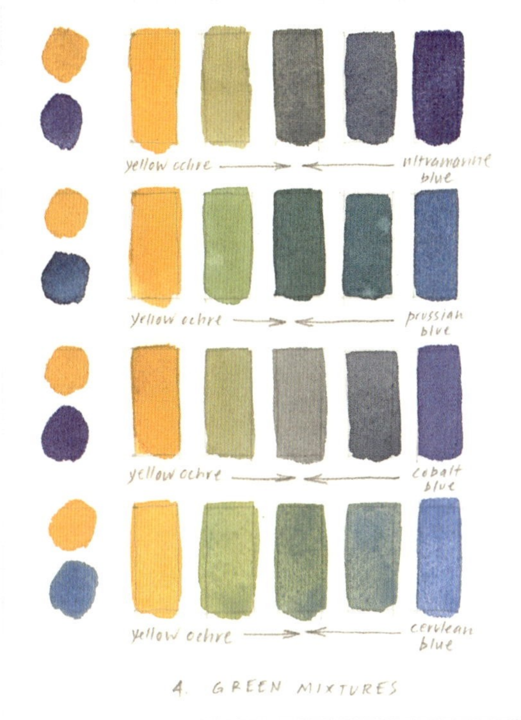

PRACTICE

- Create a chart showing all the greens you can mix from variations of just two colors, blue and yellow. Different blues and different yellows in equal amounts will produce different shades of green. Adding more blue creates one kind of green, adding more yellow creates another.
- Vary the mix to create warm and cool temperatures. Putting two opposite greens together can bring out the differences in cool and warm color and make them come alive on your palette.
- Vary the quantity of paint versus water in your green mix to adjust the value.
- Make color palettes: All of the greens you see in one landscape, in one plant, in a still life of green fruit and vegetables: limes, grapes, lettuces, chards, celery—whatever's in your refrigerator, five green shades where you sit right now

A FEW BOOKS I LIKE ABOUT COLOR AND PLACE:

- Josef Albers, *The Interaction of Color, 50th Anniversary Edition* (New Haven, CT: Yale University Press, 2013)
- Arielle Eckstut and Joann Eckstut, *The Secret Language of Color: Science, Nature, History, Culture, Beauty of Red, Orange, Yellow, Green, Blue, and Violet* (New York: Black Dog & Leventhal Publishers, 2013)
- Victoria Finlay, *Color: A Natural History of the Palette* (New York: Random House, 2003)
- Johann Wolfgang von Goethe, *Goethe's Theory of Colours*, trans. Charles Lock Eastlake (Cambridge: Cambridge University Press, 2014)
- Robert Henri, *The Art Spirit* (New York: Basic Books, 2007)
- Barry Lopez and Debra Gwartney, *Home Ground: Language for an American Landscape* (San Antonio: Trinity University Press, 2011)
- Anne Varichon, *Colors: What They Mean and How to Make Them* (New York: Abrams, 2007)
- Natasha Wing, *An Eye for Color: The Story of Josef Albers*, illustrated by Julia Breckenreid (New York: Henry Holt and Company, 2009)

AND ONE WEBSITE:

The Cooper Hewitt Smithsonian Design Museum website allows you to look at its collection through the lens of color:

- https://collection.cooperhewitt.org/objects/colors/

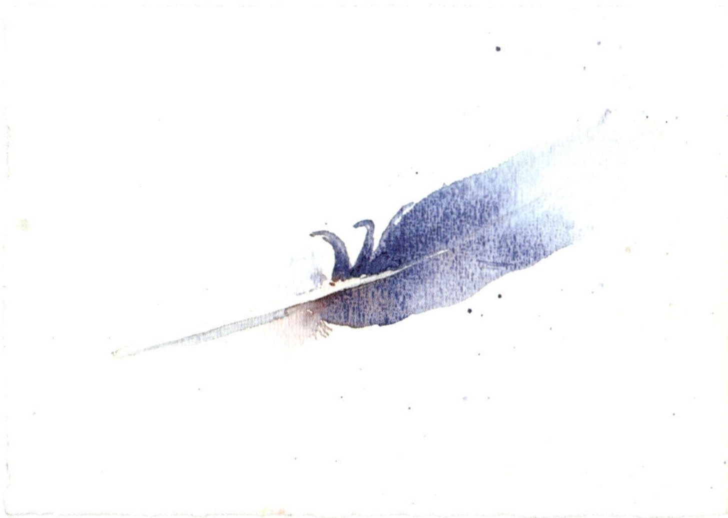

To my father, Charles Robinson, 1931–2014,
who gave me a love of art

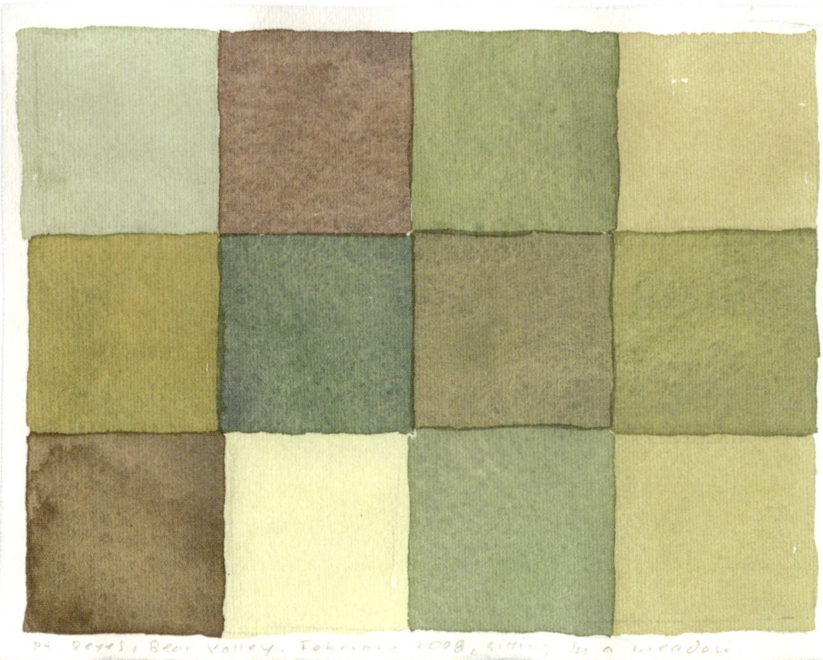
Pt. Reyes, Bear Valley, February 2008, sitting in a meadow